MORNING DECREES

A 365-DAY DEVOTIONAL OF PRACTICAL
TRUTHS FOR EMPOWERED LIVING

DR. JEFFERY A. WILLIAMS

*"You shall also decide and decree a thing, and it shall be established for you; and the
light [of God's favor] shall shine upon your ways." Job 22:28, AMP*

Morning Decrees
by Dr. Jeffery A. Williams
Copyright © 2021 Dr. Jeffery A. Williams

ISBN 978-1-63360-178-9

For Worldwide Distribution
Printed in the USA

Urban Press
P.O. Box 8881
Pittsburgh, PA 15221-0881
412.646.2780

Acknowledgement

This 365-day devotional is lovingly dedicated to the faithful partners of The King's Cathedral who have devoted their lives to following Jesus of Nazareth, the Christ. I believe one proof of passion is pursuit and your pursuit of knowing Jesus and making Him known is evident devotion. Thank you for being an unflinching witness of the living God.

Jesus Is Alive,
Jeffery A. Williams, D.Min, MPA
Bishop

How to Get the Most from Your Journal

I recommend establishing a set time and place to read your devotional, accompanied by your favorite Bible. Give yourself 15-30 minutes to read, reflect, and answer the questions. Be sure to dedicate a specific notebook for the personal insights and revelation you will receive as you read the Morning Decree Devotional. You may elect to go through the devotional in sequential order, but each Morning Decree is specifically designed to stand alone. In other words, if the title of Decree #12 speaks to your heart, by all means, read decree #12 on that particular day and choose another Decree the following day. The goal is to commit yourself to having a daily dialogue with God through His Word.

Introduction

The Morning Decree began from my desire to create a personal routine of prayer and meditation for my family. The social media distribution through Facebook, Periscope, and Free Conference Call was an effort to invite others into our struggle to establish a daily spiritual discipline. In truth, going live each morning was a way of holding myself accountable to seek God daily. Even though I am someone who has been in ministry for 35 years as I write and is proficient in sharing the Word of God with others, it became even more important that I observe a personal, rock-solid, daily "talk with Jesus." I'm deeply heartened knowing that you have decided to join Lelani (my beautiful wife) and me on our quest for real intimacy with the Lord.

Morning Decrees are a product of 1,114 consecutive mornings (over three years) when I shared the Word of God with the world simultaneously through social media and a conference call. These daily offerings are designed to deepen your spiritual relationship with Him as well as strengthen your discipline. Discipline is needed to achieve any worthwhile endeavor, especially as a follower of Jesus Christ. Moreover, no objective is more important than having a daily, meaningful, and intimate experience with God. This *Morning Decree Devotional Journal* will help you establish a routine that is vital to your spiritual growth and development.

Each decree is biblically-based and practical. Take a few minutes to read each Decree and then consider the three questions following. As you do this day in and day out, you will learn even more about God, the Holy Spirit, the ministry of Jesus, and how to express these relationships in your daily life. As you will learn, I am all about practical application. The information within each Morning Decree, though theologically "meaty," can be applied immediately to areas and issues you face in your daily life. Most of the Decrees are brief by design because it's not the volume of spiritual food we consume that matters, but rather how much we digest and live out. As you read the Decrees, take time and focus your attention on these essential questions: "How does this apply to me?" and "How can I incorporate this lesson in my life?"

Morning Decree #1
Are You Devoted?

"And he said to him, 'You shall love the Lord your God with all your heart and with all your soul and with all your mind.'" Matthew 22:37

The answer to that question depends on a number of factors. Your ability to understand the things of God has more to do with your personal hunger than anything else. If you choose to meditate on the Word of God and practice spiritual disciplines, you will automatically understand more and ultimately do more. However, with the convenience of Christian programming through the Internet, on television, and via other media resources, you can become spiritually lazy, allowing others to do the work for you. When was the last time you took what you heard from a sermon and went home to study it further? If you have, then you are among a small percentage of churchgoers who do. Jesus said, "With the same measure of thought and study you give to what you hear determines the results you get" (Mark 4:24, AMP).

As the adage goes, "talk is cheap;" therefore, what you actually do reveals what you really want or need. And what you do and how often you do it will answer today's question as to how devoted you are. Therefore, starting each day with a few minutes to pray and read the Word of God, as well as consider important questions, will yield life-changing fruit in your life. Hungry people will do almost anything to survive. The Scriptures are clear; if you love Him, you must show that to be true with all your heart, soul, mind, and strength. Just remember: The more energy you exert in study and prayer, the more your most authentic desires are revealed.

Questions for Reflections

1. Of what does your morning routine consist?

2. Do you have a set appointment with God? If so, when? If not, why not?

3. What are you willing to change in your morning routine to ensure you have time for your morning devotional?

Morning Decree #2
What's at the Top of Your List?

"There is no man that hath left house, or brethren, or sisters, or mother, or father, or children, or lands, for my sake, and for the gospel's sake . . ." Matthew 10:28

When you hear the word *devotion*, what comes to mind? Do you think about a love relationship such as marriage? The word devotion comes from the idea of making a vow or casting a vote. To be devoted to something or someone means to be so committed there is no other option to consider. It's also like someone who casts their vote for a political candidate of their choice. Once they enter the voting booth and pull the lever for their candidate, their vote cannot change—that's devotion.

Spiritually speaking, being devoted means that you have forsaken all others for the sake of Christ. You give your first and best to your relationship with God. That means time, energy, money, reputation, and dreams—everything and everyone comes in a distant second compared to your devotion to Christ Jesus, your Lord.

In what ways are you devoted to the Lord? As you undoubtedly know, it takes more than words or feelings. Does your schedule reflect your devotion to the Lord? What about your priorities? Do they demonstrate you are devoted to growing in your relationship with the Lord? Just as it is in a marriage or even a relationship with a best friend, what you do indicates more accurately how you feel than mere words.

Questions for Reflections

1. What are the first five things on your schedule each day?

2. If your family was asked about your priorities, would they say your relationship with the Lord is a top priority for you?

3. What changes are you willing to make to demonstrate and improve your devotion to the Lord?

Morning Decree #3
Pig or Chicken Commitment?

"Even as the Son of man came not to be ministered unto, but to minister, and to give his life a ransom for many." Matthew 20:28

There's a fable of a farmer who was in financial trouble. The farm animals got wind of the problem and called a meeting. In the meeting, each animal offered to help in some way. The chickens said, "We'll give some eggs." The sheep added, "We'll give some wool." They then asked the pig if he was willing to give some bacon, to which he responded, "Eggs are a sacrifice, wool is a commitment, but bacon is total devotion." That's my version of the story, but you get the point. Devotion is beyond commitment and sacrifice. It's the point of no return. Our Lord Jesus Christ was devoted to saving you by giving His life as a ransom. It's not even close to a fair trade—He died for you by crucifixion. You now live for Him. No matter how you look at it, you got the best part of the deal.

Are you living your life "devoted" to Him or is your devotion like that of some of the farm animals who were committed as long as it didn't cost them too much?

Questions for Reflections

1. Share an example of someone who demonstrated true devotion.

2. Name one relationship to which you are devoted.

3. In what ways can you further demonstrate your devotion to Christ?

Morning Decree #4
What is Your Devotion Costing You?

"These people draw near Me with their mouths and honor Me with their lips, but their hearts hold off and are far away from Me." Matthew 15:8

You have probably heard the phrase, "Talk is cheap?" There's often little sacrifice involved in simply stating our intentions unless we follow through on them. The truth of the matter is that words have more meaning when actions support them. It's effortless to say you love someone, even to say, "I love the Lord," but it's another thing entirely to back up that pronouncement with corresponding sacrificial actions.

Developing a devotional lifestyle will cost you something. It will cost you time, sleep, recreation, or at times even legitimate pleasures. If your devotion to God, or anything else for that matter, doesn't require some sacrifice from you, then you should ask yourself, "Am I truly devoted?". What's interesting is that when you devote yourself to God, you are the main beneficiary of your sacrifice. You don't lose anything. Your devotional life is for you. It empowers you. It heals you. It strengthens you.

Questions for Reflections

1. When was the last time you felt you were devoted to God? In what ways can you improve your devotion to Him?

2. Why is having a devotional lifestyle a gift to you?

3. In what ways can a devotional lifestyle negatively impact your day or life?

Morning Decree #5
How You Handle "It" Matters

"Therefore, my beloved brothers, be steadfast, immovable, always abounding in the work of the Lord, knowing that in the Lord your labor is not in vain."
1 Corinthians 15:58

Disappointment comes to all of us at different times and for different reasons. However, it's not the disappointment that makes a difference, but rather how you handle the disappointment that determines what kind of impact it has on you—for good or not so good. What's more sometimes, you may be disappointed in the Lord Himself or His response to you and your dilemma. It's at that time it's good to remember Isaiah 49:23: ""Those who hope in me will not be disappointed."

Your devotion to Christ is one way of remaining focused despite the inevitable disappointments and discouraging things that will happen. Remain steadfast to what Jesus has assigned for you to do in life and his grace will help you overcome the challenges, hills, and valleys. No one, regardless of how strong or faithful they are, can completely avoid challenging seasons. Those who have faith in Christ and follow the example of Christ are the ones who overcome the things that might overwhelm others.

Don't allow your disappointments to cause you to miss your devotional appointment with God. The power of unbroken focus can't be overemphasized. Stay focused. Remain on your knees. Continue with your plan and you shall overcome.

Questions for Reflections

1. What are the types of problems that disappoint you the most?

2. When you're disappointed, what is your usual reaction?

3. How do you think maintaining a consistent devotional lifestyle will help you overcome your disappointments?

Morning Decree #6
How to Handle the "Big D"

"He is able to exercise gentleness and forbearance toward the ignorant and erring, since he himself also is liable to moral weakness and physical infirmity." Hebrews 5:2

As stated in Decree #5, discouragement affects all of us at one time or another. We see it even in the lives of the heroes of our faith like Abraham, King David, Ruth, Esther, Nehemiah, and even the Lord Jesus Christ Himself. It isn't a matter of *if* you will be discouraged, but when. Therefore, when it occurs, you need the spiritual tools to deal with and overcome it. What is discouragement, and how can we overcome it?

Discouragement is often the result of a prolonged feeling of hopelessness or despair. Despite your best efforts, things aren't getting better. Discouragement is also the feeling you get that causes you to lose courage to keep trying—or even keep hoping. The demise of marriages, businesses, relationships (even in church), and premature death can all be blamed on discouragement. Unfortunately, feelings of discouragement are pretty common.

Aren't you glad the Lord Jesus Christ once felt the way you do? He has experienced the full range of emotions you face but yet stayed focus. You may be asking, what did Jesus focus on? Good question. He stayed focused on the promises of God and applied them to combat the thoughts the enemy was using trying to distract him. We are told, "During the days of Jesus' life on earth, he offered up prayers and petitions with fervent cries and tears to the one who could save him from death, and he was heard because of his reverent submission" (Hebrews 5:7). Because Jesus knows how you feel, He provides even more grace to help you overcome the "Big D."

Questions for Reflections

1. What tends to discourage you the most?

2. How do you usually handle the discouragement?

3. What are some spiritual things you can do to press through the difficult moments?

Morning Decree #7
How to Get Through What You're Going Through

"I have said these things to you, that in me you may have peace. In the world you will have tribulation. But take heart; I have overcome the world." John 16:33

Everybody faces challenges, tests, and trials. Jesus' words before His departure were these: "In the world, you shall have tribulation. But be of good cheer; I have overcome the world" (John 16:33). Those words have far-reaching impact and importance as you work through the issues of life.

Challenges arise from doing "right things" and for doing the "wrong things." Some challenges you are confronted with are the result of your faith in Christ Jesus. The Lord Jesus in His wisdom chose to let you know in advance what to expect, and through faith in Him, you can overcome those problems.

Sometimes, when bad things are happening, you may tend to feel like it's "all my fault." Also, when you think it's your fault, you lack confidence you may not ask for God's grace to see you through to victory. However, even though you may be suffering as the result of your actions, His grace is still available to help you through. Therefore, the next time you're faced with a life test, make the changes needed to avoid any future occurrence and count on God's grace to give you what you need to get through.

Questions for Reflections

1. When you're going through difficult times, what is typically your first response?

2. What are some of the biblical things you can do to get through what you're going through?

3. How did Jesus overcome the world for us?

Morning Decree #8
The One Thing You Need to Experience Victory

"For everyone who has been born of God overcomes the world. And this is the victory that has overcome the world—our faith." 1 John 5:4

In Decree #7, we saw that Jesus said you would face troubles in your life: "In the world, you shall have tribulation. But be of good cheer; I have overcome the world" (John 16:33). How are you able to overcome the problems you face every day? Today's Scripture reads, "And this is the victory that has overcome the world—our faith." The next verse gives you even more information: "Who is it that overcomes the world? Only the one who believes that Jesus is the Son of God" (1 John 5:5).

It takes faith to overcome life's difficulties, and not just faith that "it will all work out" or "everything happens for a reason." It is faith in the Lord Jesus that He is present, interested, and active in your life. Faith is vital because it is the knowledge that as you act in obedience to the Word of God, which also requires faith, things will work out for your good as promised in Romans 8:28: "And we know that in all things God works for the good of those who love him, who have been called according to his purpose."

Faith is more than just believing in God. Faith is acting on your conviction that God will make a way for you to overcome the uncertainties and problems of life.

Questions for Reflections

1. What is the current problem troubling you the most?

2. How do you think faith in God will help you solve the problem?

3. Faith is active trust in God's Word. What Scriptural truths are you basing your faith on?

Morning Decree #9
Are You Really Thankful?

"And let the peace of Christ rule in your hearts, to which indeed you were called in one body. And be thankful." Colossians 3:15

Sometimes it's helpful to write a list of the things for which you are thankful. It's hard to stay down in the dumps when you take time to reflect on and realize all the good things in your life. I know there are times of stress and war, seasons and events that can be hard to deal with—things that make you angry, sad, and even depressed. However, even in the midst of those periods, remembering the many blessings of God in your life is the perfect exercise.

By intentionally calling to mind the many ways in which God has blessed you, answered your prayers, and helped you and those you love, you will increase your faith ten-fold and be empowered to face the challenges of the day. With renewed and increased faith, you can fight the battles you're facing at this very moment. Unfortunately, it sometimes seems so much easier to complain about what's wrong in your life rather than choosing to praise God for what is right. Take time today to practice being thankful: "Enter his gates with thanksgiving and his courts with praise; give thanks to him and praise his name. For the LORD is good and his love endures forever; his faithfulness continues through all generations (Psalm 100:4-5).

Questions for Reflections

1. List five specific reasons you are thankful.

2. Why do think it is difficult to praise God in the hard times?

3. What are some things you can do to help you remember to be thankful to God? Spend a few minutes right now thanking God for all He has done for you.

Morning Decree #10
Thank God for This not That

"The thief comes only in order to steal and kill and destroy. I came that they may have and enjoy life, and have it in abundance (to the full, till it overflows)." John 10:10

Yesterday's assignment was to list at least five things for which you are thankful. When you stop to think about it, there are many reasons to be grateful to God. However, some people erroneously believe you should thank God for *everything*—whether good or bad. While we should give praise in all circumstances, I don't believe our Heavenly Father wants us to thank Him for things and events for which He is not responsible. Paul wrote in 1 Thessalonians 5:16-18, "Rejoice always, pray continually, give thanks *in* all circumstances; for this is God's will for you in Christ Jesus" (emphasis added).

Tragedies, sickness, and premature death—to name a few troubling things—are the kind of events for which we don't thank God. The God of the Bible as revealed in Jesus Christ is not a God who kills children and afflicts the innocent with diseases. Jesus stated in no uncertain terms that His mission was to provide an abundant life for us and we should thank God for this life.

Questions for Reflections

1. What are you thankful for today?

2. When was the last time you thanked God?

3. How does being thankful make you feel?

4. Does it help to think you should thank God *in* all things but not *for* all things?

Morning Decree #11
Fear Not

"But overhearing what they said, Jesus said to the ruler of the synagogue, 'Do not fear, only believe.'" Mark 5:36

I have read *fear not* appears in the Bible 365 times. I am reminded that I will probably face fear every day of my life. I find comfort in knowing that those same days, I need not let fear dominate me. Experiencing fear is part of our human experience. At different times for different reasons, we all become afraid. I have concluded that the opposite of faith is not unbelief; it is fear. What's more, the Bible says my fear is not a lack of faith but of love: "Perfect love casts out fear, because fear involves punishment, and the one who fears is not perfected in love" (1 John 4:18). The key to overcoming this feeling is to look to our faith in God rather than listen to the voice of fear.

For instance, you may be fearful to give a speech in public. However, with faith in God and preparation, you could learn to ignore what the fear is telling you ("don't do it"), and press forward to accomplish your assignment. While this may not be a sensational example, the principle for overcoming fear is the same regardless of the situation. When we fear something, often our first response is to get rid of fear and the thing causing the fear. The mandate "fear not" does not require that you get rid of the fear. Instead, it is a charge not to do what fear demands. Instead of doing nothing in order to avoid fear, ask yourself, "What is faith telling me to do?" Knowing that, then drag your fear with you, if necessary, so you can do the opposite of what fear is urging you to do.

Questions for Reflections

1. Name one thing you are/were afraid of? Why and when did this fear first appear?

2. How have you dealt with this fear in the past?

3. Describe how you should handle fear going forward.

Morning Decree #12
What's Fear Saying to You?

"Fear not, therefore; you are of more value than many sparrows." Matthew 10:31

Mankind is God's crowning achievement of His creation. Jesus assured His followers that God the Father was mindful of their needs and would always provide—especially if they are serving Him and doing His will. Being afraid at times is normal; however, living in fear is not—at least not for those who have their faith rooted in the Lord Jesus Christ. Often, fear is rooted in what you see happening or what you anticipate will happen. It is said that 90% of what people fear never occurs. Whether that's true or not, as followers of Christ, your focus must be on God as your Protector at all times. He knows all things. Your faith in Him enables you to walk through what might destroy others, overcome what overwhelms others, or accomplish that which fear says is impossible. Don't allow fear to be your decision maker. Let your faith determine your future.

Questions for Reflections

1. Has fear ever paralyzed you in the past?

2. If so, how would you handle such situations in the future?
What has fear been "saying to you?"

3. What has fear prevented you from achieving? What has it cost you?

Morning Decree #13
Nike

"No, in all these things we are more than conquerors through him who loved us."
Romans 8:37

Nike, the billion-dollar sports gear company, coined the phrase, "just do It." What's not known by many is that the word *nike* is a Greek word and is found in the New Testament. In Romans 8 where the verse says, "We are more than conquerors." The word for *conquerors* in that verse is *nike*. Christ's substitutional death causes us to be more than *nike*, which means more than victorious! Being in the will of God positions you to win. Still, it requires knowing who you are in Christ and to whom you belong from a spiritual standpoint.

Often, you may view yourself through the lens of your circumstances and conclude that your are a victim. It's time to see yourself in light of God's perspective and begin to declare, "I am more than a conqueror through Jesus Christ. I am *nike*."

Questions for Reflections

1. What circumstances or situations are you facing in which you feel like a victim?

2. What does God, based on the Scriptures, say about you and your situation?

3. What words have you been thinking and speaking concerning yourself and your problem?

Morning Decree #14
Failing Isn't Fatal

"...for the righteous falls seven times and rises again..." Proverbs 24:16

Failure is not a sin. Failing isn't final. Failing isn't fatal unless you decide to quit. The Bible says, "A good man falls seven times, but . . ." It's the *but* part that should be your focus. Failing is an event, a moment in time. It will happen to everyone from time to time. We may fail at a business, job, relationship, or in sports. We may fail to follow God's word regarding some area of our life. Whatever the failure is, it doesn't have to be final or fatal. For it's not the failure that is the issue; it's what you do right after the failure that will determine the ultimate outcome. Get back up, refocus, start again, and keep moving forward.

Questions for Reflections

1. What failure in your life still haunts you to this day?

2. What did you learn from it?

3. Was your "next" action the right one? What was the result?

Morning Decree #15
Course Corrections

"Behold, I am doing a new thing; now it springs forth, do you not perceive it? I will make a way in the wilderness and rivers in the desert." Isaiah 43:19

Decisions. Life is full of them along with course corrections. One study shows that in a five-mile drive, drivers will make no less than 1,000 micro-course corrections to arrive at their destination. Your life is a journey. By design, it requires course corrections. That's the way it is for everyone. Regardless of the where you are going, who you're with, your socio-economic status, gender, or even where you live, you will have to make micro-course corrections to achieve your goals in life. You can avoid the major course corrections by making the small changes often.

Questions for Reflections

1. Name a time that you had to make a change in your life in order to achieve your goal?

2. Was it a big course change or small? How did you know you had to make the change?

3. How did you know when you needed to make the correction?

Morning Decree #16
No Change, No Growth

"I fed you with milk, not solid food, for you were not ready for it. And even now you are not yet ready . . ." 1 Corinthians 3:2

Change is inevitable. Without embracing change, healthy growth is impossible. Be it a business that fails to recognize the importance of social media or a car owner who ignores the need to get new tires or change the oil. If you don't accept the need to change, even what was good quickly goes bad. Our spiritual life is very much like a car that needs regular maintenance. In order to function at your best as you were designed, change is necessary. This change isn't always a result of something going wrong or some sin, but rather a by-product of maturing. As the Apostle Paul wrote to the Corinthians, by now you should be eating solid food, not breast milk.

Questions for Reflections

1. What areas do you need changes in your life?

2. Why have you delayed in making those changes?

3. Why do you think change seems to be hard for some people? Why do you think change is difficult for you?

Morning Decree #17
Becoming Comfortable with Being Uncomfortable

"All chastening seemeth for the present to be not joyous but grievous; yet afterward it yieldeth peaceable fruit unto them that have been exercised thereby, even the fruit of righteousness." Hebrews 12:11, KJV

Name an area in your life that is important to you. If you want to grow in that area, you will have to become uncomfortable before lasting growth can take place. Growth is like a new territory; it may feel awkward and undoubtedly unfamiliar—not to mention a bit scary sometimes. Nonetheless, if you want to experience something new, being comfortable is the first thing you have to let go.

There are different experiences God has for you that cannot be attained without becoming uncomfortable. New things are uncomfortable for most people. The leadings of the Spirit take you to places that feel very much like the wilderness, but you must remember this is not forever. Soon, you will be comfortable with what once made you very uneasy. When you see someone who isn't progressing in their life, career, or relationships, it's a clear indication the person has stopped growing. Don't let this happen to you. Growth is a beautiful thing, so allow being uncomfortable be the new comfortable in your life.

Questions for Reflections

1. What about the future is making you uncomfortable?

2. What is it that you need to do, but fear is stopping you from going for it?

3. What have you lost out on by not dealing with the temporary feeling of being uncomfortable?

Morning Decree #18
What You Hear Matters

"And he said to them, 'Pay attention to what you hear: with the measure you use, it will be measured to you, and still more will be added to you.'" Mark 4:24

Growing up, my teachers would say, "Stick and stones may break your bones, but names will never harm you." I know my teachers meant well, but the truth is, words do hurt because they become the recording repeatedly playing in the person's head who hears them. Reflect for a few moments on the things you said to yourself recently. Were they empowering or destructive? Self-talk is the idea of repeating to yourself words you heard about you. For example, "I'm ugly, I'm dumb," or even worse.

These kinds of phrases are often developed by hearing someone else say them about you or directly to you. God hates gossip and lies because both hurt, destroy, and could possibly ruin relationships, businesses, and even ministries. The real danger occurs when lies are believed and then repeated again and again. These words are the words that damn you. Remember, whatever you say to yourself is a seed being planted and watered in your life. Words are powerful. Let today be the first day of reconsidering what you say about yourself.

Questions for Reflections

1. What are you telling yourself?

2. Who said to you the words you are repeating?

3. What are three lies you are telling yourself? What are three truths you can put in place of those lies?

Morning Decree #19
Put Your Back into It

"So also faith, if it does not have works (deeds and actions of obedience to back it up), by itself is destitute of power (inoperative, dead)." James 2:17, AMP

Sometimes making something work requires more effort. Sweat equity. Energy. Sacrifice. All are necessary to obtain the things for which you are praying. One wrong assumption is if you only pray about it, you don't need to do nothing else beyond that. When we read the Scriptures, however you learn there is often something you still need to do to activate your miracle. Biblically speaking, faith is not a noun but a verb—that is, faith is action. If you really want to receive the desires of your heart, what actions are you willing to take to see the promises of God manifest in your life? What effort are you willing to put forth? In order words, are you willing to put your back into it?

Even redemption, which was the Father's plan, still required something more than desire. It needed a sacrifice and Jesus was that sacrifice. Jesus literally gave His back for us. Therefore, for you to receive the untold riches of His sacrifice, you have to do and take action, not just believe.

Questions for Reflections

1. What does "faith without works" mean to you?

2. Can you share two examples where you failed to put in the necessary effort to get it? What were the outcomes?

3. What are you presently praying for? Is there some action you need to take? If so, what is it?

Morning Decree #20
What are You Bringing to the Party?

"And beside this, giving all diligence, add to your faith virtue; and to virtue knowledge"
2 Peter 1:5

Who doesn't like a good party? I was raised knowing when invited to a party, I should at least offer to bring something. When it comes to receiving miracles, you need to bring your faith to the "party." The Scriptures say, "He, Jesus, couldn't do any mighty miracles in His hometown because of their unbelief" (Matthew 13:58). As hard as it may be to accept, all too often your failure to receive the answer lies with you—not with God or the devil for that matter. Perhaps you should adopt the philosophy; if it's going to be, it's up to me!

Jesus unquestionably was, while on earth, the ultimate miracle worker. However, when He came to this hometown, He couldn't do the type of miracles He did in other areas for one reason—because of the unbelief of the people. When you study the miracles of Jesus, often Jesus would say, "According to your faith." In no uncertain terms, Jesus was telling all who would listen that their faith was required to get the result. You need to bring something to the party. Your faith may be the missing part in the miracle equation.

Questions for Reflections

1. Can you remember a time when you invited guests to your home and they offered to bring something to share? If so, how did that make you feel?

2. In what ways can you demonstrate your faith?

3. Is there a miracle for which you are in need at this moment? If so, what is it that you are bringing to the situation?

Morning Decree #21
If You Can't See It or Hear It, It Doesn't Exist

"And when Jesus saw their faith, he said to the paralytic, 'Son, your sins are forgiven.'"
Mark 2:5

I often hear people say they have "blind faith," or they are taking a "leap of faith," or they are "stepping out on faith." The challenge I have with those approaches to faith is faith is neither blind nor is faith just "going for it." Faith can be seen and heard. In other words, you can see your faith by your corresponding action and words. The Holy Scriptures show an example where a group of people, who believed Jesus could heal their friend, opened up the roof and let their paralyzed friend down to bring him into the healing presence of Jesus. In response, Jesus said, "And seeing their faith . . ." That simple statement says to us that faith is more than a concept or an idea. Faith has substance or action.

Questions for Reflections

1. In what ways can your faith be seen?

2. Describe a time when you failed to take action.

3. Has anyone ever said they can "see" your faith?

Morning Decree #22
Can Anyone Hear It?

"And the Lord answered, 'If you had faith (trust and confidence in God) even [so small] like a grain of mustard seed, you could say . . .'" Luke 17:6, AMP

Faith says something, but so do doubt and unbelief. Have you ever been in the company of someone who was so negative all you could hear was their unbelief? They needed so much from God and others, but every other word out of their mouth was doom and gloom. Such speaking does not inspire hope, let alone communicate faith. Jesus said, "If you have the faith the size of a mustard seed, you could say . . . Faith can't help but speak; it always says the right thing(s), despite the obvious circumstances. What you truly believe resides in your heart, and what is in your heart is revealed by your words. My mom would always say, "watch your mouth." At the time, I don't know if she knew how biblical she was, but they were words to live by. What do your words say about your faith?

Questions for Reflections

1. Audit what came out of your mouth for the last 24 hours. Were you speaking words of faith regarding your situation or words of doubt?

2. How do you feel when you're around someone who always speaks negative things?

3. Why is it difficult at times to speak words of faith?

Morning Decree #23
It Takes Faith, Not Money

"Since we have the same spirit of faith according to what has been written, 'I believed, and so I spoke,' we also believe, and so we also speak . . ." 2 Corinthians 4:13

Not having has more to do with faith than other factors. Often when you are experiencing lack, your tendency may be to focus your attention on what you don't have, like money, peace, or friendships. You may not have those things, but the real shortage or deficiency is faith. Faith is the currency that enables you to get the stuff of life you need. However, as long as you continue to say what you don't have, rather than speak what you want and need, lack will be your constant companion.

Words matter. The words you speak reveal what you believe. It's not possible to speak one thing and experience another, any more than it's possible to plant corn seed and harvest watermelons. Your speech determines what shows up in your life. Faith is a result of what you think and consequently speak. Therefore, faith-filled words reap the good things you desire.

Questions for Reflections

1. What needs do you have and how are your words helping or hurting your situations?

2. To whom do you complain about your problems?

3. How can you have "more faith"?

Morning Decree #24
Work Works?

"But someone will say, 'You have faith and I have works.' Show me your faith apart from your works, and I will show you my faith by my works." James 2:18

My father owned a business for many years. My brother and I had the privilege (It didn't seem like it was a privilege at the time) of working for him on weekends and during summer breaks. We soon discovered working for the owner (who was my father) did not give us special privileges. If anything, we were required to work harder, do more, and to always be on time. We were paid well, just like every other employee—but nothing more. If we didn't work or show up on time, we didn't get paid. Whether we worked or not, we were still his sons. When we got paid, it wasn't because we were His sons. We got paid only if we worked. It wasn't good enough for us to have faith that we were Al's sons. We had to prove it by working, which was a good example of faith in action!

When it comes to your relationship with your Heavenly Father, working doesn't make you children, but your work shows you are His child. You need to be confident in who you are in Christ, assured of His unconditional love toward you. Your work doesn't make you "family." Instead it is your way of demonstrating your faith in and obedience to His word.

Questions for Reflections

1. In your own words, what is the difference between being an employee and the boss' kid?

2. Can you reflect upon times when you confused your working for God with your relationship with God?

3. What "work" should you be doing to demonstrate your spiritual relationship?

Morning Decree #25
Good Farmers Always Do This First

"Do not be deceived: God is not mocked, for whatever one sows, that will he also reap." Galatians 6:7

The examples from farming like planting seed and reaping a harvest are common in the Word of God. It seems God is fascinated by the law of sowing and reaping. When you reflect on the mindset of a farmer, you have to recognize there is more to farming than just planting and watering seeds. The first thing farmers do is determined by what kind of crop they want to grow. The type of crop dictates several other decisions, such as the geographic location, soil type, irrigation needs, time of the year to plant, and many other things. Still, the type of crop they wish to grow is the first thing they decide. Every seed is pre-programmed to produce a certain kind of crop. Farmers who plant 100 acres of soybeans are expecting soy to grow, not corn. It doesn't even cross their mind anything will come up other than soy (except maybe weeds).

The same is true when it comes to the type of spiritual crop you want to grow. When you sow, you should expect nothing different than the crop from the kind of seed you sow. Therefore, if you need money, sow money. If you need forgiveness, sow forgiveness.

Questions for Reflections

1. What do you need? What seed do you need to plant to "grow" that specific harvest?

2. What are you reaping in your life now?

3. Do you remember sowing those seeds, or worse, having those seeds been planted in the garden of your life?

Morning Decree #26
You're a Creator

"Then God said, 'Let us make man in our image, after our likeness . . .'"
Genesis 1:26

Everything you say creates either a positive or negative change in your life. When your language is congruent with God's will and Word, nothing is impossible. An example of this power is the story of the Tower of Babel. "At one time the whole earth had the same language and vocabulary" (Genesis 11:1-4). Nothing, absolutely nothing, is impossible when your speech is filled with God's Words. And when at least two or three align their words with God's will and Word, then Jesus is in their midst, adding His presence to the mix. Agreement is the place of power.

Your Creator made you in His likeness and image. That means, among other things, you are also a creator. You have the ability to make things by your thoughts and words. After all, isn't that how God created everything with words? Don't underestimate the power of your words and then choose to use your words to intentionally create what you want in life. You are a creator through speech, just as your Heavenly Father is.

Questions for Reflections

1. What areas of your life lack "good fruit" and what is the root cause?

2. In what ways are your words undoing your prayers?

3. What new words (Scriptures) should you be speaking to get the results you desire?

Morning Decree #27
What's Growing in Your Garden?

"Truly I say to you whoever says to this mountain, 'Be lifted up and thrown into the sea' and does not doubt in his heart but believes what he says will happen it will be done for him." Mark 11:23

In Mark 11:12, Jesus saw the barren fruit tree and remarked, "May no one eat from you again." Jesus was looking for fruit but found none. He went to the root of the problem (literally) and spoke to it. The fig tree withered from the root up. Ask yourself, "Am I producing fruit Jesus would want?"

The root cause of any lack can be found in the type of words–seeds spoken. If you want to make things happen, you must begin with your words. Your words establish things. Speak what and only what you want to see manifest in your life. What are you creating with your words? Do not allow your confession to be based on your feelings or the current facts. Speak God's word over your life in faith and do the things you know the Word says to do. Don't abandon what you have been saying because your senses still see the mountain in plain view. Hold to your confession based on your faith and you will be able to move the mountain.

Questions for Reflections

1. What areas of your life are lacking "good fruit" and what is the root cause?

2. In what ways are your words undoing your prayers?

3. What new words (Scriptures) should you use more to get the results I desire?

Morning Decree #28
Repent

"Repent (think differently; change your mind, regretting your sins and changing your conduct), for the kingdom of heaven is at hand." Matthew 3:2, AMP

You need to be a doer of the word and not just a "seed" collector! You have heard many sermons that contained many seeds of truth, and you probably don't need to listen to another one. What you need to do is apply the truths, or plant the seeds, from the messages you've already heard and see them bear fruit. Transformation takes place when you apply the Word of God to your life. When this occurs, true repentance takes place. Just knowing something, or even agreeing with it, doesn't mean you are doing it, let alone repented or changed. Adopting Jesus' style means that how Jesus lived His life—doing only what the Father did and saying only what the Father was saying—must also become your way of living.

Change occurs when you align your actions with the Word of God. Change, also known as transformation, happens one truth at a time. Just adjusting your behavior isn't true change unless your mind is leading the change! If you really want to repent, It happens as you shift the way you think.

Questions for Reflections

1. What does your lifestyle say about what you believe?

2. In what areas do you need to "repent?"

3. How will you repent, which is change the way you think?

Morning Decree #29
What's That One Thing?

"When the young man heard this, he went away sorrowful, for he had great possessions." Matthew 19:22

In Matthew 19:22, there's the story of a rich young ruler who did not want to part with his money so much so that he actually walked away from Jesus. Is there something that stands in your way of going deeper in your walk with Christ? Maybe it's something you had or were doing that was acceptable in the last stage of your spiritual life, but it's not right for you in this next season. It can be a relationship, habit, or a "thing" that's standing between you and your next level. You need to address whatever it is, or it will stop you in your tracks. Be willing to take off the backpack of life and let go of anything things that may be a hindrance or is weighing you down as Jesus reveals them to you.

Questions for Reflections

1. What's the one thing Jesus is asking you to release in order to grow spiritually?
2. What is the reason why this "thing" has been so difficult to give up or let go?
3. What changes will you need to make to maintain your new commitment once you let go?

Morning Decree #30
Anticipate A Storm

Now when Jesus saw a crowd around him, he gave orders to go over to the other side.
Matthew 8:18

The Word of God has the power to accomplish what it says but not without some unexpected opposition or detours along the way. Whatever you are expecting for the future, whatever God has promised you, don't let the unexpected hinder your expectation! It's best to be prepared for the unexpected, and when it comes, don't let it hinder you from moving forward with hope. Sometimes you hear the command from God, but when the unexpected comes, like a storm on the lake, you can forget what you were told to do.

In Matthew 8:18, Jesus gave orders to go to the other side of the lake. Jesus got in the boat and His disciples followed. Even though they were doing the will of God, a storm still arose. When you are on our way going somewhere with and for God, you should expect opposition. Jesus asked them, "Why are you fearful, O you of little faith?" Have you stopped believing you are going to arrive at the other side of whatever it is you're facing?

Questions for Reflections

1. Is there an unexpected event that has hindered your movement toward your goal?

2. What is the thing that easily trips you up?

3. How can you better prepare for the challenges you will face?

Morning Decree #31
The Power of Expectation

"And he said to them, 'Why are you afraid, O you of little faith?' Then he rose and rebuked the winds and the sea, and there was a great calm." Matthew 8:26

What you believe is revealed by what you do. Your level of expectation is the breeding ground for miracles. God gave you a clear command to go and then assurance that you are going to "the other side" of your problem. Because He spoke it, it shall come to pass. Rebuke the wind and the waves of your situations and don't stop rowing toward your dream. Though you know everything must respond to the name of Jesus, there's no substitute for belief-in-action, also known as faith. Rebuke the impediments *and* keep moving forward. You never know how many others will be saved, empowered, or even delivered from bondage because you kept going!

Recognize that you will face opposition. Anticipate it, but keep in mind that you, through your words, can speak to your situations with confidence in the authority found in the name of Jesus and His Words. Speak to it in Jesus' name and keep moving with your eyes on the destination.

Questions for Reflections

1. Has the Lord revealed to you where you are going? If so, where is it?

2. Have you allowed a storm to blow you off course? If yes, in what ways?

3. What steps do you need to take to get back on track?

Morning Decree #32
Confidence in Prayer

"In that day you will ask nothing of me. Truly, truly, I say to you, whatever you ask of the Father in my name, he will give it to you." John 16:23

What gives you confidence that God hears you when you pray? John 16:23–24 states, "I assure you: anything you ask the Father in My name, He will give you. Until now you have asked for nothing in My name. Ask and you will receive, so that your joy may be complete." The name of Jesus is not a punctuation mark that you tack onto the end of your prayers. It is so much for when you pray in His name, you are calling on an agreement in God made long ago, something called a blood covenant

A blood covenant is an agreement between two or more parties, and states that whatever belongs to the one party also belongs to the other—and vice versa. That also includes that both parties not only share their blessings but also their enemies. When you pray in the name of Jesus, it is an invocation of the Blood Covenant. It is because of the Covenant that your prayers are answered.

Questions for Reflections

1. Why do you believe God will answer your prayers?

2. When you pray, are you mindful of Jesus' sacrifice or just His name?

3. In your own words, explain what it means to pray in Jesus' name.

Morning Decree #33
The End of Yourself

"While they were worshiping the Lord and fasting, the Holy Spirit said, 'Set apart for me Barnabas and Saul for the work to which I have called them.'" Acts 13:2

In Acts 13:1-2, we see Barnabas and Saul being set apart for ministry, filled with the Holy Spirit and power. What caused this pivotal experience to happen? They were worshiping the Lord, fasting and praying. Both instruction and the strength to do the things God requires will come out of times of worship. Worship is more than a church service or an experience; it is an internal lifestyle that shows up externally.

When you worship, there is no place for discouragement. Taking time to lose yourself in worship allows God's presence to permeate your very essence. Through the intimacy of worship, you can receive renewed strength, courage, and instruction. In a sense, you will be living off His presence, breathing the breath of God.

Worship draws you closer to God. He sees into your heart and confronts you with your true self—your past, concerns, shortcomings, and pressures. The Holy Spirit will speak to you while you are worshiping. You come to the end of yourself (your ability), therefore giving God room and time to work. Worship is a great place to be.

Questions for Reflections

1. What hinders you from worshiping the Lord the way He deserves?

2. When are the hardest times for you to worship? Why?

3. In what ways can you demonstrate that you are a worshiper outside of church?

Morning Decree #34
Hidden

"For you have died, and your life is hidden with Christ in God." Colossians 3:3

As a true follower of Jesus, you become one with Him, which means you have died, and your life is hidden with Christ in God. When He died, you died also. "If you were raised with Christ, seek those things which are above, sitting at the right hand of God. Set your mind on things above, not on things on the earth" (Colossians 3:1).

Your new life (which is your real life) is hidden with Christ in God. You get your marching orders from Him. You are an ambassador for Christ. You may be a citizen of the country in which you were born, but you're an ambassador of the Kingdom of God. He has set you free from the spiritual powers of this world, and now you represent Him here on earth. Therefore, you live by a different set of governing laws, not the rules of this world system.

In the same way that Jesus died for you, you now live for Him. You live because of Him, which is one of the great secrets to living a fulfilled and overcoming life in Christ. Until you stop living for and unto yourself and allow the Christ–like life to manifest through you, frustration will be your constant companion.

Questions for Reflections

1. What does "to die to self" mean to you?

2. What does you being an ambassador of Christ imply to you?

3. In what ways are you still living for yourself as opposed to living for Christ?

Morning Decree #35
The Place of Your Death

"And going a little farther he fell on his face and prayed, saying, 'My Father, if it be possible, let this cup pass from me; nevertheless, not as I will, but as you will.'"
Matthew 26:39

Prayer is where your will goes to die. It is also where you learn God's heart in all matters. As you get better at hearing and praying for the heart of God, your authority in prayer will rise through the roof. However, this kind of intimacy only occurs as you learn to die to your will in prayer.

I know it sounds strange to speak of prayer as being the place where death occurs, but to begin to comprehend the will of God, you must first give up your own will. Jesus demonstrated this on several occasions, but none more dramatic than His "death prayer" in the Garden of Gethsemane. That was when He surrendered His will for that of the Father's. In essence, Jesus died in the Garden first, then on the cross.

After discerning His will, your prayer becomes the moment and place when you relinquish your claims. The safest place to be is in the will of God. Let prayer be the place where you consistently yield to the will of the Father. Remember, Christ died for you and you live for Him. This can only occur as you surrender to His Will in all things, which happens in and through prayer.

Questions for Reflections

1. What do you think is the purpose of prayer?

2. Do you have a set time and place for prayer on a daily basis?

3. How often do you consciously yield your will
to the will of the Father through prayer?

Morning Decree #36
What Moves You?

"... so shall it be done to the man who kills him ..." 1 Samuel 17:27

In 1 Samuel 17, we have the story of David versus Goliath. What was David's motivation to fight this giant? David heard Goliath mock the entire nation of Israel. Then David inquired as to what would happen for the man who defeated Goliath. The answer was, "The king will make the man who kills him very rich and will give him his daughter. The king will also make the household of that man's father exempt from paying taxes in Israel" (1 Samuel 17:25). Also, David knew that if Goliath was victorious, the nation of Israel would become the slaves of the Philistines.

An important point to note is that failure to harness the power of your motivation makes you a slave to the plethora of situations that surround you. Without tapping into your inner motivation, the divine power, your "giants" that could easily be defeated loom larger than life and hold you hostage through fear.

Identify your *why*—the deepest, most compelling thing that can motivate you—and allow it to push you past your fears and into your greatest success.

Questions for Reflections

1. How would you define motivation?

2. What motivates you?

3. How do you keep yourself motivated in the face of your "giants?"

Morning Decree #37
Beware of the Un-motivators

"Why have you come down? And with whom have you left those few sheep in the wilderness? I know your presumption and the evil of your heart, for you have come down to see the battle." 1 Samuel 17:28b

You will always encounter naysayers like David's brothers who knew you "way back when" whenever you attempt to do something for the Lord. However, your movement will expose their heart toward you and reveal their own fears. Sadly, they will often try to discourage you based on their personal issues and perceptions. I call these people, Un-Motivators. An Un-motivator is someone or something that strips you of the necessary courage to fight for your dream. They will use your past, present, or even their perception of your potential against you. Moreover, if you're not wise to this tactic, you will become Un-motivated. You will fall begin to resemble those who look the part, but don't accomplish very much in life.

Pray for them but stay focused. Whatever you do, don't stop believing in yourself or your dream. David's brothers mocked him and King Saul thought very little of him, as did Goliath. However, David knew victory was assured but only if he kept his focus.

Questions for Reflections

1. At present, who are the un-motivators in your life?

2. What is the dream, goal, or vision that you need to maintain as your focal point?

3. What or who keeps you motivated?

Morning Decree #38
The Mind: A Terrible Thing to Waste

"From that time Jesus began to preach, saying, 'Repent, for the kingdom of heaven is at hand.'" Matthew 4:17

The mind is the command center for our actions, both voluntary and involuntary. As the adage goes, "What the mind can conceive, the body can achieve." This concept isn't simply a mind over matter practice, however. The mind, for the follower of Jesus, is the arena where true faith battles fear and spiritual warfare takes place. Repentance, changing the way one thinks, is the starting point for changing your life. Change your mind, you transform your life.

Your life changes according to the degree you are able and willing to change your mind. What you think today has much to do with what you experience in your life tomorrow. There is no instant way to do it nor are there any shortcuts. You must go through a process much like a butterfly and that process will make you stronger. If the butterfly does not fight its way out of the cocoon, its wings will not be strong enough to fly. That is how it is with you. Do not deprive yourself of the opportunity to become strong. Embrace the need to repent or change your mind, work through it, and growth will manifest.

Questions for Reflections

1. How have your thoughts gotten you into trouble before? How so?

2. What does the word "repent" mean to you?

3. Why do you think Jesus commands you to repent?

Morning Decree #39
Who Has the Key?

"If you forgive the sins of any, they are forgiven them; if you withhold forgiveness from any, it is withheld." John 20:23

Forgiveness is part of the process of spiritual growth and transformation. Release the past or you will be carrying it like a ball and chain into your tomorrow. Yesterday(s) can be a prison. Mourn your past, but do not allow it to turn into grief. Grief is a spirit and locks you into the negative emotions of the past that prevent you from moving forward. Grief causes you to replay the pain of past experiences.

The act of forgiving others is mainly for the benefit of the offended person and not just the person that hurt us. If we hold on to their sins, we become the keepers of the pain and anger while they have gone on with their lives. Release those who have hurt you in Jesus' name. Remember it's a faith exercise, so don't expect a particular feeling. Do it in obedience. Do it by faith. Sometimes, you will have to "forgive them" several times before healing occurs in your heart and mind.

Questions for Reflections

1. Describe in your own words how unforgiveness has affected you.

2. Are you holding unforgiveness against anyone?

3. Why is it so hard for you to let it go?

Morning Decree #40
It's Always a Choice

"And whenever you stand praying, forgive, if you have anything against anyone, so that your Father also who is in heaven may forgive you your trespasses."
Mark 11:25

When someone injures you through words or actions, it can be painful and challenging to overcome. What's more, the lasting damage isn't in the sin committed against you, but in the unforgiveness which you harbor. Unforgiveness is like an infection left behind after an injury. Unless it is treated and removed, it could compromise every other biological function in your body. Forgiveness is a divine antiseptic and antibody. As you yield to God, you will gradually recover and detox from the poison of unforgiveness.

To forgive is a conscious, deliberate decision on your part. You must make a choice to forgive. Ask God to help release the sins of others away from your life. Again, it's by faith and it's a choice. It's a decision which requires courage and determination. This decision becomes easier when you remember that forgiveness is a command and benefits you the most. Choose to forgive. Do it today.

Questions for Reflections

1. What do you think is the purpose of forgiveness?

2. How do you practice forgiveness?

3. Have you forgiven yourself of the past mistakes? If not, why?

Morning Decree #41
It Shall Come to Pass

"The earth produces by itself, first the blade, then the ear,
then the full grain in the ear." Mark 4:28

Waiting for the manifestation of promise from God is indeed a test of our faith. It doesn't require a ton of faith to believe God for a promise that, in reality, doesn't matter that much to you. However, when you really need a breakthrough, sometime it feels like an eternity during the waiting period.

The faith process involves staying in a posture of expectation while waiting for something to happen. It's similar to when a farmer plants a seed. The farmer waits in expectation for the maturing of that seed. There are things they do in the waiting season that are similar to what you should do in your spiritual waiting period. Sadly, many unfulfilled dreams are the result of neither understanding nor cooperating with how seedtime and harvest work and part of that is a waiting period. You need to learn how to wait without worrying yourself sick. The seed will produce. It's just a matter of time.

Questions for Reflections

1. What prayer requests, like seeds, have you sown that have yet to produce?

2. Why does it seem more difficult for our generation to wait than previous generations?

3. What are some things you, as the farmer, can do during this waiting period?

Morning Decree #42
Keep Doing It Anyway

"... for we cannot but speak of what we have seen and heard." Acts 4:20

When you are trying to do the will of God, there will be opposition, hindrances, and persecution. You can count on it. Acts 4:13-14 shows how Peter and John were doing God's work and the Sanhedrin had taken notice that they had been hanging with Jesus. In verses 16-17, they asked, "What shall we do with these men? For indeed a notable miracle has been done through them that is evident to all who dwell in Jerusalem, and we cannot deny it. Let us severely threaten them."

"But Peter and John answered them . . . we are unable to stop speaking about what we have seen and heard" (Acts 4:19-20). Peter and John did not back down and neither should we. Don't stop doing the thing you have been assigned to do. Do what is in front of you. Do what you know to do and don't give up. However, when you realize that trouble comes with the territory and remember that God will ultimately deliver you, you will have a much easier time during the drama. Whatever you do, don't stop what you have been tasked to accomplish.

Questions for Reflections

1. What are you doing right now that is drawing the attention of adversaries?

2. Have you ever quit doing something because of criticism or persecution?

3. What would you be doing at this stage of your life
if you felt you had sufficient support?

Morning Decree #43
Obey the Instructions

"And he said to them, 'How many loaves do you have? Go and see.' And when they had found out, they said, 'Five, and two fish.'" Mark 6:38

The first step to a miracle is to assess the situation as it presently is. Jesus asked the disciples, "How many loaves do you have?" He told them to "go look." The disciples obeyed the instruction. Miracles occur when instructions are followed. The Word of God is replete with examples of miracles of all kinds: provision, healing, commanding nature, etc. Have you ever noticed that in almost every case the "miracle" was preceded by an act of obedience?

Such was the case when thousands of people needed to be fed with minimal provisions on hand. When being obedient to Jesus' instructions, and not before, the needed miracle came to pass. Our challenge, however, is that we either want guarantees that our actions will make the miracle happen, or we get lost in trying to figure out how God will perform the miracle. You job is to believe and obey, how it happens is God's part.

Questions for Reflections

1. What need(s) do you have?

2. What resources do you have on hand to meet that need? Be specific.

3. What have you been instructed to do from the Word of God with the resources you presently have under your control?

Morning Decree #44
Are You Out of Order?

"Then he commanded them all to sit down in groups on the green grass. So they sat down in groups, by hundreds and by fifties." Mark 6:39-40

After having an accurate accounting of the resources on hand, Jesus gave further instructions to the disciples. He said, "Have all the people sit down in groups on the green grass." The disciples sat them down in ranks of hundreds and fifties. God is a God of order so order precedes your overflow. You need to be in order before He can bless you as He wants to, and how you need Him to. Every miracle is a result of a decision to obey a seemingly insignificant unrelated directive. In this case, it was *sit down in groups*. There's nothing particularly supernatural about sitting down but unless those innocuous instructions were followed, the rest of the miracle process would have been aborted.

The obedience asked of you is rarely something overwhelming, nor is it something you can't do—though it will require faith and courage, His commands are doable by His grace. He is going to take your little (micro-obedience) and multiply it. In the process, God will be glorified and you will blessed. Order first, then overflow.

Questions for Reflections

1. What are some examples where being in order is important?

2. What's another name for failing to do what someone asks?

3. Are their areas of your life that are out of order?

Morning Decree #45
Our Rights in Praying

"Pray then like this: 'Our Father in heaven, hallowed be your name.'" Matthew 6:9

Have you been praying earnestly but not receiving answers to your prayers? There are some rules found in the Word of God governing successful prayers that must be followed. You have been taught that praying is merely talking to God. While in a genuine way that's true, but that's not all it is.

You should be praying the Word of God. If you are praying the Word, then you know you are praying the Father's will and He will always honor His will. However, if you don't know what is written, you can't pray what is written. I cannot overemphasize enough the importance of praying with the Word of God. Knowing and praying the Word of God is like reading the last will and testament to see if your loved has bequeathed something to you. You have a right to the contents of the will if your name is in the will. The one hindrance may be not knowing your legal rights and what belongs to you! The Word of God is the will of the Lord Jesus Christ. Once you know and pray in accordance to the contents of His will (the Word), you can have confidence you will receive that for which you are praying.

Questions for Reflections

1. How's your prayer life? On what basis should you judge its success?

2. Why does God the Father answer our prayers?

3. What are you claiming belongs to you from the will of God?

Morning Decree #46
The Legal Side of Prayer

"Consequently, he is able to save to the uttermost those who draw near to God through him, since he always lives to make intercession for them." Hebrews 7:25

A will does not go into effect until someone dies. Where a will exists, one must establish that the death has occurred. When Jesus died, for three days the courts of heaven established His death. He rose from the dead and then became the executor of the will, His will. Therefore, His will is in effect.

When you are praying, you are asking that the provisions contained in the will, established by the death of Jesus, be released to you. The granting of the request isn't because of need, race, geography, or self-righteous, but because the legal requirements have been satisfied. Jesus Christ did that for you. He advocates on your behalf. He's your lawyer who has never lost a case.

Your prayers are in a sense a legal transaction. The enemy of your soul, who brings accusations against you to the court of heaven, loses whenever you make your petition based upon what Jesus Christ accomplished for you. Pray in the name of Jesus. God the Father, the Judge of all Creation, has ruled in your behalf.

Questions for Reflections

1. Do you know the parts of the will that pertain to your specific situation?

2. How does not knowing your rights affect the outcome of your prayers?

3. How does the feeling of condemnation affect your confidence in getting your prayers answered?

Morning Decree #47
Self-Selection

"... for we walk by faith, not by sight." 2 Corinthians 5:7

Life, especially your life in Christ, is a series of decisions. You can choose to accept Jesus Christ as your Savior or not, and then you can choose to believe His Word or not. You have the power of choice. However, when you decide to doubt, or to worry rather than remain steadfast in your faith in the integrity of God's word, you forfeit the right to have God's best for your life. Did you realize you can self-select right out of the next level of your faith by allowing fear to decide at what stage you will stop growing? At that point, you allow your emotions to rule and block your ability to receive God's best for your life.

The prophet Moses told the people he was leading, "Choose life." He knew that it was a choice. You and I must choose to believe God instead of circumstances, symptoms, and feelings. It is the Word of God that remains unchanging and immutable. whereas situations and emotions are subject to change like the wind. Remain in faith and self-select to go on to the next level as a way of life.

Questions for Reflections

1. In the past, how have your emotions affected your decisions?

2. Have you ever made a decision based on emotions, which in retrospect was the wrong decision?

3. What emotional situation are you presently facing? How will you handle it knowing that emotions are not always (or rarely are) reliable indications of what action you should take?

Morning Decree #48
You Possess What You Confess

"Death and life are in the power of the tongue and those who love it will eat its fruit."
Proverbs 18:21

You are the sum total of your thoughts and words. What's living in your life, is what has come out of your mouth. The words you speak are the building blocks of the edifices that make your life what it is. Your words created everything in our life—everything. As the Scriptures show us, "The things that appear were created by things which are *not* visible" (Hebrews 11:3, Emphasis added).

What you speak over time, is what shows up in your life—either for your good or detriment. Words, and more specifically, the words you speak impact your life and the lives around you. Like your Creator, who created through words, you too possess the unique ability to build or destroy, unify or divide, bless or curse with the words you speak. You will possess what you confess. You will see what you say. Words, though invisible, take shape, substance, and form in time. As my mother often told me, "Watch what you say."

Questions for Reflections

1. Are the words you're speaking creating life or releasing death?

2. Can you remember a time when words were spoken to you, and even though they were not true, they still hurt you deeply?

3. Have you ever spoken words intentionally to someone that you knew would hurt that person?

Morning Decree #49
Words Are Like Feathers

"There is one who speaks rashly, like a piercing sword; but the tongue of the wise brings healing." Proverbs 12:18

The power of words is often understated because they are a commodity, to which almost everyone has unlimited access. It costs a person nothing to say something. Free speech, which is a protected right under the Constitution of the United States of America, is something that most people exercise generously—and without much thought. The problem is that those readily available words, though free, can inflict significant damage or provide much comfort. They can destroy or heal.

Just like the feathers in a pillow, words are very light and go wherever the wind blows. Therefore, you must not be fooled or indifferent to the power of words, because just like the feathers you sleep on, they also can give you rest. However, those same feathers, when released to the wind, cannot be recaptured, and neither can the words you release out of your mouth. Speak what you want the wind to carry. Speak for intentional, predictable, and beneficial results.

Questions for Reflections

1. Can you describe a time when you said something you later regretted?

2. What, if anything, could you do (or did you do) to rectify the situation?

3. How easy is it for words to be forgotten?

Morning Decree #50
Learning to be Led

"When the Spirit of truth comes, he will guide you into all the truth..." John 16:13

Often it is said that a baby will fall on their rear end at least 300 times before learning to walk. It is the same when being led by the Spirit of God: Mistakes are inevitable. Just as a baby is encouraged to try again, you too must remain in a growth posture and then means you will stumble as you learn to walk. This growth posture may at times be frustrating and full of errors. Nevertheless, if you stay teachable, you will get the hang of it, and after a while, being led by the Spirit will be as natural as breathing air.

One of the most important elements in being led by the Spirit of God is knowing the Word of God. The Word of God will be the boundaries, or the guardrail, as you learn. It's the foundation for all activity of the Holy Spirit. The leading of Holy Spirit will never, ever lead you away from the Word of God. At all times and in all ways, the Word of God and the Holy Spirit will be in total agreement.

Questions for Reflections

1. Why does it seem so difficult to be correctly led by the Holy Spirit?

2. Can you describe a time when you thought you were following the Holy Spirit, but later realized you were not?

3. What did you learn from that experience?

Morning Decree #51
Working Together

"When the Spirit of truth comes, he will guide you into all the truth, for he will not speak on his own authority, but whatever he hears he will speak, and he will declare to you the things that are to come." John 16:13

The Holy Spirit will lead you appropriately if the Word of God is in you. As you talk it, speak it, live it, you will know the right way to go. The Holy Spirit only leads according to the precepts and principles of the Word of God. When the Holy Spirit richly dwells in you, you will be able to discern and see more clearly as well as be guided much more easily—knowing right from wrong. Nonetheless, the Word of God is not the letters in a book, but rather it is the person of Jesus Christ: "And the Word became flesh . . ." (John 1:14). "Jesus is the Word of God . . ." (John 1:1-3). You get to know Jesus through study and practice of the Word of God.

Also, the Holy Spirit, who is One with Jesus the Son and God the Father, responds to the direction given by the Word which is Jesus. As you come to know the Word more intimately, you will know the desires of the Holy Spirit. It is through this level of intimacy that you learn how to be led, or I should say, follow the leading of the Holy Spirit.

Questions for Reflections

1. Why has it been hard for you to follow the Holy Spirit in the past?

2. What changes do you need to make to be led by the Spirit?

3. What mistakes have you made because you failed to follow the leading of the Holy Spirit?

Morning Decree #52
Is Your Faith Strong?

"Finally, be strong in the Lord and in the strength of His might." Ephesians 6:10

Several things can make or break your faith. You must follow the example of Jesus. You cannot expect God to answer you if you are choosing to ignore His voice or His Word. You cannot expect to be blessed beyond measure if you do not do what He has told you to do. Obedience builds strong faith and confidence in hearing the voice of the Lord.

Do things seem a little chaotic right now? What was the last thing God told you to do that you have not gotten around to doing yet? If you believe He is God, then you will do whatever He says. Very simply put, to disobey God is a sure sign of lack of faith in Him. Who would defy the living God of the Bible? Only those who don't truly believe He is God. You must ask yourself, "Am I doing the last thing God told me to do?"

Questions for Reflections

1. Why has it been difficult for you to obey God's Word for your life?

2. How do you think God feels about your disobedience?

3. Why is it that people believe they will still get blessed despite living in unrepentant sin?

Morning Decree #53
Your Miracle Is in Your Seed

"While the earth remains, seedtime and harvest, cold and heat, summer and winter, day and night, shall not cease." Genesis 8:22

God has not left us without answers to our problems. Our God works through small, seemingly insignificant things, like seeds. Because seeds are small, their level of impact is deceptive. The power of a seed is independent upon its size. Truth be told, everything is a byproduct of something very small.

Because your problems seem so big at times, you may find it hard to believe that something as small as a "seed" can make the difference. The fact is that when God wanted to change a situation, whether it was the environment or even the course of humanity, He used a seed, Words. Hidden in a seed is the answer to a barren life. Contained in a seed, is your future. More specifically, you possess the seed that contains your future. You are not without hope, for hope is divinely wrapped in the seed you presently have in your possession.

Questions for Reflections

1. Can you describe a time or an event in which a little action yielded a huge result?

2. What problem(s) are you facing that seem to be beyond natural solutions?

3. What do you see as 'seeds,' if planted, that could produce a change in your situation?

Morning Decree #54
Have You Planted Enough Seeds?

"And Elisha said to her, 'What shall I do for you? Tell me; what have you in the house?'
And she said, 'Your servant has nothing in the house except a jar of oil.'"
2 Kings 4:2

There are many types of seeds, too many to name or catalog I would imagine. Every living thing you see came from a seed of some kind. Indeed, every fruit or vegetable you purchase at the supermarket, if it isn't genetically modified originated, is from a seed. Seed types produce a predictable fruit or harvest. Spiritually speaking, there are four categories of seeds, and each of us has one or more of these seeds at any given moment: The seeds of time, money, words, and thoughts.

How we invest (sow) those precious seeds is the determining factor in what we are experiencing in life. *Words*: What you say structures your future. Your words matter. Your words become matter. *Thoughts*: Your thoughts become your words. You may not always be able to control what comes to your mind, but you can determine those upon which you meditate. *Money*: You have something we trade for something else. It may not be dollars and cents, but rather some form of currency or other valuables (I'm calling this *money*). *Time*: You are given 24 hours, 14,440 minutes each day for every day you live.

Questions for Reflections

1. How do you view your seed account? Abundant or lacking?

2. Which seeds (words, thoughts, money, or time) do you intentionally invest in your life?

3. Which of the seeds have you neglected?

Morning Decree #55
Is It a Seed?

"He told them many things in parables: 'A farmer went out to sow his seed.'"
Matthew 13:3

God uses nature and agricultural metaphors to get His points across. In doing so, He gives us unique insight into how the Kingdom of God operates. Jesus introduced one the most famous parables by saying, "A farmer went out to sow…" (Luke 8:5). I consider this the master plan parable because as we understand the meaning of this parable, we can more easily understand other teachings of Jesus and how the Kingdom of God operates.

When you look at the four types of seeds—thoughts, words, money, and time—in light of the question, is it a seed?, you can quickly understand that at our disposal, at any time, is the opportunity to plant a seed for a future harvest. Whether we are conscious of the laws of seedtime and harvest or not, you can sow one or more of these seeds every day. An underutilized strategize to combat a lack of seed is sowing in order to get even more seed. The key, however, to producing perpetual harvests (harvests of your design) is understanding that you are "seeding" something, somewhere every day and doing so on purpose.

Questions for Reflections

1. What and when was the last time you intentionally planted seeds?

2. What is your harvest expectation?

3. What would it require for you to be a consistent sower?

Morning Decree #56
Where Does Your Seed Come From?

"He who supplies seed to the sower and bread for food will supply and multiply your seed for sowing and increase the harvest of your righteousness." 2 Corinthians 9:10

There's one thing we cannot accuse God of not doing, and that is not supplying us with seeds. God as the supplier of your seed is one of the most important revelations a follower of Jesus can have. God has and will always supply you with the "seed" for your next harvest. According to this Scripture, He will even multiply your seed for sowing. Still, when you are in immediate need, it's hard to think of the answer to your need being "planting a seed." Found in the mystery of "how the Kingdom works" is an understanding of the law of seedtime and harvest

The answers you will need are like the harvest the farmer hopes to reap in due time. However, no farmer would fail to plant and still expect a harvest. The answer to his or her barren fields is in the bags of seed in the barn. Unless and until those seeds (the seed you now have) are planted, the needed harvest will not come.

Questions for Reflections

1. Would you consider yourself as one who has a farmer's mentality? Why or why not?

2. What actions can you take right now to begin setting yourself up for multiple harvests?

3. What has been the biggest hindrance to you sowing enough seed for an abundant harvest in the past?

Morning Decree #57
What to Do When You Don't Know What to Do

"We do not know what to do . . . but our eyes are on you." 2 Chronicles 20:3,12

Are you in a "wilderness" right now? What is it that worries you? Worry and worship can't co-exist at the same time. Looking at the story of King Jehoshaphat, you learn what to do when life is overwhelming. Second Chronicles 20:3 reads, "Jehoshaphat was afraid, and he resolved to seek the Lord. Then he proclaimed a fast for all of Judah, who had gathered to seek the Lord." The first thing you need to do is acknowledge that you don't know what to do! It is such a simple response, but often we don't do it.

It's only human to be frightened when faced with a serious and unexpected situation. However, as a follower of Jesus, a believer in the all-powerful, loving God, you need to train yourself to look toward heaven in times of stress. King Jehoshaphat's strategy for approaching a daunting problem is still relevant today. Recognize from what source your help comes, seek God for answers, and in the meantime decide to worship rather than worry.

Questions for Reflections

1. What's your default reaction to sudden trouble?

2. Is worry a sin? If so, why?

3. What are some practical things you can do to help defeat worry in your life?

Morning Decree #58
What Does It Mean to Worship?

"You will not need to fight in this battle. Stand firm, hold your position, and see the salvation of the Lord on your behalf." 2 Chronicles 20:17

In the Hebrew language, the name Judah means praise. Sometimes, you may stop worshiping during challenging times. However, if you fail to worship, then you will fail to win. Worship is a response to who God is. You must discipline yourself to seek the Lord, regardless of the situation. Worship positions you to receive God's strategy for a breakthrough. The Scriptures read,

> The Spirit of the Lord came on Jahaziel. "Listen all Judah carefully. This is what the Lord says: Do not be afraid or discouraged because of this vast number, for the battle is not yours but God's. You do not have to face this battle. Position yourselves, stand still, and see the salvation of the Lord. He is with you. Do not be afraid or discouraged. Tomorrow, go out to face them, for Yahweh is with you" (2 Chronicles 20:14-17).

This Word came only as the people focused their intentions on pursuing God in the midst of what must have been a very stressful situation. How you respond in times of testing will determine how long the trial will last and what the outcome may ultimately be. Choose worship over worry.

Questions for Reflections

1. How does a stressful situation affect you physically, emotionally, and spiritually?

2. When was the last time you worshiped God rather than worry about a problem? What was the issue and how did you worship Him?

3. What can you do to discipline yourself to respond with worship instead of fear?

Morning Decree #59
Number One Dream Killer

"But overhearing what they said, Jesus said to the ruler of the synagogue, 'Do not fear, only believe.'" Mark 5:36

Many things can kill yours dreams. However, one thing that will snuff it out quicker than most anything else is stress. Stress, especially prolonged stress, will strip you of motivation, energy, and strength. It can affect your vision, and even physically constrict blood flow throughout your body. If you want to see your vision manifest in your lifetime, correctly dealing with stress is not an option.

The chief cause of stress isn't bad news, relational dysfunction, or money problems. It's not sickness, or rejection, or even losing a job. The number one cause of stress is the failure to see God as God in your situation. Why would anyone worry if they knew, from God's perspective, how things will turn out for their good? You never see God the Father or even Jesus the Son worry and that's because of their perfect view of tomorrow.

If you knew shortly after receiving a proverbial "pink slip" from your employer that you would receive a new job with better benefits, stock options, six-week paid vacation, company car, signing bonus, etc., would you worry even though you were holding a dismissal notice in your hand? The answer is a resounding no—you wouldn't be worried at all. The point is that you calculate stress in your mind so if you can align your thoughts correctly with the truth that God is working all things for your good, then your stress would dissipate and you could carry on with your life's work and vision undeterred by minor, or even major, setbacks.

Questions for Reflections

1. What are the three major causes of stress in your life?

2. How do your problems affect your vision for your life?

3. What does your response to stress say about your view of God?

Morning Decree #60
Blind with 20/20 Vision

"Here is a call for the endurance of the saints, those who keep the commandments of God and their faith in Jesus." Revelation 14:12

Sight is precious and often taken for granted until illness or accident threaten it. Spiritual blindness is even more common than we might think and is a result of sin or other problems eclipsing your view of God or His Word. In other words, when problems come, we tend to forget that God is God, *and* He is our Father. Whatever the issue is, the matter has not caught Him off guard.

Issues in life cause many to forget the sun still shines even on cloudy days and that's easy to do. From God's perspective (which must become your perspective), you know that all things are working out for your ultimate good. As you accept this, you will worry less and less and worship more and more. Don't let what you can't see blind you to the truth that the Son is still shining in your life. Nothing and no one can prevent that—except you. The challenge is to maintain that perspective even in the dark times.

Questions for Reflections

1. Why do people lose sight of God during difficult seasons?

2. What is the one aspect about God you forget when in crisis?

3. What are some ways you can retain your spiritual sight, even in dark times?

Morning Decree #61
The Power of Knowing Why

"For God so loved the world, that he gave his only Son, that whoever believes in him should not perish but have eternal life." John 3:16

Motivation is the thing that makes you move. Knowing your *why* is of the utmost importance. The w-h-y is anything that causes you to do something, to go for it, and to keep going for it again and again. Your *why* is your deepest motivation for doing something. God so loved the world He gave His son as our substitute and that makes us God's *why*. His love for us is His motivation to save us. He gave His only begotten son as proof of His commitment to restore us.

Your *why* is already in your life. Your *why* won't allow anything to stop you. It's something, someone, or some goal that already exists in your mind or heart. You may not even be conscious of it, but it's there. When you discover and then focus on it, you will never again have a problem with motivation.

Questions for Reflections

1. What's your *why*?

2. What's stopping you from pursuing your most important goals?

3. What goals do you need to restart or resume?

Morning Decree #62
See Past Your Problems

"And he said to his servant, 'Go up now, look toward the sea.' And he went up and looked and said, 'There is nothing.' And he said, 'Go again,' seven times."
1 Kings 18:43

Problems are like walls and fences that prevent you from seeing beyond the immediate. Instead of being able to see or plan for the future, you are stuck reviewing or fretting your present circumstances. If this lingers, you become discouraged. When discouragement persists for a long time, you may quit or, at a minimum, stop believing that there is *more* for you than what you are experiencing.

Focus that is broken or fragmented is one of the main reasons we fail as believers despite being "more than conquerors." You need to learn how to see as Jesus saw. He saw past your problem and instead saw the Father's plan for you. Don't focus on the obstacle, focus beyond the problem. Your ability to remain steadfast and unmovable concerning the work of the Lord is critical to your success in your chosen area. Keep the faith and stay focused on your vision.

Questions for Reflections

1. What's currently blocking your view of your goals?

2. How does this obstacle affect your emotions and your motivation?

3. What are three things could you do to keep the vision in plain view despite the obstacles in your way?

Morning Decree #63
Even More Grace

"But by the grace of God I am what I am . . ." *1 Corinthians 15:10*

When we say people are "graceful," we often mean they can do a certain thing effortlessly—or at least it appears effortless to the observer. Whether it's as easy as it looks is another story, but the divine element of grace takes the difficult, even the impossible, and causes it to happen.

I define grace as God's ability and power made available to you through Christ Jesus. It is an intangible force that enables you to go through life supernaturally. While it's infinitely more complex and all-encompassing than that definition, grace is nevertheless a force that enables things to happen in your life. Becoming increasingly aware of God's grace will reduce your daily level of anxiety. That's why I urge you to receive the grace of God through Jesus Christ today. It will make all the difference in your life.

Questions for Reflections

1. How do you define the grace of God?

2. Identify people you know and describe what they do with grace.

3. What do you need to do to get more grace?

Morning Decree #64
Don't Work for It

"And his grace toward me was not in vain. On the contrary, I worked harder than any of them, though it was not I, but the grace of God that is with me."
1 Corinthians 15:10b

Grace is free, meaning you don't have to work or earn it. Grace has no price and God gives it whenever it is needed. Grace is like currency. For example, say you need to buy something, but you don't have the money. It would be grace that someone gave you the money. You didn't earn it; it was offered to you and you received it. That's grace. Keep in mind you don't earn grace; you learn Grace. You don't purchase grace; you receive grace.

You have more grace than you will ever need. You have more grace than you will ever want. It may be hard for you to believe sometimes that grace is free when you live in a world where everything is based on performance. God's grace, even His saving grace, can't be earned, and on no occasion is it ever based on merit. By faith, grace is received and comes from God's unfathomable love for you.

Questions for Reflections

1. What was the last thing you were given that had nothing to do with your performing for it?

2. Why does it seem so difficult for believers to receive the grace of God?

3. When was the last time you gave someone grace?

Morning Decree #65
Without Even Asking for It

"... so that in the coming ages he might show the immeasurable riches of his grace in kindness toward us in Christ Jesus." Ephesians 2:7

Our minds will quit before our grace ever runs out. Despite our sin and rebellion, God wanted to show His love for us. He did so by sending Jesus Christ to die for us. "If God is for us, who can be against us?" (Romans 8:31). God gave us grace when we knew we didn't deserve it. He gave us grace before we were conscious of our need for it. It's like parents who anticipate the full length and breadth of their children's needs before the need ever arises. Therefore, they make provision for that need, bank it, and when the child becomes aware of their need, the parent makes it" available—that's grace.

It's mind-blowing to think, let alone receive, such a marvelous thing as the grace of God. Grace is available to you regardless of your present spiritual status. Grace would cease being grace if the precondition was your goodness. Grace is unearned. Grace is learned.

Questions for Reflections

1. Read Romans 8:32-39 and list what you fear might cause God to turn away from you.

2. After listing those fears, re-read Romans 8:32-39. Hear the words as you read and think about which words or phrases mean the most to you.

3. If nothing will separate you from Christ's love, then why do you choose to let obstacles keep you living below the level of grace afforded to you?

Morning Decree #66
It's a Grace Thing

"For by grace you have been saved through faith. this is not your own doing; it is the gift of God . . ." Ephesians 2:8

God gave you grace before you knew you needed it. He answered "it" and solved "it" before "it" ever existed. The Scriptures reveal, "For you are saved by grace through faith . . . it is God's gift" (Ephesians 2:8). Salvation pertains to more than the afterlife, but is also for the here and now. This salvation includes deliverance from temporal evil and provision for prosperity, healing, peace, and eternal life. All these things and more are made available to you by the grace of God. You can't earn these magnificence benefits. No amount of goodness would cause you to merit such wonders. Faith in Jesus Christ acquires the blessings of God. It was His "work" that made them possible. That is why call it *amazing* grace.

When you lose sight of this bonanza, which is grace as revealed in Jesus Christ, you will invariably struggle. It's like repeatedly telling a person, "Go into the bedroom" when the person is *already* in the bedroom. All one has to do is acknowledge they are present in that room. They "have it" or "they are there." They need not do anything except believe and receive the benefits of being "there." You are "there" which is placed in the manifold grace of God. Believe and receive it.

Questions for Reflections

1. Describe a moment in which you were looking for something only to find you had it all the time.

2. What is it that you are dealing with in your life that is frustrating to you?

3. How can experiencing the grace of God elevate your frustration?

Morning Decree #67
It's a Faith Thing

"For in it the righteousness of God is revealed from faith for faith, as it is written, 'The righteous shall live by faith.'" Romans 1:17

Like young children, we tend to need proof that what is promised to us is going to actually take place. Just tell a five-year-old child they are going to Disneyland for Christmas, and count how many times they'll ask you, "When are we going?" "How many more days until we leave?" Until the child rests in knowing that the promiser will make good on the promise, they will not rest. They must learn to receive the "trip" by faith, trusting that it will manifest as promised.

It's that way for you. You must learn to receive the promised benefit by faith, resting in the integrity of the One who promised. He can be trusted to fulfill His Word concerning you. You often fail to "go to Disney" not because the promise isn't valid, but because you refuse to believe it until you see it.

Questions for Reflections

1. What are the top three promises for which you are still awaiting fulfillment?

2. In what ways are you showing faith in the Promiser to make good on the promise?

3. Name a few things that have made it difficult for you to believe today.

Morning Decree #68
True Faith

"So also faith by itself, if it does not have works, is dead." James 2:17

The word *faith* is often used without any biblical support or focus. For example, some say they have faith because they believe in a set of doctrines or teachings. Others say they are of the Christian faith because they believe in Jesus Christ, pertaining to the fact that He lived and died for humanity. This kind of faith, although it is a start, is not true biblical faith.

True faith is that which is grounded in the Word of God and through corresponding actions prove one's beliefs. For instance, if you believe a chair can support your weight, but are unwilling to sit in that same chair, do you have faith in the chair? You do believe, but in this example, faith gets demonstrated by the action of sitting down in that chair. Without that step, or in this case, the act of sitting, biblical faith does not get released.

Essentially, biblical faith either says something, does something, or thinks something—in addition to believes something. It's never blind. It's never stagnant. Faith must have corresponding action(s), or it's not biblical faith.

Questions for Reflections

1. List at least three things for which you are believing God.

2. On what Scriptural basis do you have confidence in the fulfillment of your belief?

3. What actions are you putting forth as a demonstration of your faith?

Morning Decree #69
Real-Life Faith

And the men marveled, saying, "What sort of man is this, that even winds and sea obey him?" Matthew 8:27

Jesus posed a question to His disciples amid a storm: "Where is your faith?" It seems harsh to ask them about their faith when they were facing a life-threatening storm. However, it appears the Lord Jesus was asking them for something they should have had. He would have known, for He taught them what faith *does* in the middle of difficulties. It would be similar to a weather forecast calling for rain, and getting caught in the storm without an umbrella. You knew it was going to rain. You were even given an umbrella but chose not to bring it with you. The disciples had been taught to have faith but, in a sense, they neglected to bring their umbrella.

What was He expecting the disciples to do that would have demonstrated they had their faith ready? He spoke to the problem. Rebuking the storm was a demonstration of belief-in-action. The disciples could have done that. Jesus did in that storm what He expects you to do in yours—have real-life faith.

Questions for Reflections

1. What actions are you ready to take to demonstrate your faith?

2. Since the basis of faith is the Word of God, do the Scriptures support your actions?

3. How do you know you are in or have faith regarding a particular issue?

Morning Decree #70
Faith Spice

"... if you have faith like a grain of mustard seed, you will say to this mountain, 'Move from here to there,' and it will move, and nothing will be impossible for you."
Matthew 17:20

It doesn't take a lot of spices to make or break a meal. Too much of this or not enough of that can spell disaster. Our approach to the problems of life gets seasoned with faith. This right kind of faith spice is more than a psychological agreement but includes corresponding action demonstrating what you believe.

Jesus let us know that a little faith spice, the size of a mustard seed, is all that's needed to handle our problems. Typically when quoting today's verse, it is overlooked that we must speak our faith.

Faith speaks. Faith does more than think about the size of the mountain, it speaks to the mountain. I've come to realize that unless I'm speaking to the problem utilizing what God's Word says about it, I'm really not in faith yet. My words often reveal my faith and it doesn't take many words, or much faith, to season my life in a way that tastes good to God.

Questions for Reflections

1. What words come out of your mouth when you're facing a mountainous problem?

2. Describe in your own words the difference between belief and faith.

3. What are some things you might say to a problem when you have faith?

Morning Decree #71
God Is for You

"What then shall we say to these things? If God is for us, who can be against us?"
Romans 8:31

God is for me. It wouldn't hurt you to say that multiple times a day. This knowledge will settle your heart and mind even during the most trying times. Often, you may forget that God demonstrated His love and support for you by sending Jesus to die in your place. There is no situation or failure that you could experience that changes the truth of God being on your side.

Though He doesn't approve of what we do or say at times, His commitment to you never diminishes, not one single degree. *God is for me* is more than a slogan; it's a reality. Embrace this truth, regardless of how you feel. If God is for you, no one or no thing can be against you. Don't allow the issues of life to cause spiritual amnesia causing you to forget that God is for you.

Questions for Reflections

1. What are your thoughts about God in moments of personal trials?

2. In the past, what has made you question whether or not God was on your side?

3. What are some of the proofs of God's love for you?

Morning Decree #72
God Is Your Source

"And my God will supply every need of yours according to his riches in glory in Christ Jesus." Philippians 4:19

Sources and resources aren't necessarily the same thing. In fact, they are quite different. For instance, my job isn't my source of income; it's a resource. My source is the loving God who saved me. My job is the conduit for God's source of blessing and provision to flow to me.

Another example is found in your homes. The faucet is not the source of your water. The faucet is the resource or the vehicle through which water gets to you. The source isn't even the reservoir or the water company. The source of your water is the heavens, practically speaking. Water comes from precipitation, the collection of moisture in the clouds that falls to Earth.

When you think that a thing or person in front of you is your source and they don't come through for you, then you are greatly disappointed in them—and many times with God also. That person may be a resource. Do not get it confused. God is your only Source.

Questions for Reflections

1. Recount a time when you thought someone or something other than God was your source and it went badly.

2. How did you feel? How did you feel toward God?

3. What may be the reasons why you look at others as your ultimate source rather than your Heavenly Father?

Morning Decree #73
Your Source

"I lift up my eyes to the hills. From where does my help come? My help comes from the Lord, who made heaven and earth." Psalms 121:1-2

Adjust your focus and recognize that God is your source for all things you need and want. He will never leave you or forsake you. It can be difficult to keep looking up to Him when in need, rather than looking to people, but for the follower of Jesus, this is the difference between experiencing peace and depression. Whatever your need at this very moment, trust God to show you what resources are available to you. Never lose sight of the truth that God is your ultimate source.

I have found that those whom I thought might be a source turned out not to be what I thought. Often, I think God conspires to teach us this all-important truth—He is my source. Instead of being upset with and disappointed by others who failed to meet your expectation, look unto the Hills (Calvary) from where your help comes.

Questions for Reflections

1. How does your body posture change when you're under stress? Do you look down?

2. What does the above verse imply that you should do in times of need?

3. How are your needs being met by looking at Jesus on the Cross?

Morning Decree #74
His Grace Is All Sufficient

"But Noah found favor in the eyes of the Lord." Genesis 6:8

God's grace is available for you. His grace is continuous. Grace is God's unmerited favor, powerful beyond measure, the ability made available to you, given to you by Jesus Christ. Noah found grace in the eyes of God and you too have favor in the eyes of the Lord Jesus. We surmise that Noah may have had an alcohol problem. God knew this but still gave him favor in the midst of his struggle. He didn't earn that grace just as you don't earn grace. You learn grace (God's favor) because race is a revelation. You cannot lose grace.

You may not think you deserve them, but *grace* and *truth* came through the finished work of Jesus Christ. They are the gift of God. Romans 5:8 says, "That while we were yet sinners, Jesus died on our behalf." That is grace. Receive the grace of God in your present situations. His grace is all sufficient. Ask God for the revelation of His grace.

Questions for Reflections

1. Has anything happened in your life causing you to think you aren't eligible for the grace of God?

2. Why do you think God is interested in maybe meeting your needs, but not your wants?

3. What can you do to get more grace?

Morning Decree #75
Your Real Need

"I am the vine; you are the branches. Whoever abides in me and I in him, he it is that bears much fruit, for apart from me you can do nothing." John 15:5

Everyone on earth has needs that could lead to a better life. Some needs are a matter of life and death, while some would simply make existence a little better. However, when we strip away all the superficial ideas and cosmetic things, the real need every human being has is to be reconnected to the Creator through Jesus Christ the Son.

Sin separates you from God, and that is an incontrovertible truth. It is because of this separation that you have been cut off from the life-giving presence of God. In essence, you are very much like a branch cut from a tree. Although for a little while the branch seems to be full of life, the truth is that the branch died the second it got severed from the rest of the tree. Until it is reattached or grafted back to the tree, it will decay more and more, with no hope of producing fruit of any kind. The same is true for you. You need to get reconnected to the life that is in Jesus Christ.

Questions for Reflections

1. In your own words, describe what happens to a flower after it's plucked from the soil.

2. What parallels are there between the flower and your life?

3. What do you think you should do to get and stay connected to life?

Morning Decree #76
It's In the Bag

"Then he took his staff in his hand and chose five smooth stones from the brook and put them in his shepherd's pouch. His sling was in his hand, and he approached the Philistine." 1 Samuel 17:40

You have power and the ability not just to withstand a spiritual attack, but to be ultimately victorious. In order to overcome, however, you have to begin with the knowledge that you will come out on top. Military science teaches that you don't fight battles you can't win. If you do proceed knowing that you can't win, it's called a suicide mission. No general approaches a fight with a suicide in mindset.

However, as a follower of Jesus, you know you are more than a conqueror through Him. You know you have the authority and the tools required to meet any challenges you may face. The young shepherd boy named David knew this. Armed with that revelation and a bag of rocks, he approached his giant with absolute confidence. He knew victory was in the bag. You need to have the same kind of confidence when you face the giants in your life. Remember, it's in the bag!

Questions for Reflections

1. What's giant are you facing right now that seems unbeatable?

2. How have you dealt with giants like this in the past?

3. What rocks do you have in your bag, along with God's power, that you can sling at your giant?

Morning Decree #77
The Weaker, The Better

"But he said to me, 'My grace is sufficient for you, for my power is made perfect in weakness.' Therefore I will boast all the more gladly of my weaknesses, so that the power of Christ may rest upon me." 2 Corinthians 12:9

The power of His grace becomes evident in your moments of weakness. The personal realization of how weak you are gives rise to more and more grace to work on your behalf. It seems like a contradiction (no, it *is* a contradiction) to feel more hopeful the more helpless you feel. However, the King's way is exactly that—going up starts by going down, increase starts when you deplete your resources, and you find yourself when you lose yourself. His ways are different than your ways for sure.

The more you declare your need for help, the more God's power rests upon you. The more you rely on the grace of God—His power and ability—the more you move right through obstacles that would have stopped you in the past. Confessing that you need more grace to compensate for your weaknesses is the way to sweet victory. Actually, the weaker you feel, the more conscious you should be of His ability and His wisdom at your disposal.

I know it sounds too good to be true, but it's true—His grace is amazing.

Questions for Reflections

1. In what areas do you feel less capable of overcoming than others?

2. In what ways do you try to compensate for those weaknesses?

3. How can you demonstrate that you depend upon God's ability rather than your own?

Morning Decree #78
A Perfect Credit Score

" . . . who was delivered up for our trespasses and raised for our justification."
Romans 4:25

There's an important theological concept to understand and it's *justification*, which basically means you are off the hook although *you are guilty* of sin. An easy way to remember what justification means is through the phrase "just as if I never sinned" before. The death of Jesus made it possible for you to go before God without feeling the guilt of your sin and without suffering the consequences. That's because Jesus was your Savior and substitute. He took the judgment on Himself that really belonged to you.

Justification is like using someone else's credit card who has a perfect credit score. When you use it, you enjoy the benefits of their score. You can go right up to the sales counter and throw down their credit card without fear of it not working or being accused of fraud.

The same is true when you pray in Jesus name. When you pray to the Father using "Jesus Credit" (His Name and what it represents), the Father responds to you the same way He would respond to Jesus.

Questions for Reflections

1. What's your spiritual credit score? How do you feel it affects your prayer life?

2. How should your confidence be affected when you take on Jesus' credit score?

3. What big spiritual "purchase" are you trying to make now for which you know you don't have the spiritual credit score to make? How will your faith be affected as you switch cards with Jesus?

Morning Decree #79
Not Being Good Enough is a Good Thing

"... for all have sinned and fall short of the glory of God, and are justified by his grace as a gift, through the redemption that is in Christ Jesus..." Romans 3:23-24

Your best behavior does not give you access to Jesus, miracles, or answered prayers. Doing good and your goodness will never be good enough. Your access to God is because of His grace as evidenced through Jesus Christ—period. You are justified through His Blood. When you come to God, your Father, you do so based upon the merits of Jesus, not your own—regardless of how great you may be.

Being clear within yourself that the reason for answered prayer is never based on your personal righteousness is liberating. Instead of performing for God's approval, you'll simply receive it as a benefit of being a follower of Jesus. Though the Father Himself loves you, He still deals with you on the basis of Jesus' goodness and His righteousness—not yours.

Questions for Reflections

1. Why do you feel you need to be good in order to earn God's love?

2. What are some of the actions you do to prove to God that you're worthy?

3. How will knowing you can never be good enough but by God's grace to change your prayer life?

Morning Decree #80
Compared to Who?

"For those whom he foreknew he also predestined to be conformed to the image of his Son, in order that he might be the firstborn among many brothers." Romans 8:29

Until there is a radical submission of heart to live out the Word(s) of God, your so-called relationship with God will not be much more than a religious exercise. Quite frankly, the essence of what is called Christianity rests on the degree to which you are submitted. The Word of God is the final authority and absolute rule of conduct for Christians—or at least it should be. Rather than judging "how well you're doing" by comparing yourself to others, you should use the standard of the Word of God as your measuring stick. Jesus is your example. "I have no one is outside of Jesus Christ" is your ultimate goal. Others can provide examples to follow, but only to the extent that they are modeling Jesus for you.

Questions for Reflections

1. Who, in the body of Christ, do you admire? Why do you admire them?

2. What characteristics of Jesus do they embody for you?

3. How can you represent or express those same qualities?

Morning Decree #81
Process Before Productivity

"...so that you may not be sluggish, but imitators of those who through faith and patience inherit the promises." Hebrews 6:12

You will never develop or reach the full potential the Father has for you without submitting to a process—His process. This process is usually not quick or easy. As a matter of fact, it requires patience, diligence, and endurance. Every year in the spring months, I become an amateur botanist. I start planting this and digging up that, all in the hope of producing a beautiful vegetable garden. One year, I thought about planting fruit trees. Upon further research, however, I discovered it could be years after planting the tree before I would *start* enjoying any fruit that was edible. It was so disappointing that I decided to abandon the project. I simply wasn't willing to submit to the process. No process, no produce.

Here's the moral of that story: If I really wanted fruit, I would have to be willing to work through the process. Fruit was possible. Growth was possible. But I didn't have the required faith and patience to fulfill my desire.

Questions for Reflections

1. What does it take to produce real and mature fruit in your life?

2. What is it that you desire to produce but involves an unpleasant process?

3. What part of the process are you struggling with and why?

Morning Decree #82
Growth Stinks

"And he answered him, 'Sir, let it alone this year also, until I dig around it and put on manure.'" Luke 13:8

In real estate, I'm told what matters most is location, location, location. But in the Kingdom of God, process, process, process is critical. What I mean by process is the fact that true, legitimate maturity takes time. What's more, it's accomplished best when it's intentional. For anyone who endeavors to grow their business, strengthen their relationships, or become healthier, it can be an arduous and messy work—but worthwhile.

Science speaks to the need for manure to be applied to bring about healthier plants—and Scripture corroborates that fact. If you know anything about manure, you know it has a distinct odor that is impossible to miss. Manure is unpleasant to work with, to say the least, but if you want good, strong, healthy plants, using manure or some other compost is an absolute necessity.

Your personal growth is the same way. It requires unpleasant periods that quite frankly stink. It's hard, it's messy, it's uninviting. However, successful people all have stories of the unpleasant seasons that were part of their journey. Growth stinks.

Questions for Reflections

1. What is the hard, potentially stinky work you are avoiding?

2. What specific areas in your life require process?

3. What are some possible support systems you can engage to help you complete the process of growth?

Morning Decree #83
Transformation

"Do not be conformed to this world, but be transformed by the renewal of your mind."
Romans 12:2

There is something about the process of a caterpillar being transformed into monarch butterfly that is borderline mystical. A worm-like creature vanishes and then reappears as a completely different being. That's a perfect picture of transformation. It's precisely what being reconnected to the Father through Jesus Christ will do to you. The goal of being a Christian was never to be "a rehab" project or "a paint job." In Christ, you become a new creation, one that never existed before. It's a miracle of the highest magnitude.

Transformation is a process with specific steps that must happen in succession for it to take place. Nothing is more important in the transformational process than changing the way you think. Don't settle for information or being more knowledgeable. With effort, you can become like that monarch butterfly who emerges as a whole new creature. Transformation is the will of God for your life.

Questions for Reflections

1. What do you think are some of the steps you need to take to experience true transformation?

2. What is the difference between the rehabilitation of an old building and new construction? How does that relate to your personal spiritual life?

3. How would you describe the metamorphosis a caterpillar undergoes?

Morning Decree #84
One Truth at a Time

" . . . and to be renewed in the spirit of your minds . . ." Ephesians 4:23

The process of transformation occurs first in your mind. How you are "educated" to think determines how you think. I know that sounds like double speak, but the reality is that what you are taught has a lot to do with what you do and how you behave.

The Word of God actually gives you a clear instruction on how to transform your entire life, which is through changing or renewing your mind. The way you think right now is the cause of the life you are living now. If you want to live a different type and quality of life, learning to think different thoughts is the most important thing you can do.

Change occurs one truth at a time. You change our mindset by intentionally inserting "new and improved" thoughts. One new thought replacing an old is how transformation ultimately happens. Reading, reciting, meditating, hearing, and doing the Word of God is how new thoughts—God's thoughts—shift your mind in the right direction. You are what you think about.

Questions for Reflections

1. What do you want to change about your life?

2. What are the thoughts/mindsets that create the life you're experiencing now?

3. What are some new thoughts you will need to meditate on to begin the transformation process?

Morning Decree #85
Confession or Quotation?

"Let us hold fast the confession of our hope without wavering, for he who promised is faithful." Hebrews 10:23

As one who makes Morning Decrees, you know the importance of speaking the Word. As the Scriptures teach, "life and death" are in your speech. However, just saying the right words or quoting the right verses, no matter how loudly or sincerely you do it, isn't by itself going to change your situation. *Confessing* Scripture means that you are agreeing with God regardless of the circumstances you are facing; *quoting* Scripture is simply saying the right thing. The first is about agreement, while the second is only about memorization.

You should be a confessor, someone who is in lock-step with the Father and determined to see His Will done in your life and the world around you. You create our heaven on earth by the Words you confess into your world. To agree with God and speak accordingly is one of the most powerful things you will ever do.

Questions for Reflections

1. What key Scripture do you regularly confess over your life and family?

2. How have words affected your life—either positively or negatively?

3. What makes it so difficult to change the words you speak?

Morning Decree #86
Did You Mean to Say That?

". . . but no human being can tame the tongue. It is a restless evil, full of deadly poison. With it we bless our Lord and Father, and with it we curse people who are made in the likeness of God." James 3:8-9

"Open mouth, insert foot," as the saying goes when you say the wrong thing at the wrong time. It's happened to all of us. It's usually under pressure or duress when you speak things that you might not normally say. Tragically, those words that you really didn't mean to say, can't be recalled. Because words carry power, damage is done, even though you didn't mean to do harm.

Such utterances are seemingly harmless, but the real problem is that many times we have ignored the power of words—even words said in haste, anger, or without thinking. When you fail to use the right words, namely the Word of God, your forfeit the chance to send situations in the proper direction. Words can heal. Word can hurt. What would happen if you treated every syllable as precious and life-altering? How would that change the content of your conversations, even what you say to yourself?

Questions for Reflections

1. Have you ever said something that as soon as it came out of your mouth, you realized it was the wrong thing to say?

2. Can you recall a time when words were spoken directly to you that were laced with anger? How did it affect you?

3. What are some habits you could develop to ensure that your speech is exactly what you mean to say?

Morning Decree #87
Are You Spending or Investing Time?

". . . making the best use of the time, because the days are evil." Ephesians 5:16

There's a difference between spending money and investing money. While in each action you are "giving something up," spending implies loss (or at least less money) but investing implies a hope for return on investment (ROI).

One commodity that every person has is *time*. You are gifted 24 hours per day to use as you wish. What you do with the gift called *time* determines what you have in the end to show for it. If you treat time like money and spend it on something you want in the moment, you will wake up one morning with zero to show for all the "time currency" that slipped through your hands. On the other hand, if you invest *time* on activities that will produce a lasting return than that's a different story.

God wants to invest *time* with you and in you. You are wise if you invest *time* in Him. Investing *time* (time comes from God) enables you to re-calibrate your heart, thoughts and words. There are real, tangible returns from your time investment with God. Invest more, get more.

Questions for Reflections

1. Express what ways you're willing to rearrange your day in order to invest more time with the Father.

2. In what ways have you been spending instead of investing (time, money, etc.)?

3. Regarding yesterday, how much of your activity was spent as opposed to invested?

Morning Decree #88
It's a Matter of When, Not If

"And when you fast, do not look gloomy like the hypocrites . . ." Matthew 6:16

When you pray, give, or fast, you become stronger. This "triple play" contains indispensable disciplines for any serious-minded follower of Jesus. Let's take fasting for instance; Jesus said *when* you fast, not *if* you fast. It was assumed by the Master that His followers would practice the discipline of denial.

Fasting is an intentional decision to forego food for the purpose of prayer. Actually, the very act of fasting is a prayer. Fasting increases your sensitivity to the things of the Spirit and reveals things that dominate your flesh. Besides the many physical and health benefits of fasting, the resulting spiritual power makes any temporary discomfort unimportant.

How and why fasting is so effective are really a mystery. It hardly matters how long you fast, unless specifically directed by the Lord for a pre-determined number of days. The most important element is that in place of eating, prayer and reading of the Word of God take priority.

Questions for Reflections

1. When was the last time you fasted intentionally for spiritual purposes?

2. Why is it hard for you to fast?

3. List three things (prayer needs) you have for which you are willing to fast?

Morning Decree #89
Be a Giver

"But when you give to the needy, do not let your left hand know what your right hand is doing…" Matthew 6:3

The way of the Kingdom is based on certain laws. One such law is the Law Giving. Jesus said, "When you give." Followers of Jesus are givers. God the Father is a giver, Jesus is a giver. And as followers, we should practice giving as a lifestyle.

God the Father gave His Son. With that, He demonstrated just how important giving is. Giving has so many benefits; it's hard to know where to begin. But one such benefit is that it forces us to remember that which we have and hope to have comes from the Source Himself. Giving breaks the greed spirit, that the lust for more that so easily attaches itself to us. Giving to others makes their dreams happen that otherwise might not. Giving causes the receiver to give God praise.

Questions for Reflections

1. Why do you think God requires you to give during times of plenty *and* scarcity?

2. Why is it so difficult to do either?

3. How can you develop a giving lifestyle?

Morning Decree #90
It's a Two-Way Street

"And when you pray, do not heap up empty phrases as the Gentiles do, for they think that they will be heard for their many words." Matthew 6:7

Jesus was a man of prayer while on earth, and now, seated at the right hand of the Father, He's still making intercession for us. When Jesus said, "When you pray," He was teaching His listeners (and us), what He did as a lifestyle. There are numerous examples of Jesus' prayer life. He showed us how, why and when to pray. It's been said that Jesus went from one place of prayer to another and did miracles in-between.

Prayer is more than talking to God or just telling Him about your problems. Prayer is a dialogue. Prayer is communing, listening, and obeying. In other words, prayer is a two-way street. You must learn to drive on the highway of prayer. As you do, you will go places you never dreamed of going. May you learn the power and discipline of prayer. Then you will live a life of miracles.

Questions for Reflections

1. Do you observe a daily dialogue with the Father?

2. If not, why not? What's the main challenge you're facing with being disciplined in prayer?

3. What changes are you willing to make in order to ensure that prayer is a daily part of your life?

Morning Decree #91
Attitude Matters

"For if the [eager] readiness to give is there, then it is acceptable and welcomed in proportion to what a person has, not according to what he does not have."
2 Corinthians 8:12

Who wants a gift from someone who has a mean or nasty attitude? Or a gift given out of mere obligation or with an "I have to do it" spirit? Most people like to receive gifts when they are offered with joy and gladness. Often, the act of giving a gift is less important than the attitude in which the act is performed. Although both the act and attitude are both essential, the heart is what's more important to God.

In the Scripture above, the Apostle Paul indicates God is more interested in your intention and even gives you credit for the desire to do something noble, even if you lack the means or opportunity to do so. Therefore, whatever it is that you are doing in the name of the Lord, first check your attitude because it's your attitude that gets God's attention, even before you accomplish your task—or give your gift.

Questions for Reflections

1. Can you recall a gift you receive from a person whose attitude was off?
How did that make you feel?

2. Can you remember a time, maybe even in church,
when you gave a gift out of obligation and not from your heart?

3. Why do you think a person's attitude is important when giving or serving another?

Morning Decree #92
Giving is a Choice

"Let each one [give] as he has made up his own mind and purposed in his heart, not reluctantly or sorrowfully or under compulsion, for God loves . . . a cheerful (joyous, 'prompt to do it') giver [whose heart is in his giving]." 2 Corinthians 9:7, AMP

Yesterday, we saw how a person's attitude about giving is more important than the gift they present. Jesus didn't die for us "sinners" all the while complaining and saying, "Why do I have to do this for those ungrateful human beings?" Instead, it was an unconditional love that compelled Him to lay down His very life for us. For His decision to love, we should be forever grateful.

Jesus exercised the power of choice. He has given you the same power of choice of whether to be givers or just takers. When it comes to caring for others, giving to others, and even serving others, it all comes down to a choice—a conscious decision. It's a decision that should be rooted in love for another's well-being. It must not be done in selfishness or out of obligation. God the Father has determined that you retain your free will in all matters regarding the Kingdom of God and this is also true in the matter of giving as well. He loves a cheerful giver, whose heart is rooted in His giving. Choose to be a cheerful giver.

Questions for Reflections

1. Why is giving difficult at times?

2. Why is it more blessed to give than receive?

3. What do you hope another person feels when you give something to them?

Morning Decree #93
Is It More Blessed to Give than Receive?

"In everything I have pointed out to you [by example] that, by working diligently in this manner, we ought to assist the weak, being mindful of the words of the Lord Jesus, how He Himself said, It is more blessed (makes one happier and more to be envied) to give than to receive." Acts 20:35, AMP

At first glance, it may not seem to add up. It's counterintuitive to think that one is better off giving rather than receiving gifts. How can a person benefit more by losing something than by getting something? This idea would be strange if it were not for the fact that the Kingdom of God works based upon the spiritual Law of Sowing and Reaping. The finest example of this is when God the Father gave His son—like a seed to the ground—so He would regain an innumerable number of sons and daughters, of which Jesus was the firstborn.

When a person receives a gift, something they truly wanted and needed, it enriches them. However, the blessing ends with the receiving part. But, when a person is a giver, just like a farmer, his gift keeps on producing continual harvests/blessing. So, in truth, a giver is positioning himself to receive continuously, whereas a receiver gains just that single time. By being a giver, I am a receiver as well.

Questions for Reflections

1. Describe a time when you realized that giving worked better for you than just receiving?

2. Why does it seem difficult for many believers to be givers?

3. Can you name a harvest you received that was directly related to seeds you have sown?

Morning Decree #94
How Much Is Too Much?

"[Remember] this: he who sows sparingly and grudgingly will also reap sparingly and grudgingly, and he who sows generously [that blessings may come to someone] will also reap generously and with blessings." 2 Corinthians 9:6, AMP

The real question is how much you want to receive, not how much is too much to give. The Laws of Seedtime and Harvest or Sowing and Reaping are what some call universal laws. In other words, these laws work for or against anyone whether they are conscious of their existence or not. If people unknowingly drop a seed in the ground, they will have planted a crop although unintentionally. This is the Law at work.

The Apostle Paul uses the metaphor of sowing and reaping plants to illustrate how your giving of financial resources benefits you, the giver, as well as the recipient. However, He challenges you to be intentional about how much of a harvest you want to receive. He makes it clear: you receive in direct proportion to how and what you give. If you sow a little, you will reap accordingly. Conversely, if you plant a bunch, you will receive bunches. We determine the amount of harvest we receive at planting time. You must be understand and embrace this law. If you want a big harvest, sow the best you can, every time you can.

Questions for Reflections

1. At what point during the planting season does a farmer decide what kind of crop they want to harvest?

2. Who determines what is grown?

3. Are you planting with a focus on what and how much you want to receive?

Morning Decree #95
No More Needs

"And God is able to make all grace (every favor and earthly blessing) come to you in abundance, so that you may always and under all circumstances and whatever the need be self-sufficient [possessing enough to require no aid or support and furnished in abundance for every good work and charitable donation]." 2 Corinthians 9:8

What a promise! We can have our needs met if we are sowers of financial seeds. We should be like a farmer who during planting season, looks out over her farm and thinks, "if I sow seeds, I will have a harvest and be able to be self-sufficient during the winter months." However, often when we are faced with a shortage, we think of holding back rather than sowing what we can. I'm not suggesting you give away everything you have, especially during times of struggle. At the same time, the law of seedtime and harvest requires that you re-plant some of your harvests to ensure future harvests.

Sadly, you can give in to the voice of fear that says if you give, you won't have enough for tomorrow. It's true for a period of time you will be without the amount you sow, but when your harvest shows up, and it definitely will, you will have many times more than you gave in the first place. Be a good farmer and focus on getting your seed in the ground. Seed in the ground eventually becomes harvest in the barn!

Questions for Reflections

1. What needs do you have right now that you can't meet or fulfill?

2. What financial resources do you have that you can sow into a worthy Kingdom-based ministry?

3. What is stopping you from sowing today so you can be sure to reap in your tomorrows?

Morning Decree #96
You Don't Have Anything to Give?

"And [God] Who provides seed for the sower and bread for eating will also provide and multiply your [resources for] sowing and increase the fruits of your righteousness [which manifests itself in active goodness, kindness, and charity]." 2 Corinthians 9:10

Having more month than money is, unfortunately, a common occurrence. When your income does not exceed your expense, stress is often the result. This stress is equally real for believer's who say, "God is my source." If that's the case and God is their source, then why is it that most Christians are not able to meet their monthly financial obligations, let alone save money or take a vacation?

While many factors may have created the problem in the first place, at the top of the list is violating the Law of Sowing and Reaping. I'm not diminishing the need for proper stewardship or employment, but the real problem is that most do not trust God's Word in the matter of giving. This is especially true when it comes to giving for the support and advancement of the Kingdom of God.

Regardless of your present income, whether it's fixed, inconsistent or not enough, if you obey the Law of Sowing and Reaping, you will begin to see harvests of financial resources along with other blessings—things which money can't buy for you.

The truth is you have seed right now, enough to prove you take God at His Word. Even if you really don't have anything to give, ask God for seed to sow. He will provide you with seed money to get your harvest season under way. God has you covered. Just ask. Then plant a portion of it, stand back, and watch the Law of Sowing and Reaping go to work on your behalf.

Questions for Reflections

1. What seed do you have right now? Alternatively, what can you sell to get seeds to invest in your future?

2. What negative thoughts have stopped you in the past from being a consistent giver?

3. Find at least three biblical references that teach the Law of Sowing and Reaping?

Morning Decree #97
What's in Your Garden?

"The earth brought forth vegetation: plants yielding seed according to their own kinds and trees bearing fruit in which was their seed, each according to its kind. And God saw that it was good (suitable, admirable) and He approved it." Genesis 1:12

As many different types of plants as there are on the planet, that's how many kinds of seeds there are. A farmer, hobbyist, or a commercial landowner determines the type of crop they want to harvest at the time of planting based upon the seeds they plant. This Law of Sowing and Reaping has at its core the understanding that apple seeds will only produce apples. The apple is hardwired into the seed, so once the conditions are right (namely, the planting of seed), the DNA hidden within the seed goes to work. The results never vary; apple seeds produce apples—never oranges, pumpkins, or broccoli.

If you consider what type of harvest you're looking for, be focused on planting those type of seeds. Though it takes faith in the process, the production of a specific harvest is not a hit-or-miss proposition. Growing corn is a direct, indisputable result of planting corn seeds. Plant what you want to harvest.

Questions for Reflections

1. What do you lack in your life at this present time?
2. What seed actions do you need to take to produce the thing you are lacking?
3. What do you see in your life that you can now attribute to certain seed actions?

Morning Decree #98
Harvests Are Predictable

". . . for whatever a man sows, that and that only is what he will reap." Galatians 6:7b

You reap what you sow. Therefore, sow or plant what you want to grow. This is irrevocably true in agriculture as well as when it comes to your actions. For a farmer, harvests are very predictable. No farmer plants corn and believes wheat is going to show up in a couple of months. There is never a question of what will grow. The seed sown will produce based on its genetic makeup. No amount of wishing or hoping will change the outcome. They reap what the sow.

Farming and agricultural examples were often used by the Lord Jesus Christ to illustrate in simple terms how the Kingdom of God operates. Whatever it is you need or want, there is a specific seed that, when planted, will produce exactly that but nothing else because the type of seed sown at the moment of planting determines the kind of harvest. This is a simple, but profound truth. When this truth is activated, the response is predictable, unbiased, and unprejudiced. The seed has no regard for gender, race, nationality, height, weight, or one's history. Plant only what you want to harvest and you will eventually reap.

Questions for Reflections

1. How would you describe a farmer who expects carrots but plants watermelon seeds?

2. Name one thing you need or want. What type of seeds do you need to plant for the thing you need or want to manifest?

3. Why are corn farmers called corn farmers and wheat farmers called wheat farmers?

Morning Decree #99
The Stuff from Which Miracles Are Made

"And He said, The kingdom of God is like a man who scatters seed upon the ground, And then continues sleeping and rising night and day while the seed sprouts and grows and increases—he knows not how." Mark 4:26-27

As stated in a previous Morning Decree, miracles are mysterious. They are by definition something that defy logic or explanation. Yet countless miracles are occurring every second of every day! How a seed after it is planted in the proper soil actually becomes something else is a mystery. A botanist can explain what happens but can't tell you "how" it happens. This is even truer when it comes to the mystery of life—it's marvelous, glorious and remains in the realm of the miraculous.

With that said, there are elements common to all miracles of "harvest—specifically seed, soil, and the most important element,, which is faith. Of course, weather, water, and temperature all play a role, but the essential elements are the same—seed, soil, and faith.

Faith is the one aspect over which you have control. Faith can be defined as active trust in God's Word. In other words, when you have faith, it means you are acting in accordance with what God's Word says. Consequently, you demonstrate faith by planting or sowing a seed. To believe you reap what you sow, but then elect not to actually sow something, is not really faith.

Questions for Reflections

1. In what areas of your life have you been saying you're in faith, but lack corresponding action (like sowing seeds)?

2. What element of the miracle process are you lacking (seed, soil, or sowing/faith)?

3. What miracle(s) do you need?

Morning Decree #100
It Takes One to Grow One

"He who goes forth bearing seed and weeping [at needing his precious supply of grain for sowing] shall doubtless come again with rejoicing, bringing his sheaves with him."
Psalm 126:6

We tend to forget in the dark times what we heard in the light. Often in our difficult moments of lack, we can quickly lose sight of the Laws of Seedtime and Harvest. God in His compassion and wisdom prearranged it so whenever there is a need in our lives, we only need to plant a seed, the right seed to begin to turn things around.

Seeds can be many different things. Time, actions, words, money, thoughts are all seeds, just to name a few. In the midst of your present trouble, decide to find a seed to sow to jumpstart your miracle. Everything living began with a seed. Grow what you need. Sow what you want to grow. Be intentional concerning what you say, what you do, and what you give and where you give it. You're just one seed from making a comeback.

Questions for Reflections

1. What are your most significant personal problems?
What was the seed that started the issue?

2. Regardless of how small you may perceive it to be,
what seed can you plant now to begin your miracle?

3. What keeps you from sowing the seed(s) you need to prepare for a new harvest?

Morning Decree #101
Your Benefits Package

"Bless (affectionately, gratefully praise) the Lord, O my soul, and forget not [one of] all His benefits." Psalms 103:2, AMP

The benefits of being a child of God are beyond explanation. The natural mind can no more fathom the depth of God's love for you any more than you can put the Atlantic Ocean in a teacup. However, you are admonished through the Word of God not to forget all His benefits.

It takes study, relationship, practice, and, most important, revelation to begin to appreciate all that comes with being in the family of God. It includes healing, deliverance, prosperity, forgiveness, restoration, peace, and so much more. If you only see your benefits through the lens of other people's experiences or religion, you could erroneously conclude that your benefit package is a meager handout, barely sufficient to keep you satisfied, when in reality, it is a sumptuous feast.

Questions for Reflections

1. Have you read your health, dental, or life insurance benefit packages?

2. What good things could you be missing by not fully exploring your benefits package?

3. Name three benefits you think you have but may also doubt they are for you? How can you be sure? What do you need to do once you are sure they are yours?

Morning Decree #102
The Forgiveness Factor

"Who forgives [every one of] all your iniquities . . ." Psalms 103:3, AMP

The most important of all our spiritual benefits is the forgiveness of our sins, for it is sin that separated us from God our Father. No amount of good deeds, or being nice or kind, will close the gap between a Holy God and us. Sin is the great divide. It required a Divine act to remove the sin and bridge the gap that stood between us. It took Jesus' death by crucifixion to take away our sins. He became our scapegoat to square things with God. Without forgiveness, which means to remove sin, relationship with God would be impossible. Access to the many benefits and blessings of God would also not be available to us.

That is the reason forgiveness of sin is the chief benefit it positions you for all the others. Consequently, without understanding and appreciating the forgiveness factor, nothing else in Christianity will work.

Questions for Reflections

1. Do you know that you have been forgiven of your sin?
   Or do you still wonder if forgiveness is for you?

2. Do you feel guilty when you pray today because of "yesterday's" sin?

3. How do you think the feeling of unforgiveness affects your prayer life?

Morning Decree #103
Your Healer

"Who heals [each one of] all your diseases..." Psalm 103:3, AMP

All means all. Therefore, when the Word of God says, "who heals *all* your diseases," that literally means there is no disease God does not heal. The medical profession's diagnosis of incurable means absolutely nothing when it comes to God's willingness and ability to heal whatever ails you.

Salvation comes from the idea of salvage and restoration. As a follower of Jesus, the miracle of salvation entitles you to a spiritual benefits package, which includes healing. The Jesus in whom you believe has forgiven you of sin is the same Jesus who heals your body and mind. Through your faith in Jesus, you can receive healing from your physical and emotional infirmities. It's only because we don't hear that truth preached much (if at all) that we think salvation and healing are two different dimensions.

The God who heals is the God who saves. The God who saves is the God who heals. What's more, He accomplished both at the same time. Isn't it about time you claimed the full benefits of your salvation? Bitterness, unforgiveness, and a lack of knowledge are a few things that can keep you from receiving your benefits package. Ask God today to reveal to you anything that may be hindering your being healed.

Questions for Reflections

1. Did you know healing was part of your spiritual benefits package? Why do you think most Christians are unaware of this blessing?

2. Does receiving healing require a different faith than receiving salvation? If so, why? If not, why not?

3. Do you need healing in your life? If so, just as you received salvation by faith, do the same for your healing.

Morning Decree #104
Moon Walkers

"Surely He has borne our griefs (sicknesses, weaknesses, and distresses) and carried our sorrows and pains [of punishment], yet we [ignorantly] considered Him stricken, smitten, and afflicted by God [as if with leprosy]." Isaiah 53:4, AMP

What does walking on the moon and healing have in common? Actually, more than you may think. The word English word *borne* is translated from a Hebrew word which means to *lift off*. The actual transliteration of that word in Hebrew is *nasa*—just like National Aeronautic and Space Administration! *Nasa* in the Book Isaiah 53:4, means that Jesus through His death on the Cross, *nasa* (lifted off) your sicknesses, weaknesses, and distresses. Glory to God.

The next time you think of the late Michael Jackson's Moonwalk, remember that Jesus lifted disease off your life. Since Jesus bore it for you, you need not bear it.

Questions for Reflections

1. What does it mean to you now that Jesus bore your sickness and disease?

2. Do you think it was God's plan for you to bear sickness and disease although Jesus already bore (*nasa*) it for you?

3. Since Jesus bore it, should you bear it also?

Morning Decree #105
Read the Fine Print

"Jesus answered him, 'I assure you, most solemnly I tell you, that unless a person is born again (anew, from above), he cannot ever see (know, be acquainted with, and experience) the kingdom of God. "You search and investigate and pore over the Scriptures diligently, because you suppose and trust that you have eternal life through them. And these [very Scriptures] testify about Me!'" John 3:3, AMP

I miss many details when I read things I think I already know. That it is even more prevalent when I read the Bible. There are things that I have heard about since I was a young child in Sunday School, things like Jesus saves, Jesus is a healer, or Jesus will be a friend who sticks closer than a sibling—to name few. I assume it is the same with you. We often miss the truth behind the truths we read because we are either too familiar with them or, quite frankly, too lazy to dig deeper.

The Word of God is not something that can be understood, let alone embraced, without intentionality and effort. Simply put, if you're not hungry for truth, you won't be fed from the Word. There are details, (the "fine print") that unless you're looking for them, you won't see them. When that's the case, what you don't know, or in this case see, will hurt you by default.

One part of the fine print is that Jesus Christ came to completely, totally, and irrevocably remove the destructive impact of the devil. Did you know this? Can you find those details in the Word of God?

Questions for Reflections

1. Recall a time when you failed to understand the fine print in the assembly or directions of a project, and as a result it didn't come together?

2. On a scale of 1 to 10, ten being red hot, what is your intensity level when it comes to studying the Word of God?

3. What changes can you make to your daily routine to maximize your study opportunities?

Morning Decree #106
You're Loaded

"Blessed be the Lord, who daily loadeth us with benefits,
even the God of our salvation. Selah." Psalm 68:19, KJV

Benefit defined: "something that is advantageous or good; an advantage".

The long-held idea that following Christ means living in poverty in every way (physically, financially, emotionally) except spiritually is not what the Bible teachers nor the Will of God for anyone's life. Benefits are advantageous; they are good; poverty, brokenness, and lack are not good.

Taking a fresh look at the Scriptures, understanding what Jesus Christ actually purchased, you can't help but conclude that you are loaded down with blessings. As a good Father, God wants your life to be full of beneficial things, things that will fulfill you.

These benefits are part of your salvation. They are not extra add-ons for a select few, but instead they are available to all who have the faith to receive them. It's a tragedy to live without that which Jesus Christ has died for you to have. Benefits are your inheritance because you are an heir of God, according to the Scriptures (see Romans 8:17).

Questions for Reflections

1. Why do you think many people equate Christianity with poverty?

2. List some benefits a person receives from their employer.

3. What would a person be losing out on if they were not aware of their benefit plan?

Morning Decree #107
Pray Specifically

"If you then, evil as you are, know how to give good and advantageous gifts to your children, how much more will your Father Who is in heaven [perfect as He is] give good and advantageous things to those who keep on asking Him!" Matthew 7:11

Breakthrough is a result of sustained, focused pressure on a barrier. From a spiritual perspective, faith pressure breaks down doors, walls, and moves mountains. All hindrances succumb to faith pressure. The more focused your prayers are, the more pressure is released. meaning you need to be intentional about exactly what and for whom you are praying.

God is really into details and specifics. Pray about matters with as much specificity as you know. You're not directing or bossing God around when you pray specifically. Rather you are merely expressing the desires of your heart. Your heavenly Father likes to hear directly from you. If you want a specific blessing, be specific in your request. General pray requests, don't seem to get answered in my experience. God's knows what you need before you even ask, but He still wants to hear your heart.

Questions for Reflections

1. What do you exactly want God to do for you?

2. What are your most sincere prayer requests?

3. How can you know if God answered your prayers
if you are not specific when you prayed?

Morning Decree #108
Prayer and Fasting

"And Joshua said unto the people, 'Sanctify yourselves: for tomorrow the Lord will do wonders among you.'" Joshua 3:5

Through prayer with fasting, you make your intentions known to the Father, indicating you serious about the things for which you are praying. No one fully understands how fasting works or why it effective. It's somewhat of a mystery, but the power of it cannot be denied. Fasting reveals the hindrances within and around you that must be addressed by your faith-in-action.

Fasting has a unique way of preparing you for what is to come or what should happen in the future. During times of intense prayer and fasting, listen for the correcting voice of the Holy Spirit. He will work on the matter for which you are enduring hunger pangs, but will also detox your life. Keep praying for your family and others too, but keep in mind God is also preparing you for much more than you are presently experiencing.

Questions for Reflections

1. What is it about the preparation that scares you?

2. Can you remember an event in your life in which you were underprepared?

3. How do you feel knowing that you are well-prepared rather than under or ill-prepared?

Morning Decree #109
Don't Give Up; It's Coming

"Then he said to me,' Fear not, Daniel, for from the first day that you set your mind and heart to understand and to humble yourself before your God, your words were heard, and I have come as a consequence of [and in response to] your words.'"
Daniel 10:12, AMP

The power of fasting with prayer is incontrovertible. Simply put, it works. However, the waiting period between the time you make the request and your prayers getting answered can be challenging to negotiate. Take solace in the fact that Daniel prayed for 21 straight days before getting a response from Heaven. Precisely as the Angelic Messenger stated," . . . from the first day . . ." Daniel's prayers were heard and your prayers are listened to as well.

Do not give up because the answer has yet to get revealed. Press forward. Stay on your knees. Regardless of the circumstantial evidence, keep praying. Continue to thank God for the breakthrough you seek. Your sacrifice will surely be rewarded.

Questions for Reflections

1. What are some practical things you can do to stay encouraged?

2. What are the reasons many people give up too soon?

3. Can you recall a moment when quitting would have been easier but you didn't?

Morning Decree #110
What Are You Focusing On?

"... looking to Jesus, the founder and perfecter of our faith, who for the joy that was set before him endured the cross, despising the shame, and is seated at the right hand of the throne of God." Hebrews 12:2

When I lose focus on why I'm fasting, it becomes a chore. Each hunger pang reminds me what I'm losing out on, rather than what I'm gaining. By staying focused on the reason I'm fasting, or my why, I "almost" look forward to fasting with prayer. There's much power in fasting. It's somewhat mysterious, not knowing how it changes things, people and situations, but somehow it does. As you focus on for whom your fasting and praying, you will discover a determination that will push you right through the uncomfortable moments. It takes a vision of what "can be," that gets you through "what is."

I recall what is said about Jesus Christ in the book of Hebrews – "that how He endured the Cross because of a future joy" (see Hebrews 12:1-2), I believe the joy that was "set before Him," was you and I, safe and secure, prosperous and healthy, joyful and peaceful. I thank God for Jesus' sacrifice. His focus is what got Him through. Keep in the forefront of your mind who and what you're sacrificing. There is incredible power within a focus that is unbroken.

Questions for Reflections

1. How does what you see affect your motivation?

2. What is the "joy" that will cause you to push past the difficulties of prayer?

3. What have been the distractions that have broken your focus in the past?

Morning Decree #111
It's Not Waiting For You

"My times are in your hand." Psalm 31:15

Neither time nor the tides of the ocean are waiting on you. They move as they have been designed regardless of your wants, needs, or desires. Both time and tide have power. Depending on how you use them, they can be an asset or signal your demise.

Everyone one of us is given the exact same allotment of time each day when twenty-four hours are deposited into your life account. Regardless of your race, gender, nationality, spiritual state, we all get the same amount of time. What differentiates people is how they invest their twenty-four-hour allotment of time. For the most part, you determine how your time is spent.

Time is a gift. It's doesn't stop for anyone. It's doesn't discriminate or show any favoritism. As you endeavor the best usage of your time, first consult the Creator of time. Every day is a gift from Him. He knows what is the best and most judicial use of the time He has graced you with. Be a good manager of time and you will be rewarded in this life and the next most handsomely.

Questions for Reflections

1. What grade would you give for your time management?

2. Name a few instances when you didn't manage your time well and it cost you something very important?

3. What are some of the ways you can improve the usage of your time starting today?

Morning Decree #112
The End is in Sight

"Looking away [from all that will distract] to Jesus, Who is the Leader and the Source of our faith [giving the first incentive for our belief] and is also its Finisher [bringing it to maturity and perfection]. He, for the joy [of obtaining the prize] that was set before Him, endured the cross, despising and ignoring the shame, and is now seated at the right hand of the throne of God." Hebrews 12:2, AMP

The end is nearer than you think. I know that sounds ominous, but I'm not talking about the end of the world. What I am referring to is the end of the trial you're facing; the fruit of your tears released in prayer. Anyone who tells you victory comes swiftly and easily all the time has never been in a real trial. It takes faith, vision, and a willingness to endure until the breakthrough comes.

Still, there is one way to make even the most difficult journeys a bit easier. It's realizing God is the ultimate finisher. When you come to the end of yourself, then you will find God. You will see His power, wisdom, and grace. He will do what you cannot. "The end of self is the beginning of God."

Questions for Reflections

1. Are you in the midst of a trial that doesn't seem like it will end? Have you lost hope?

2. If so, what can you to find hope again today?

3. Do you have a similar situation in your past on which you can focus today to give you hope that He "saved" you once before and will do it again?

Morning Decree #113
The Value of Being a Hardhead

"And be constantly renewed in the spirit of your mind [having a fresh mental and spiritual attitude]." Ephesians 4:23, AMP

A mindset is an established way of thinking. Much like cement, a mentality is hard to reshape once hardened. However, when the Word of God creates a mindset, it provides a consistent framework for the plan of God to be fulfilled, but it takes a certain mindset to operate in the realm of the Spirit. The carnal mind, which means, "a thought process that is based on the six senses," works against the Spirit-led life. A person who attempts to operate in the Spirit based upon the natural/carnal mind will fail miserably.

Mindsets are all based on a clear and ever-increasing revelation of who Jesus Christ is and what He came to do for you, in you, and through you. Please re-study those truths and discover the many others that reveal the living Christ.

Questions for Reflections

1. Do you know anyone you feel is set in their ways?
How do you think that is hindering their growth?

2. What areas do you think you are stubborn or slow to change

3. In what ways can you improve your life if you changed the way you think?

Morning Decree #114
Change is Hard Work

"For this very reason, adding your diligence [to the divine promises], employ every effort in exercising your faith to develop virtue (excellence, resolution, Christian energy), and in [exercising] virtue [develop] knowledge (intelligence)..." 2 Peter 1:5, AMP

Not only is change uncomfortable, but it also takes real work. It takes a *new* level of commitment and focus. One of the most important revelations you can receive is that you are under construction by the Lord. Because of sin and the condition of the world in which we live, there is a requirement for reconstruction. Failure to recognize this fact is one of the main reasons why so many Christians do not mature in their faith, relationships, or purpose.

Even Jesus Christ had to mature. Of course, He was sinless. Still, it was required of Him to be raised in complete submission to His earthly parents. I'm sure there were times He was expected to do something He did not want to do but did it anyhow.

Questions for Reflections

1. Why does change seem so difficult for you?

2. What areas do you feel you need to change the most? List at least three.

3. What steps are you willing to take to make the changes you listed above?

Morning Decree #115
Are You Really a Child God?

"But to as many as did receive and welcome Him, He gave the authority (power, privilege, right) to become the children of God, that is, to those who believe in (adhere to, trust in, and rely on) His name— Who owe their birth neither to bloods nor to the will of the flesh [that of physical impulse] nor to the will of man [that of a natural father], but to God. [They are born of God!]" John 1:12-13, AMP

In today's society, it seems everyone says they are a child of God. Usually, what they mean is that all human beings are God's children. While this may sound good and even be comforting, the Bible doesn't support that way of thinking. There is a difference between a child of God and God's creation. God created all people, for only God can create life. However, a child of God is different. They are given privileged status, not by natural birth, but spiritual rebirth.

According to the Bible, only those human beings who receive Jesus as their Lord and Savior are children of God. Family members have privileges and access to the blessings of the family, so knowing you are a child of God and then living as one is very important.

Questions for Reflections

1. Are you a child of God based upon the biblical requirement?

2. What benefits can you think of that a child has that just a kid down the street might not enjoy?

3. Once becoming a child of God, can you lose your status as a son or daughter?

Morning Decree #116
Who's Your Dad?

"Jesus answered him, 'I assure you, most solemnly I tell you, that unless a person is born again (anew, from above), he cannot ever see (know, be acquainted with, and experience) the kingdom of God.'" John 3:3

Being a child of God is a spiritual matter. From a purely biological perspective, a child takes on the DNA of both parents, but the father contributes the blood. It is also true from a spiritual perspective. It is the seed (sperm) that is the Word of God that re-creates a person's human spirit. This miracle as described in the Bible is being born-again or born from above.

When a person receives the Word of God, the miracle of inner transformation occurs. That's when a spiritual conception takes place making one a child of God, who is the seed/word giver. It is a great mystery, but those who have experienced such an experience will confirm it is the best and most important decision they could have ever made.

Questions for Reflections

1. Are you born again? If so, how do you know?

2. What does being born again mean to you?

3. What characteristics of your parents do you exhibit the most?

Morning Decree #117
Do You Need to Be Born Again?

"Marvel not [do not be surprised, astonished] at My telling you, 'You must all be born anew (from above).'" John 3:7, AMP

Isn't believing in Jesus enough? Doesn't going to a Christian church count for something? These are common questions that many good, well-intentioned people ask. However, the answer is something that is not so readily accepted because religion teaches us to just "believe." The problem is that believing in the reality of Jesus is not uncommon or just something only Christians do. There are other religious groups that also believe in the historical fact of Jesus. However, that's not enough.

Since we all have sinned, our spirit, the real us, is corrupted. We need to be born a second time. Of course, this isn't a physical rebirthing, but rather a spiritual one. Everyone, regardless of age, race, gender, or societal status must be born a second time to be a child of God. That's not opinion; it's what Jesus said and the Bible teaches. You must be born again.

Questions for Reflections

1. Do you believe you have sinned and therefore need to be born again?

2. Is there any kind or amount of good deeds that can make up for your sins?

3. Can you save yourself? Or do you need a Savior?

Morning Decree #118
Are You Authorized?

"Behold! I have given you authority and power to trample upon serpents and scorpions, and [physical and mental strength and ability] over all the power that the enemy [possesses]; and nothing shall in any way harm you." Luke 10:17-19, AMP

The ability to use power is different from the right or authorization to use power. As the youngest of four, I was always the one my parents would send to get my brother and sister for dinner or the one to tell them to clean up their rooms. However, when I would say, "time for dinner," my siblings would look at me as if I had two heads and ignore me. However, when I'd say, "Mommy said it's time for dinner," the older siblings would obey my words. The difference was they knew I had the authority to tell them what to do because of whom I was representing.

Recognize that you have authority because you are a child of God, given the right to use the name of Jesus. That name is even more powerful than saying "Mommy said"—if you can believe that. You are authorized.

Questions for Reflections

1. In your own words, describe the difference between power and authority.

2. Name at least two people (professions) that exercise authority over people.

3. What does it mean to have delegated authority?

Morning Decree #119
What Are You Authorized to Do?

"And Jesus summoned to Him His twelve disciples and gave them power and authority over unclean spirits, to drive them out, and to cure all kinds of disease and all kinds of weakness and infirmity." Matthew 10:1

Authority is for a specific purpose. Having authority—the right to use power—is of no value unless it is directed for godly purposes. Jesus gave His disciples, which includes you and me, authority over demons and unclean spirits. However, it would be tragic for the disciples of Jesus to have all that authority and merely sit in the pews of the synagogue. As ludicrous as that seems, that is exactly what happens every week in most churches.

We have power and authority, but we are not using it for the common good of all. Most Christians sit and observe problems and issues, but few understand they have the authority and responsibility to do something about it. It's time, really far past the time, to use the authority given to you by Jesus Christ. It's time!

Questions for Reflections

1. Why do you think most Christians are bored with their spiritual life?

2. Can you think of people who need to be touched by God in their body or mind, or family?

3. What is your role in helping others?

Morning Decree #120
What Are You Making?

"Go then and make disciples of all the nations..." Matthew 28:19-20

Christianity is a "do" thing, not just a "believe" thing. Jesus commanded His disciples to go and make—not just come and sit. Going to Church is extremely important. Nonetheless, coming to church is not the end, but it's the launch pad for ministry inside and outside the building.

Jesus said to go and make disciples. That's a pretty specific command. Sadly, we don't think of making disciples as our personal responsibility. It's not the pastor's job or the church's job—it's everyone's responsibility. Just praying for people to receive Jesus is not enough. The goal is to make disciplined learners and followers of Jesus. Let's do what Jesus commanded us to do.

Questions for Reflections

1. Have you ever prayed with someone to receive Jesus Christ as their Lord?

2. Do you consider yourself a disciple?

3. Are you personally discipling someone? If not, why?

Morning Decree #121
What Did You Get for Christmas?

""Now about the spiritual gifts (the special endowments of supernatural energy), brethren, I do not want you to be misinformed ... But to each one is given the manifestation of the [Holy] Spirit [the evidence, the spiritual illumination of the Spirit] for good and profit." 1 Corinthians 12:1, 7, AMP

The essence of Christmas speaks to the worship of Christ. The holiday is also marked typically by the giving and receiving of gifts. While there is much to comment on regarding the commercialism of Christmas, the gift we should focus on is the present(s) the Holy Spirit has given us to help others.

The stated purpose of the gifts of (from) the Spirit is to help others. It's the supernatural endowments that are never earned or bought. Instead, the gifts are learned and freely given for the benefit of humanity. The real problem though is many are unaware that the Holy Spirit has gifted them. As a matter of fact, everyone who is a true follower of Jesus Christ has been gifted! That means you, me, and the person in the pew next to you. You are in the presence of many gifts. What's your gift?

Questions for Reflections

1. What qualifies you to receive a gift of the Spirit?

2. What happens when people don't know they are gifted by God?

3. How has your life been affected by not knowing what your gifts are?

Morning Decree #122
What's Your Gift?

"Now there are distinctive varieties and distributions of endowments (gifts, extraordinary powers distinguishing certain Christians, due to the power of divine grace operating in their souls by the Holy Spirit) and they vary, but the [Holy] Spirit remains the same." 1 Corinthians 12:4, AMP

Getting up early Christmas morning is a tradition in many households. It's when the family rushes to the holy site called the Christmas tree because under that tree are *gifts*! Trying to determine what's inside based on the size or shape of the package is part of this magical exercise. Without the benefit of x-ray vision, however, the only way to really know what's contained in the box is to open it.

The same is true as to how we can determine what our gift are. We have to open the box. In this case, the box is a book called the Bible. And studying the gifts, how they function, what the specific purpose is for each of the individual gifts is how you can know what gift(s) you were given.

Questions for Reflections

1. With what gifts do you think you have been endowed?

2. Do you know what types and kinds of gifts are available from the Holy Spirit?

3. What have you done to understand your gifts and how best to utilize them?

Morning Decree #123
Naughty or Nice?

"Since all have sinned and are falling short of the honor and glory which God bestows and receives." Romans 3:23

A gift by definition is something given, not something earned or bought. The idea that God gives us something for which we don't deserve is still hard for many to accept. This is probably due to the fact we live in a performance-based society. In other words, our value to a company is based on our performance, or how well we perform based on our job description.

However, when it comes to the gifts of the Spirit, they are never earned. They can't be earned. The Holy Spirit can't be bribed or manipulated. He decides what gifts you need based on the assignments that have been predestined for you to have. Actually, when you think you qualify for a particular gift because of some ability you have, you are devaluing the gift and are sure to misuse or abuse it eventually. It's a gift, not a reward.

Questions for Reflections

1. Name at least three areas where you feel you must perform to be rewarded?

2. Since the gifts of the Holy Spirit are given and not earned, what's your responsibility regarding them?

3. How can you develop your gifts so you are more effective?

Morning Decree #124
You Can't Lose It

"For God's gifts and His call are irrevocable. [He never withdraws them when once they are given, and He does not change His mind about those to whom He gives His grace or to whom He sends His call.]" Romans 11:29

When God gives you something, He doesn't take it back. This is equally true when it comes to the gifts of the Holy Spirit. You never have to worry that you're going to wake up one morning and the gift is going to be missing! However, that doesn't mean you can ignore or misuse them without penalty. The gifts of God are so precious and vital that they come with a tremendous amount of responsibility. Though they are gifts, they are to be valued, prized, guarded, and used properly.

God won't take the gift away, but He certainly can decide no longer to provide the power source, which is the Holy Spirit. He does not work with anyone, regardless of how gifted they are if they persist in ignoring Him by acting or speaking in ways that dishonor Him. Integrity and godly character are two fundamental requirements to operate the gifts of the Holy Spirit. Failure to do so is tantamount to having a luxury vehicle without gasoline or electricity to operate it. The cleanness of your hands and heart matter.

Questions for Reflections

1. What gifts do you feel you have been given by God?

2. Have you ever met someone who was gifted by God but was a poor steward of their gift?

3. How can you ensure you will remain honorable as well as gifted?

Morning Decree #125
Stewards Not Owners

"And if you have not proved faithful in that which belongs to another [whether God or man], who will give you that which is your own [that is, the true riches]?"
Luke 16:12

Have you ever met someone who thought a bit more highly of themselves then they probably should? Usually, that's because the individual has a misunderstanding when it comes to their real role or status. As a follower of Jesus, we should recognize what we have, especially when it comes to the divine enablements, comes from God. They are not something we own or earned. We are the containers, the vessels, not the very gift to the world.

There is a huge difference between owning something and managing it. When you own it, let's say your car (free and clear), you can decide what you are going to do with it. You can give it away, throw it away, or do whatever you want. However, when you are still making payments, you can't just do what you want with it. You are bound by a contract with the owner—usually a bank or some other finance company.

The same is true when it comes to every area and aspect of your life. You are a manager of the gifts of Holy Spirit. You do not own them. They came from God and they belong to God. You have the right, privilege, and responsibility to use them for the benefit of all.

Questions for Reflections

1. What's the role of humility when it comes to being used by God?

2. What do you have that came from God, either directly or indirectly?

3. How can you remind yourself that you are a manager and not an owner?

Morning Decree #126
USPS

"For I passed on to you first of all what I also had received . . ." 1 Corinthians 15:3

Each week, millions, if not billions, of letters and parcels are delivered to homes and businesses around the world. The Postal Service is a fine-tuned machine that ensures our packages arrive at their intended destination. I can't quite imagine what life would be like if such a service did not exist. In a like manner, the gifts of the Spirit which you carry are to do similar work. We are "mail carriers" like a divine postal service. We are working for the Kingdom of God, commissioned to deliver gifts to others.

As a carrier of the gifts, it's your responsibility, rain or shine, to deliver what others need and often are expecting. Though you have gifts, the truth is you only have the gift to give to someone else. As the mail carrier never thinks of him or herself as the owner of the letters they are to deliver, you should recognize you are not an owner of the gifts you carry. Your job is to ensure the packages get delivered as quickly as possible and to the person to whom they are addressed, in the same condition they left the Giver.

Questions for Reflections

1. Relate an experience in which the mail service you were expecting was below your expectation.

2. Recall a time when you were very blessed by a package you received.

3. How would you feel if you could be the delivery person of a gift that literally could save someone's life?

Morning Decree #127
Somebody Is Expecting You

"So then, whatever you desire that others would do to and for you, even so do also to and for them, for this is (sums up) the Law and the Prophets." Matthew 7:12, AMP

Like it or not, somebody, actually a lot of somebodies, are expecting you to show up with the goods. Just like when you are awaiting the arrival of goods, good news, or some gift, which most likely will be delivered to by someone just like you, others are waiting on you. Sometimes while waiting on your package, you fail to deliver the packages you have for others. Without question, you have "goods" for someone today. Despite how your feeling or what's going on in your life, you still have a job to do. Do your job and deliver your gifts to others. Your rewards will be in doing your job of delivering as you serve someone else.

"What about me?" is a question often asked when a person has their own needs that need to be met. However, what the Bible teaches is that by doing for others, it creates a "must show up in my life" effect. In other words, when you, regardless of your own glaring needs, do what you can to help someone else, it obligates God to supply what's lacking in your life. The Law of Seedtime and Harvest come into effect here as well. Seed your gift into someone else and watch God do that and more for you.

Questions for Reflections

1. Recall a time you expected something to be delivered to you that was very important, but the person failed in getting it to you. How did it make you feel?

2. What "goods" do you have that could benefit others?

3. Name a time when you didn't feel like "it" but did "it" anyhow and it proved to be a significant help to someone?

Morning Decree #128
What's Your Address?

"But I have prayed especially for you [Peter], that your [own] faith may not fail."
Luke 22:32, AMP

"And He said to them, '[Why are you so fearful?] Where is your faith (your trust, your
confidence in Me—in My veracity and My integrity)?'" Luke 8:25, AMP

Being in the publishing business, I'm sending out books and other products daily. Sometimes the books are returned to me because the incorrect address made it "undeliverable." This is frustrating because it costs time and money to resend it. Unfortunately, this is true when it comes to the blessings that have your name on them—but the address is not right.

A wrong address in this instance is when you are not in the position of faith. You have a need and made a request, but did not remain in faith until the product was delivered. Maybe because the request took longer than you expected to arrive, or perhaps you didn't believe it would happen in the first place.

When it comes to the mail, if it has the proper postage and correct address, it will be delivered. Just be home to sign for the package—both in the natural sense and spiritual. Faith is not just a belief, it's a place, a position. God's answers are delivered to specific people at a particular address: Faith Lane.

Questions for Reflections

1. Have you ever missed a delivery to your home? What did you have to do to get the package?

2. Remember a time when you sent a family member a gift, but it never arrived because you had the wrong address. How did that make you feel? How did they feel?

3. Faith is more than a belief system, it's a place. Are you at the location of faith awaiting the arrival of what you ordered?

Morning Decree #129
Spend It

"But if God so clothes the grass of the field, which today is alive and green and tomorrow is tossed into the furnace, will He not much more surely clothe you, O you of little faith?" Matthew 6:30

Money, money, money, as the song goes, is what makes the world go 'round.' Whether that's true can be argued, but what can't be argued is to transact in heaven, you need faith. Faith is a currency. It's what one must have to do business with God on behalf of the Kingdom of God. However, if you don't have biblical faith, you can't spend what you don't have.

Many confuse believing the right things with faith. You can't have faith without believing the right things, but you can believe and still not have faith. Belief, in modern culture, is an intellectual agreement that something exists or is true. However, biblical faith is taking what one believes to be true and connects it with actions that support it.

For instance, a person can believe that a bed will support their weight—a correct belief. However, faith is expressed when a person actually lays down on that bed. That's faith. Belief won't get you a good night's sleep, but faith will. You demonstrate your faith by your actions in concert with what you believe to be true. If you've got faith, then spend it and you spend it by doing, not by merely believing.

Questions for Reflections

1. Reflect upon a time when you arrived at the checkout counter only to realize you didn't have enough money to pay for what you had in your basket. How did it make you feel?

2. Whose fault was it that you didn't have sufficient currency to purchase those items?

3. Did the store let you take home those things, or did you have to come up with the money?

Morning Decree #130
You Need More to Get More to Get More

"The apostles said to the Lord, 'Increase our faith!'" Luke 17:5

Saving money is remarkably difficult for many people, perhaps even you. This is especially true when you barely have enough money to meet your current needs. However, it's believed by many economists and pragmatists that having a savings account is critical to overall financial and emotional security. Furthermore, without more than enough in the bank, it's next to impossible to get the things you desire—a parallel truth when it comes to having faith. Although you can never stockpile faith, you certainly can have the amount required to get what you need or want.

Faith is like money. It doesn't discriminate against individuals because of race, gender, or nationality. If you got it, it would work to "buy" what you need. If you don't have it, you can't get the same. Faith is unemotional, and it's not affected by the whims of people or the current cultural malaise. Instead, faith is always up for the task—providing you have enough of it. Just like money faith can increase, and it can decrease. If you have needs, build your faith and then go buy what you need.

Questions for Reflections

1. Identify a time when you wanted something, and you saved up for a long time until you were able to purchase it. How did it make you feel?

2. When you were focused on buying that particular item, how did you treat the money you were making?

3. What did you do to save more money? What can you do now?

Morning Decree #131
Give "It" Away to Get More of "It"

"She did as Elijah said. And she and he and her household ate for many days."
1 Kings 17:15

It's counterintuitive to think that the way to get more is to give more. It's just not logical, but the ways of God often don't make sense to the natural mind. As seen in the above story, the way that this single mother and widow was able to thrive in the midst of a drought was by giving what she had. She gave to the prophet in this case, but the Law of Sowing and Reaping works for everyone, anyone, every time.

What you lack is what you need to give away. When farmers need a harvest of a particular agricultural product, they sow that specific seed. It's so simple that you can overthink it. You need love, give *agape* love to others. You need friends, be a better friend to someone else. You need favor, do a favor for someone who needs one. You have in your present possession something that can be used as a seed to meet your need.

Questions for Reflections

1. Why is it hard for us to give when we have needs?

2. When is the last time you intentionally gave away something expecting a return on your giving?

3. Do you have a giving plan?

Morning Decree #132
What's Your Credit Score?

"Thus Abraham believed in and adhered to and trusted in and relied on God, and it was reckoned and placed to his account and credited as righteousness (as conformity to the divine will in purpose, thought, and action)." Galatians 3:6, AMP

A credit score is used to determine many things, least of which is your ability to purchase things or acquire loans. Merchants, Insurance companies, and several other industries use a credit score to determine if they are willing to do business with you. Little did you know that there is a spiritual credit score you need to be conscious of as well.

This spiritual credit score is what gives you the right to ask the Father for things you both need and want. It's a score that is based on worthiness to even be on speaking terms with God. The problem with your score is that just one ding on it completely disqualifies you from any hope of being qualified. God knew this would be the problem and gave you His credit status—it's called righteousness.

Simply put, Jesus became your righteousness. You have access to the Father through Jesus' status as righteous. Perfect credit—it's glorious, undeserved, and unearned.

Questions for Reflections

1. Do you know you credit score? Has your credit ever negatively affected you in the past?

2. Have you ever felt you were not good enough to receive a blessing from God?

3. What do you think will be the result when you "use" Jesus as your credit score in prayer?

Morning Decree #133
Your Past Is Passed

"If You, Lord, should keep account of and treat [us according to our] sins, O Lord, who could stand?" Psalms 130:3, AMP

Many times when I pray, I'm flooded with all the things that, in my mind, should disqualify me from getting the blessing I seek. Whether it's for me or someone else, thoughts of unworthiness, condemnation, and regret try to make me feel like giving up. At that point, the thing I need to remember is that my past is not the determining factor of whether or not the Father hears my prayer. Righteousness and faith are what really matters.

On your best day, when you have done everything right, you still do not meet the holy standard that qualifies you to approach a holy God. To think otherwise is self-righteousness and is an exercise in futility. The reason why you can approach God in prayer is because of what Jesus Christ accomplished for you. It's not how good you have been, or how much money you give to the church, or how much you are willing to suffer for Christ. Your prayer and relationship with God are through Jesus Christ. To remember this will give you both peace and comfort when you pray.

Questions for Reflections

1. When you pray are you reminded of why it won't be answered? If so, what in your past does the enemy use to disqualify you?

2. How can you develop more confidence in your prayers in Jesus' Name?

3. Is there anything you can do to qualify for access to the Father?

Morning Decree #134
The More You Do, the Less God Does

"For if because of one man's trespass (lapse, offense) death reigned through that one, much more surely will those who receive [God›s] overflowing grace (unmerited favor) and the free gift of righteousness [putting them into right standing with Himself] reign as kings in life through the one Man Jesus Christ (the Messiah, the Anointed One)." Romans 5:17, AMP

The way of the Kingdom of God is seemingly upside down. Give to get. Forgive to be forgiven. Bless instead of cursing your enemies. Strange. The more we try to earn from God, the further we move away from the things we need and want. God favor can't be bought. God can't be bribed or manipulated. He can be worshiped, but that isn't a way to get Him to bless us His blessing is based upon an unearned and undeserved gift.

Righteousness, which means "right standing with God," is a gift. A gift by definition is not something you can earn or even qualify for. It can and must be received, but it can't be earned. Yes, we need to pray, fast, give, love, forgive, and many other spiritual and practical disciplines, but none of them buy the favor and blessing of God. The gift of being "right" with God through Jesus Christ is what places you in such a marvelous position.

Questions for Reflections

1. Why is it so hard for many people, maybe even you,
to receive something you know you didn't earn?

2. How would you pray if you were conscious of His righteousness
rather than the lack of yours?

3. What does it mean to you to be righteousness conscious
as opposed to. sin conscious?

Morning Decree #135
Boldness Is Beautiful

"Let us then fearlessly and confidently and boldly draw near to the throne of grace (the throne of God's unmerited favor to us sinners), that we may receive mercy [for our failures] and find grace to help in good time for every need [appropriate help and well-timed help, coming just when we need it]." Hebrews 4:16, AMP

Boldness is necessary when pursuing God. It's important to note, however, that this boldness is not bravado or pride. The boldness that gets things done is because of what Jesus Christ accomplished by dying in our place on the Cross.

I see this boldness in approaching God in prayer like my daughters did (and still) do when they need money from me. Because of their security in knowing that they are my flesh and blood, coupled with the revelation of my love for them, they ask without hesitation! I find it refreshing to know that they are secure in the reality of our relationship.

When you fully grasp the truth of Jesus being your mediator with the Father, reconciling you through His own blood, you will also have a boldness to approach the throne of God without hesitation or reservation. He's proven that His love for you is not based on your works or good deeds. God loves you just because you exist in His heart. Boldness is beautiful thing.

Questions for Reflections

1. What's the difference between being bold or brazen?

2. What stops you from being bold in your prayer requests?

3. How would your confidence in your relationship with God be affected if you understood the reason you have for being bold?

Morning Decree #136
Don't Forget Your Luggage

"For you have need of steadfast patience and endurance, so that you may perform and fully accomplish the will of God, and thus receive and carry away [and enjoy to the full] what is promised." Hebrews 10:36, AMP

Recently, I received a very expensive piece of luggage as a gift. Never would I have solicited such a gift nor decided to buy it. It's beautiful and even has my name on it. It's a piece of travel art. But it's for a clear purpose—to transport stuff I want to carry. Confidence is that inner quality that will empower you to carry what you need all the way to see your goals and dreams accomplished. Confidence is needed in times and seasons when it looks improbable that you will achieve the dream. Having confidence, though, will cause you to more patiently endure the vicissitudes of life.

Dropping your confidence is like forgetting your luggage. Confidence carries what you need—both patience and endurance—so you can arrive at your intended destination. Hold on to your confidence. Don't allow anything or anyone to drain it out of you. You need it.

Questions for Reflections

1. Can you describe a situation that built your confidence?

2. Who do you have in your life that maybe hindering your confidence?

3. What activities strengthen your resolve, and which ones weaken it?

Morning Decree #137
Do the Right Thing

"The wicked flee when no man pursues them, but the [uncompromisingly] righteous are bold as a lion." Proverbs 28:1, AMP

Have you ever loaned a friend some money and they just seem to have forgotten it was a loan? And every time you run into them, they can't look you in the eye or they try to avoid you altogether? You were once confident in your relationship with this person, but because they did not do the right thing, your confidence in them and the relationship has weakened.

This also applies to your relationship with God through Jesus Christ. When you are not doing the right things, you usually know it, and when you pray or need something from that relationship, you lack the required confidence to approach God. This lack of confidence is directly tied to your behavior and not God's rejection.

The truth is, whether you are doing what's right or wrong, the only way you can come to the Father is in the name of Jesus. However, the Holy Spirit convicts your conscience and won't allow you to continue with business-as-usual with God. You will be timid, reserved, and unsure unless and until you own the truth of your unrighteousness. Conversely, when you are doing as the Word of God demands, you will have no reservations coming to God.

Questions for Reflections

1. On a scale of 1-10, 10 being most confident, how would you score your confidence in prayer?

2. What is the main reason for your lack of confidence in approaching God?

3. What is it that you need to do to increase your boldness?

Morning Decree #138
You Didn't Ask for It

"You do not have, because you do not ask." James 4:2

It's remarkable to think that one reason you don't have what you want or need can be simply because you failed to ask for it. Often, in prayer, you spend your time talking to God about the problem, sharing all the challenges and complaining about the people involved, instead of asking the Father in Jesus' Name for what it is you desire.

Elder James in this Scripture reminds you of this simple, yet profound, reality that you don't have "it" because you didn't ask for it. Jealousy and envy rise up within you when you look at what others are enjoying, mistakenly thinking that they took what belongs to you. While the reason for the deficit in your life goes back to your failure to ask in faith with the right motives. Could it be you don't have that outstanding need met simply because you failed to ask the Source Himself for it?

Questions for Reflections

1. Are you jealous of someone else?

2. What is it that they have or are doing that you feel you should be doing?

3. Have you asked the Father for what you need and/or want?

Morning Decree #139
What's Really Motivating You?

"[Or] you do ask [God for them] and yet fail to receive, because you ask with wrong purpose and evil, selfish motives. Your intention is [when you get what you desire] to spend it in sensual pleasures." James 4:3, AMP

Motives matter. Motives, like motivation, can be understood by thinking about what is the thing that makes you move or take action. By definition, it is the reason for doing a certain thing. However, when it comes to praying, I don't think we often think about our true motives for making the request in the first place. There's nothing wrong with asking God for something that benefits or blesses you. The problem arises when we are unaware of the real motivation behind our prayers.

Be honest about why you want that "thing." Without that level of personal awareness, your prayers get blocked. Don't pretend to want that new big house so you can take in homeless people when you really don't plan to operate a rooming house. Be clear with your plans. If you want a big house because you want to enjoy a spacious living space, then say so. God wants you to enjoy life, just be honest with yourself and God.

Questions for Reflections

1. What is it that you really want, but feel bad about wanting it?

2. Do you secretly envy other followers of Jesus for what they have?

3. What's stopping you from asking your heavenly Father for those same things?

Morning Decree #140
Why Not You?

"Keep on asking and it will be given you; keep on seeking and you will find; keep on knocking [reverently] and [the door] will be opened to you." Matthew 7:7, AMP

Limitations are a man-made construct, usually something that we finite human beings have concluded are reasonable. However, the God of the universe is a limitless, infinite Being. That doesn't translate into limits on his children in terms of what's possible or acquirable. The only caveat is that what they desire will bless and do no harm. The truth is that most believers live with a self-imposed, limiting belief system. It's not something God the Father declared, "You shall go this far and no farther." We did that do ourselves or allowed society to put those limitations on our thinking.

Who said you couldn't be healed? Who said you can't be happy and joyful every day? Who said you couldn't prosper? Consider the source, but I assure you, it wasn't you Creator. Who said you couldn't ask for this or that?

Questions for Reflections

1. What happened in your life that caused you to downplay your dreams?

2. Can you remember a time in your life when you dreamed bigger dreams than you do now?

3. What can you be doing now to recapture a limitless mindset?

Morning Decree #141
Who Clipped Your Wings?

"You were running the race nobly. Who has interfered in (hindered and stopped you from) your heeding and following the Truth?" Galatians 5:7, AMP

Everyone is born to soar above the storms and circumstances. Your destiny is to thrive in life, not just survive life. However, stuff happened to you that can ground you when you were born to fly. People, situations, money challenges, and the expectations of others, just to name a few, have a tendency to be weights around your ankles that make it nearly impossible to fly above the average life.

Identify what clipped your wings that now keeps you just pecking around instead of flying around. What happened to create this "groundhog day type" movie/nightmare that keeps playing in your mind?

You are designed to soar. You are created to fly. You are designed to live above, not be tied to, the ever-changing winds of life. Flying is more fun than trudging through mud.

Questions for Reflections

1. What was the dream before "life" happened to you?

2. What is your expectation of yourself at this point in your life?

3. What's your real dream—the thing you would do if you had the money, time, and support?

Morning Decree #142
Nightmares or Dreams?

". . . and we shall see what will become of his dreams!" Genesis 37:20, AMP

Dreams are a picture of a future reality. This is even more powerful when the dreams are from God, but just because you have a dream is no guarantee that it will become a reality. As a matter of fact, dreams from God are often resisted by it seems like Hell itself. At that point, what was a dream turns into a nightmare—a nightmare from which you have no hope of waking.

One failure that even believer's often experience occurs when they allow the inevitable obstacles because of the dream to distract them. Many simply give up pursuing their goals, only to end up living a life well below their privilege. Instead, you should recognize anything worth having will require supernatural persistence.

Continue working toward the fulfillment of the dream by accepting the rain and the sun, the support and obstacles, as just part of the process. Determine today that you will live your dream. What comes of your dreams have more to do with how you respond to frustrations along the way than anything else.

Questions for Reflections

1. Describe how you will feel when your dream becomes a reality?

2. What are the issues that are hindering your dream from coming to pass?

3. How have you allowed the obstacles to stop the pursuit?

Morning Decree #143
Who's Starring in Your Dream?

"Now Reuben heard it and he delivered him out of their hands by saying . . ."
Genesis 37:21

God has so rigged life that no one can reach their full potential without the help of others. Even Jesus Christ had folks who helped with the administration of His ministry, not to mention those who funded the mission. Being aware of our need for others is the first step in accomplishing the dream, whatever it may be.

When God wants to bless someone, He usually brings someone into your life situation. Conversely, when the devil wants to sabotage someone, he usually uses someone to do his dirty work. It's not always clear, at least not initially, who is on your side. The key to finding out is to recognize that there are people God has assigned to your life to bless you, to encourage you, to rescue you, and even correct you when you're wrong. Learning how to incorporate them into your dream may be the difference between being frustrated or seeing it fulfilled. Thank God for the Reubens who will deliver you out of harm's way.

Questions for Reflections

1. Who has been your go-to person in your past?

2. On a scale of 1 to 10, how open are you to the support of others?

3. Can you recall a time where you failed to recognize
the God-sent people in your life?

Morning Decree #144
Dreams Work

"He becomes poor who works with a slack and idle hand, but the hand of the diligent makes rich." Proverbs 10:4

Dreams are easy to come by, but they take work to make a reality. Many people have a vision or desired goals. Dreams are a dime a dozen. The question isn't whether or not you have a dream, but rather what are you doing about it? Contrary to popular belief, dreams—even when they are from the throne room of God—require your partnership and cooperation.

Dreams work when dreamers do to their work. When is the last time you scheduled time to work on your dream? What resources are you allocating to support your plan? Who are you meeting with to learn more about how to make your dream a reality? The idea that dreams just happen is more like a fantasy. If your dream means a lot to you, then invest the sweat necessary to make it happen.

Questions for Reflections

1. What's your dream, the *big* dream?

2. What are the steps you've taken to make your dream a reality?

3. What's are three obstacles you're facing to manifest your dream?

Morning Decree #145
The Deceived Dreamer

"But be doers of the Word [obey the message], and not merely listeners to it,
betraying yourselves [into deception by reasoning contrary to the Truth]."
James 1:22, AMP

We erroneously think that being deceived is a mystical magic occurrence or that only the really spiritually weak fall prey to the wiles of the devil. Deception is evil, but to be self-deceived is the worst kind of deception. No wakes up one morning and says, "Today, I'm going to deceive myself." Deception is sneaky; it doesn't announce it's coming. This is even more evident when it comes to being self-deceived.

Self-deception occurs when we fail to adjust our life according to what the mirror of the Word of God shows us. To think that just seeing the need, problem, or, in this case, the dream, is enough for it to become a reality is the essence of deception. Don't allow yourself to be a deceived dreamer by thinking more than doing.

Questions for Reflections

1. Can you remember a time when you thought something to be true only to find you were deceived?

2. As you reflect on the Word of God, what are you seeing that needs to change in your life but you have failed to take action to make it so?

3. What do you call someone who sees the truth but fails to obey it?

Morning Decree #146
Your Foundation Matters Most

"So everyone who hears these words of Mine and acts upon them [obeying them] will be like a sensible (prudent, practical, wise) man who built his house upon the rock." Matthew 7:24, AMP

Any builder will tell you that the most important part of an edifice is the foundation. The foundation, unlike the color of the front door or the type of windows used on the house, cannot be seen. As a matter of fact, there's really no esthetic value placed on the foundation whatsoever. Nevertheless, more time and sometimes money is spent on getting the foundation laid correctly than any other part of the building.

When it comes to our "faith," sometimes little thought is given to ensure that it's built on right Scriptural truth. Many, when speaking about their faith, only have a cursory understanding. Perhaps this is why the majority of people in the United States claim to have Christianity as their faith but in practice demonstrate very little evidence to support such a claim. Consequently, when the storms of life blow against their faith, few are able to whether the storms. Evidence of having the right foundation is seen when the storms passes by and the person of faith is still standing.

Questions for Reflections

1. Describe a situation so difficult that it really tested your faith in God?

2. Explain what the foundation of your faith is based on Jesus Christ?

3. What are the types of storms you've faced that having a sure foundation is vital to victory?

Morning Decree #147
A Common Problem

"Whom resist steadfast in the faith, knowing that the same afflictions are accomplished in your brethren that are in the world." 1 Peter 5:9

To believe that as a follower of Jesus, you won't experience seasons of difficulty is naive at best. As the Bible teaches, in the world you will have tribulation. The question then is not if you will have trouble, but when and what to do when it comes. Knowing what do before the storms, during the storm and after the storm is critical to survive the hard times.

One of the critical keys to get through hard times is realizing your situation is not unique and you are you alone. While you are special, your situation is not. In fact, it's actually rather common. Understanding that others have gone or are going through nearly identical challenges in their faith is comforting. Success leaves clues. Finding out what they did to win their faith fight will save you time, energy, and sleepless nights. Others won, why can't you?

Questions for Reflections

1. Why do many people feel alone when they are going through a difficult season?

2. Do you feel no one understands how challenging the problem is that you're facing?

3. Would hearing about other people's problems and solutions be helpful to you?

Morning Decree #148
Remember the Last Time?

"So He replied to them, Go and tell John what you have seen and heard: the blind receive their sight, the lame walk, the lepers are cleansed, the deaf hear, the dead are raised up, and the poor have the good news (the Gospel) preached to them."
Luke 7:22, AMP

Hard times can make almost anyone question their faith. John, Jesus' second cousin and the one who identified Jesus as the Lamb of God (John 1:29), questioned whether or not Jesus was who John thought he was. When John's disciples came to ask Jesus whether or not He was the One, Jesus reminded them of what He had done and sent them back to John with that information and assurance.

When your back is up against the wall, remember what Jesus did for you and for others in the past. Recalling past victories, deliverances, even miracles will serve to strengthen you when facing emotionally-draining problems. Jesus Christ never changes. As the Bible reminds us, He is the "same yesterday, today and forever" (Hebrews 13:8). Your memory is a blessing. Use it.

Questions for Reflections

1. How does hearing a testimony affect your emotions? Your faith?

2. Recall at least three times when God made a way for you.

3. What are some things you can do to make it easier for you to recall past victories?

Morning Decree #149
Choose to Remember, Choose to Forget

"Brethren, I do not count myself to have apprehended; but one thing I do, forgetting those things which are behind and reaching forward to those things which are ahead . . ."
Philippians 3:13, AMP

The mind is a powerful organ and has the ability to determine how your life actually shapes up. Life transformation starts between your ears, much like the operating software runs a computer. The computer is only as good as the software used to run it.

There are things that you should choose to forget, like mistakes of yesterday. Once you have confessed your sins, you, like the Father, should elect to choose to forget about them and move forward. Sadly, we often don't do that but instead drag the dead weight of past failures into our present and future. Not only is this common practice unprofitable, it's also unbiblical.

Choose the selective amnesia option when it comes to sin and failures. Choose to remember the promises of God, the grace of God, and the mercy of God. It's only when you choose correctly that you experience the blessing of God in your life which will include making the right choice when it comes to what you should remember.

Questions for Reflections

1. When you hear the word *choice*, what three words come to mind?

2. What are your dominant thoughts about yourself?

3. In what ways do you feel your thought-life has impacted you either positively or negatively?

Morning Decree #150
Who's in Control?

"For as he thinks in his heart, so is he. As one who reckons, he says to you, eat and drink, yet his heart is not with you [but is grudging the cost]." Proverbs 23:7, AMP

Understanding who's in control is of supreme importance. To assume someone or something else is the boss of your future is tantamount to slavery. A slave simply does as they are told, exercising very little, if any, freedom of choice. Who's your boss determines the life you lead.

Your mind and thought-life runs your life. You are all the sum total of what you have thought or meditated on over the years. Garbage in, garbage out is what has been said about computers. You've heard the saying, "You are what you eat." More accurately, you become what you think about the most. As one preacher once said to me, "You can't control what birds fly over your head, but you sure can determine if they build a nest and lay eggs!"

It's critical that you take responsibility for your thoughts, realizing just because a thought enters your mind doesn't mean you must accept it, let alone meditate on it hour after hour. You're the boss of your mind. Take control of your thought life today.

Questions for Reflections

1. What are the main sources that feed your thought life?

2. Identify some of the most recurring thoughts that are hindering your progress?

3. What counter-thoughts can you meditate upon to eliminate the negative thinking cycle?

Morning Decree #151
Who Are You, Really?

"Therefore if any person is [ingrafted] in Christ (the Messiah) he is a new creation (a new creature altogether); the old [previous moral and spiritual condition] has passed away. Behold, the fresh and new has come!" 2 Corinthians 5:17

Identity theft is a real big deal nowadays. Multiple billions of dollars are stolen every year by first stealing someone's identity. This same crime is perpetrated on human beings, especially Christians. I'm not talking about the theft of someone's Social Security check, but rather their personal understanding of who they are in Christ.

Who you are (who you became) by receiving Jesus Christ as Lord is much more than a philosopher or a new religion. Actually, you became a new species, a new creature. As the Scripture states, you are a new creature in Christ. Though your physical appearance doesn't change, meaning you don't change eye color for instance, the essence of who you are from the inside certainly does. The importance of this cannot be understated, for true transformation is first an inside job.

Questions for Reflections

1. What does being a new creation mean to you?

2. How should an inner change affect the outside life of a person?

3. What's the difference between religion and relationship when it comes to God?

Morning Decree #152
What Are You Made of?

"... and may your spirit and soul and body be preserved sound and complete [and found] blameless at the coming of our Lord Jesus Christ (the Messiah)."
1 Thessalonians 5:23, AMP

You are more than a pretty face. You are more than a collection of cells, blood, and bones. In actuality, that's not who you are at all. You have a body and a soul, but you are a spirit. The body is where your spirit resides, but you are not a body. According to the Scriptures, you are a tri-part being (three part); you are spirit and you have a soul (mind, will, emotions), living in a physical body.

In our society, there is much emphasis on body or the physical appearance. Very little attention is paid to the health of the body, unless of course there is pain or some obvious sickness. While it's extremely important to take care of one's body, the most important part of a person is their spirit and soul. The body, over time returns to dust, but the spirit and soul of a person will live eternally. So your spirit life must be a top priority, for you are spirit not a body.

Questions for Reflections

1. Is saying body, soul, spirit the same as spirit, soul, body?

2. Why is there so much emphasis on appearance?

3. How would you describe the condition of your spirit and soul?

Morning Decree #153
Who Do You Look Like?

"...because as He is, so are we in this world." 1 John 4:17

"For whom He foreknew, He also predestined to be conformed to the image of His Son, that He might be the firstborn among many brethren." Romans 8:29

Image is everything to some people. It's actually very important to God, too. The Scriptures declare we are made in His likeness and image. But what does God look like is the next logical question. The challenge is that God's image is spirit manifested in flesh. And since we are made in His Image, then we too are spirit. Spirit has no physical features. By definition, it can't be seen. But why then is there so much emphasis on one's physical appearance? There's actually very little in the Bible about physical appearance and by no means is it more important than the spirit and soul of a person.

Who you look like is still a valid question however, but the "look like" element is more about how you are living and talking like Jesus rather than resembling Him from a physical perspective. The ultimate goal you should have is to be conformed into the image of the Son. I want the entirety of my life to "look like Jesus." I hope you do as well.

Questions for Reflections

1. Who do others say you favor in your family?

2. In what ways to you "look like" them other than physically?

3. Has anyone every commented to you about your resemblance to Jesus? If so, in what ways?

Morning Decree #154
Like Father, Like Children

"If I do not do the works of My Father, do not believe Me; but if I do, though you do not believe Me, believe the works, that you may know and believe that the Father is in Me, and I in Him." John 10:37-38

Jesus is like the Father. The Holy Spirit is like both the Father and the Son. The oneness, the unity of the Godhead is incontrovertible. If you really want to know what God the Father is like, just take a good long look at the Son of God. He only did and said what was in complete agreement with the Father.

Likewise, the Holy Spirit only behaved in ways that were in perfect concert with Jesus. As a matter of fact, a good way to determine if your actions or the actions of others are righteousness, just compare them to what Jesus would do. If He would not do it, then neither should you.

Jesus is our Lord, Savior, and elder brother. His is the firstborn and knows the will of our Heavenly Father better than you and I ever will. If we are desiring to know the heart, character, and will of our heavenly Dad, study Jesus. Look at His life, His approach to things, His reactions, and His priorities and then imitate them. This is one time when being a copy-cat is right, proper, and expected.

Questions for Reflections

1. Name someone you know who you sought to emulate while you were in high school. What was it you did to be like them?

2. What were the main characteristics to which you were drawn and why?

3. What are the characteristics of Christ you feel you most lack?

Morning Decree #155
Consider the Source

"There we saw the giants (the descendants of Anak came from the giants); and we were like grasshoppers in our own sight, and so we were in their sight."
Numbers 13:33

Believing, let alone repeating, what you hear can be a self-defeating and self-deceiving proposition. Just because it was said to you or about you doesn't make it true, even if it comes from someone who you respect and look up to. The source and motivation behind what is said is as important as what is said. You need to think, speak, and believe the Word of God regarding every and all matters of your life.

Often the enemy plays word games with you, floating thoughts your way. It's like throwing mud against a wall to see if it sticks. And if you aren't diligently guarding what gets thrown in your direction, your judgment gets murky. What you allow to stick in your mind is exactly what you will become over time.

You shouldn't draw any conclusions based on what you hear or see unless it's coming from God. Otherwise, just like Israel, you will see giants and can erroneously conclude that you are already beaten. If God didn't say it, if God didn't send it, reject it. Period.

Questions for Reflections

1. Share a time you have been intimated by something you heard or saw, only to find out later it wasn't worth another thought?

2. What could happen to a person's dreams if they allow "sights and sounds" to paralyze their movements?

3. Why is it important to consider the source of the information given to you?

Morning Decree #156
Don't Give Up

"He said to them, 'An enemy has done this.' The servants said to him, 'Do you want us then to go and gather them up?'" Matthew 13:28

Many times when we are doing the right thing, the right way, we lose sight of the reality that there are forces at work attempting to sabotage our efforts. And when we realize what is going on, we are disappointed and disillusioned. While those emotions are understandable, our energy would be better spent safeguarding our efforts, rather than questioning why things are going poorly.

Just because something goes wrong when you are doing what's right is no excuse to get out of character or worse, lose faith. Know, from the very beginning, there will challenges to impede your progress. When you understand there is a real possibility that headwinds are in the forecast, you will neither lose heart nor abandon ship. Such challenges are often a sign you are marking more progress than you realize. Get going. Don't slow up. Be resolute.

Questions for Reflections

1. Describe a project that despite your best efforts, someone or some effort hindered it?

2. What happens to your morale when you discover not everyone is on your team or in your corner?

3. What can you do going forward to bolster your chances of success despite the negative forces swirling around you?

Morning Decree #157
What You Believe Is More Important

"When Jesus came into the region of Caesarea Philippi, He asked His disciples, saying, 'Who do men say that I, the Son of Man, am?'" Matthew 16:13

Everyone who knows you has an opinion about your potential. Whether or not they ever voice it to you, they have made an assessment of your abilities. I think it's human nature. What's more, your true friends and family probably believe in you more than you do. Although is a plus to have such support, the most important person in your network of believers is you. What you believe about you is what really counts.

In our culture, even within the ranks of the Church, many have given too much thought to the opinions of others in forming their own opinion about themselves. We ask things as innocuous as, "How do I look?" to "What's my purpose in life?" to form our opinions about ourselves. While it's important to ask for advice on important matters, you should know what you believe first. There is no shortage of "talking heads" out there, but be sure you're secure in your beliefs about who you are and what your potential is.

Questions for Reflections

1. Looking back, whose opinion of you has most shaped your thinking about yourself?

2. In what ways did their thoughts about your potential impact your decisions?

3. From what source should you rely most heavily upon
in developing our belief system?

Morning Decree #158
Did You Forget Who You Are?

"And the Angel of the Lord appeared to him, and said to him,
'The Lord is with you, you mighty man of valor!'" Judges 6:12

It happens to the best of us. Due to a series of disappointments, setbacks, and tragic events, self-doubt can creep in. You may even start to feel that you are what your circumstances are. For instance, say you filed bankruptcy, you can start thinking, "I am bankrupt." No, you're not bankrupt, but your situation required you to take advantage of the system that allowed you to petition for the bankruptcy. You are not your situation.

If those unfortunate situations occur, you must remember from where your help comes. God's thoughts about you and your situations are more important than what anyone else says. If you lose sight of this, you will by default start to identify with your problem. You are not an event, a tragedy, a disappointment. You are who God says you are. You can do what God says you can do. You can have what God says you can have. You are a child of God. You are an heir of God. You are a joint heir with Jesus Christ Himself. You are special.

Questions for Reflections

1. What event in your life have caused you to think less of yourself?

2. In what ways did your attitude and behavior change for the worse?

3. What things can you start doing today to rediscover the real you?

Morning Decree #159
Come Back to Yourself

"But when he came to himself, he said . . ." Luke 15:17a, NKJV

Pride, selfishness, and impatience are just some of the reasons why we mess up. Failure to listen, lack of self-control, the unbridled lust for freedom have cost many Christians much money, time, and, in some cases, their very lives. These character issues can only be resolved by deep repentance, but the start of the turn-around is recognizing you were created for better than where you are.

The prodigal son, as he is known in the gospels, came to the realization that his life had taken a turn for the worse due to his own decisions. The story records the moment when he "came to himself." In other words, he was living outside of his true identity. Truthfully, any time you do something that is contrary to the Word of God, you are living outside your true self in Christ just like the prodigal.

The prodigal son came back to his true self, which gave him the courage to return to his father's house. Undoubtedly, he returned to the same house with the rules, traditions, and responsibilities firmly in place. Don't you think it's time to return to the Father's way of living and doing life?

Questions for Reflections

1. Can you recall a period in your life where you just "lost your mind?" What were some of the consequences you had to endure?

2. What happened to cause you to wake up and come to you senses?

3. In what ways did you lose yourself? How did you recover from that season?

Morning Decree #160
You're Better Than This

"Now David was greatly distressed, for the people spoke of stoning him, because the soul of all the people was grieved, every man for his sons and his daughters. But David strengthened (encouraged) himself in the Lord his God." 1 Samuel 30:6, AMP

One valuable principle I discovered through advising thousands of people over the years is that encouragement brings out their better sides. There's something about acknowledging someone's good efforts, as opposed to always at picking up on the wrong things, that makes them want to try harder the next time. Correction is often needed in all of our lives, but there is a deep hunger in people to be told good things about themselves. It's been my experience that even God sees our future and encourages us to pursue it, knowing we will have to grow past the immature behaviors of the past in order to realize it.

Encouraging yourself with the thoughts and words of God is the place to start learning the power and encouragement from the Word. There will be things that happen in your lifetime through which you will need to encourage yourself onward through deep waters. Positive, God-breathed truths will enable you to traverse the toughest times. To harness the power of encouragement requires a knowledge of God's thoughts concerning you. Bible reading, study, and the hearing of sermons is never wasted time, providing you realize at some point you will need every Word you have heard.

Questions for Reflections

1. Describe a situation when someone gave you hope through encouraging words?

2. How did it make your feel? How did you respond?

3. When was the last time you intentionally gave someone an encouraging word?

Morning Decree #161
Ask the Designer

"For I know the thoughts that I think toward you, says the Lord, thoughts of peace and not of evil, to give you a future and a hope." Jeremiah 29:11

If you want to know the original purpose of a thing, just ask the one who created it. It really is that simple because the person who created it knows what their intention was in the beginning. Tragically, over time, situations, experiences, and the hands of others can mar the article, obscuring its original purpose. This has happened to all of us. Sin, whether those we committed and or those committed against us, have all served to deface God's original purpose for our lives. The uniqueness of each snow fake and fingerprint confirm the originality of each person. Life has marked us, actually scarred us. And as a result, we rarely understand God's original thoughts for us.

One of the most important things you need to do is rediscover God's purpose for your life. The best way to achieve this is by asking the Creator Himself what that purpose is. His thoughts about you are more beautiful than you can imagine.

Questions for Reflections

1. What were your thoughts about yourself before "life" happened?

2. Because of your "yesterdays," is it hard for you to believe good things about your future?

3. Ask the Creator for His thoughts about you. What is He saying?

Morning Decree #162
Broken is More Valuable

"He who did not spare His own Son, but delivered Him up for us all, how shall He not with Him also freely give us all things?" Romans 8:32

Just because something is broken now doesn't mean it's no longer valuable. A very expensive, luxury car that isn't working properly isn't discarded, it's repaired. The same is true for you and me. Despite our brokenness, Jesus came to restore us to pristine order. He knows our inherent value and looks past our present issues. It's not that our problems, sins, and failures don't matter to Him, but His grace is greater.

Stop looking at yourself as damaged goods. You, me, and the rest of the human race, have all been molested by life—but that's not a surprise to God. Actually, it's the scarring that makes you even more precious in His sight. Think about it. You are so valuable that God the Father sent His Son, Jesus, as the ransom for your future.

Questions for Reflections

1. Name at least three things that are more valuable because they are "old"?

2. How do you think a person's self-esteem is affected by negative experiences?

3. From where should you get your sense of personal worth?

Morning Decree #163
Stay Flexible

"Look, as the clay is in the potter's hand, so are you in My hand . . ." Jeremiah 18:6

Being flexible is an important quality when it comes to growth and personal development. The transformation process that all of us must undergo requires us to be flexible and malleable. Failure to bend when a bend is needed results in one of two things: 1) a misshapen life; 2) being left to our own ways. I'm not sure which of the two is worse. One thing is certain, however, and that is we can't experience God's best for our lives unless we work on our flexibility.

Transformation is the goal. As the Scripture reminds us, we are "transformed by the renewal of our minds" (see Romans 12:2). That means our lives takes on a new shape as we submit to the potter's touch. Resisting His touch is tantamount to disobedience and rebellion, and the end result is never pleasing. It's much better to bend and bow now so your best life can be enjoyed to the fullest.

Questions for Reflections

1. Do you know someone who lacks flexibility in their relationships?
In what ways are they inflexible?

2. Has anyone described you as being inflexible?

3. Are you malleable and teachable when it comes
to your spiritual life and development?

Morning Decree #164
Embrace the Shift

"Behold, I will do a new thing, Now it shall spring forth; Shall you not know it? I will even make a road in the wilderness and rivers in the desert." Isaiah 43:19

Anything that is growing is by definition changing. Therefore, growth is really a healthy part of life and living. When you stop growing, you start dying. Spiritually, this principle is also relevant. To mature spiritually demands intentional development. The best way to develop begins with the recognition that change is an absolute necessity. It is not an option, it is expected.

Embracing this reality is a sign that you are ready for change. Thankfully, the Lord accepts you the way you are. However, He doesn't leave you the same way in which he finds you. Your growth and maturity are of the utmost importance to Him, and should be to you as well. Don't fight change; embrace it.

Questions for Reflections

1. How would describe your tolerance for change?

2. In what ways do you feel God pushing you to "shift?"

3. How will you strengthen your ability to shift those areas in your life?

Morning Decree #165
Will the Real You Please Step Forward

"And He said, 'Your name shall no longer be called Jacob, but Israel; for you have struggled with God and with men, and have prevailed.'" Genesis 32:28

Change can be difficult, but change is necessary. Giving your life over to the Lordship of Jesus demands change. The changes required are far from just being cosmetic. This type of change is at the spiritual cellular level that affects your very character.

Christianity as a "religion" is about what you do, much more than who you are. While being a follower of Jesus is about transformation from the inside out, what you do is a byproduct of who you are. Character matters. Deep transformation is the job of the Holy Spirit but only with your cooperation. Work on the inside person. The outside, the public presentation of ourselves to others, changes as you undergo an inner metamorphosis. Don't settle for acting, be transformed.

Questions for Reflections

1. Who are you when no one is watching?

2. Is your character in alignment with the Word of God?

3. What areas of your "true self" need to undergo character transformation?

Morning Decree #166
Don't Give Up

"Therefore do not cast away your confidence, which has great reward."
Hebrews 10:35

Everyone who has attempted anything significant in life has faced the overwhelming temptation to quit. Pressures, setbacks, disappointments, and hard times all contribute to the feeling like "giving up." The old saying goes, "Winners never quit, quitters never win" still rings true today. Wanting to quit is a natural response under certain circumstances. Ultimately, however, quitting because its hard is an unacceptable response.

As a follower of Jesus, faith is the antidote for a virus I call "giving up." This virus attacks the emotions, dreams, and goals of a person, causing them to abandon all hope of ever being successful. Faith, on the other hand, sees a future unaffected by the present problems. Building your faith is the first step out of the dungeon of discouragement.

Questions for Reflections

1. Can you recall a time when you quit too soon?

2. What were the reasons you quit things in the past, only to realize you should have stuck it out?

3. What things can you do that will help you overcome the pressure to quit?

Morning Decree #167
He Started It; He Will Complete It

"...being confident of this very thing, that He who has begun a good work in you will complete it until the day of Jesus Christ." Philippians 1:6

The "it" in the title is you and me. We are the "it" that God started. All life, regardless of the conditions under which conception occurred, is a God-life. Neither devil nor science can give life and since God is the creator of your life, the pressure is really on Him to make it work. In no way, however, does this exempt you from doing your part.

In the period between your first heartbeat and your last breath, you have things to do. There are biblical laws and principles that once you embrace them will yield beautiful results. The power, however, of following the biblical mandates is in how well you cooperate in your own shaping of your life. The erroneous idea that "God is in control" without your active participation is one of the main reasons for frustration. What He has started (which is you) includes a plan to empower you to be the best version of yourself as possible.

Questions for Reflections

1. Do you feel God is for or against you?

2. What are you in the "middle of" that doesn't seem like will ever be accomplished?

3. What steps can you take to get back on track?

Morning Decree #168
Get God's Attention

"Then those who went before warned him that he should be quiet; but he cried out all the more, 'Son of David, have mercy on me!' So Jesus stood still and commanded him to be brought to Him. And when he had come near, He asked him . . ."
Luke 18:39-40

Have you ever been in a difficult situation and wondered if God even knows you're going through a hard time? Often, when under a lot of circumstances, you can tend to think that God doesn't realize just how bad things are. Rest assured, God knows and God cares, and God is working on your behalf. He's actually walking in your direction right now.

A blind man named Bartimaeus heard Jesus was in the neighborhood. He took full advantage of the opportunity and began to cry out to get Jesus' attention. There are times when nothing short of crying out to God will get the job done. This man's cry was so desperate for change He lost consciousness of the opinions of others. He needed a miracle. He cried out to Jesus. You should do the same if your need is like his was.

Questions for Reflections

1. What are you desperate to receive from God?

2. In what ways do you demonstrate your desperation?

3. How can you demonstrate, on a daily basis,
that you are awaiting a miracle from Jesus?

Morning Decree #169
Positioned for a Miracle

"And He said to him, "Go, wash in the pool of Siloam" (which is translated, Sent). So he went and washed, and came back seeing." John 9:7

Many people think that "miracles" are only given at the whim of God. However, the Bible gives us a different picture. Certainly, miracles are a supernatural occurrence and the word *supernatural* provides us with a hint as to how miracles happen. The word *super* speaks to the God's role, while the word *natural* refers to the part that you play. Therefore, in a very real sense, the miraculous is a by-product of your obedience to God. Without obedience to God's direction, miracles are predictably absent.

Discovering the role you need to play in obtaining a miracle is critical. Though prayer is a key, it's also important to hear what the Father says during prayer. When you need something from God, listening for specific instructions is the first step to getting your petition met. God has made the first move, but the breakthrough is contingent upon your response to His command. Make you follow through on what you hear.

Questions for Reflections

1. Is there something you have been "led" to do, but have failed to do to date?

2. What's the miracle you need?

3. What steps will you take today in obedience to receive your miracle?

Morning Decree #170
Seed-Minded, Not Need-Minded

"Now may He who supplies seed to the sower, and bread for food, supply and multiply the seed you have sown and increase the fruits of your righteousness."
2 Corinthians 9:10

When you have a problem, your tendency may be to focus on getting it solved. That seems logical, but God's way is different. As needs and even wants show up in your world, you need to shift your thinking to answer, "What seed can I plant to produce the harvest to meet my need?" Farmers, who need a harvest of corn, don't focus on the fact they have no corn. Instead, they put their energy and money into preparing the soil and plant every seed they have. By focusing on seeds, they position themselves for multiple harvests of miracles.

What is it that you need? What seed do you have to sow for a harvest? Those are just two questions you should ask yourself when you are faced with lack. Lack doesn't respond to your tears, but only to faith. What's more, the faith required isn't just a mental or knowledge thing. Faith demands action. Faith isn't faith without action. If you need something demonstrate your faith by sowing a seed. Seeds meet needs.

Questions for Reflections

1. How does worry affect your mind, movement, and faith?

2. What is the most pressing need you have right now?

3. Instead of looking for answers, look for seed. What seed do you have to sow?

Morning Decree #171
It's Easier the Next Time

"Therefore take heart, men, for I believe God that it will be just as it was told me."
Acts 27:25

Who doesn't like "easy" when it comes to accomplishing their goals or dreams in life? However, when you quit because it's hard, the next time a problem arises in your quest for success, it will be easier to quit than the first time. Human nature seems to gravitate towards the path of least resistance. When it comes to achievement, the path with obstacles is the way to your pot of gold.

Use each challenge you face as an opportunity to develop resilience. The pressures, the negative environment, or the lack of resources can all be used and viewed in a positive manner. However, if you see quitting as a viable option, you will never see the mighty hand of God mark a way for you. It's usually when you come to end of your own resources—knowledge, support, finances etc.—that you experience divine intervention. Trust the invisible God to make His provision visible to you. Quitting is not an option.

Questions for Reflections

1. When you were younger, do you remember a time when you quit something because it just seemed too hard at the time? Was it the right decision?

2. Why does it seem easier to quit the "next time" than the first time?

3. What resources are at your disposal to give you the push you need to hang in there?

Morning Decree #172
What's In Your Hand?

"So the Lord said to him, 'What is that in your hand?' He said, 'A rod.'" Exodus 4:2

Common, everyday things are often overlooked as the means to solving problems. Things around you that are seemingly insignificant are many times the very things God will use to do incredible things. Being aware of what's in your hand—or within your reach—is the key to understanding how God will deliver you.

In Moses' case, he didn't realize the piece of wood, his walking stick, would be the tool God would use to set him, along with several million other people, free after 400 years of bondage. It's the common, used at the command of God, through which supernatural things will occur. The secret didn't reside in Moses' rod, but in his trust in God who could turn a piece of wood into a symbol of power. What have you been leaning on all these years that might be used for God's glory? Your heavenly Father can use anything to work miracles in your life.

Questions for Reflections

1. Take a look around you right now. What common everyday items are within your reach? List them?

2. How they might be used as a tool for your deliverance? Maybe it's something that could be sold or given away as a seed.

3. Describe a time when you obeyed God concerning something seemingly significant and it turned out to be a great blessing in your life or in the life of someone you knew?

Morning Decree #173
Cake Batter

"And as she was going to get it, he called to her and said, 'Please bring me a morsel of bread in your hand.'" 1 Kings 17:11

It's amazing what a little flour can become in the right hands. The hands I'm referring to are not the prophet's hands, but the widow's and single parent's hands in 1 Kings 17. In this story, it's all this woman had to give—a morsel of fresh-baked bread. We make a big mistake when we diminish what we have, fearing it's not significant enough to get what we need or want.

This scenario seems a bit far-fetched to most of us today. But the truth is, many people are facing situations in which they lack the necessities of life. To add insult to injury, they lack the wherewithal to purchase them. The wonder of God is that He never leaves anyone without something that can be used to jumpstart their needed miracle. The key is nestled in obedience to the Word of God. Doing what the Word says to do in that moment is what releases the miracle.

This widow, despite her hopeless situation and meager resources, obeyed the prophet. When she did as the prophet requested, supernatural provision was made. Who knew a cake would be the answer?

Questions for Reflections

1. Why is it so difficult sometimes to trust God?

2. What do you have in your "cabinet" that if God asked you to give, you would be hesitant to do so because you need it yourself?

3. How would you, having read this story, react if God asked you to give your "last?"

Morning Decree #174
The Oil in Your House

"So Elisha said to her, 'What shall I do for you? Tell me, what do you have in the house?' And she said, 'Your maidservant has nothing in the house but a jar of oil.'"
2 Kings 4:2

It's no mistake the Word of God highlights the most vulnerable when teaching lessons on provision. Women, widows, and children are often the stars of these stories. In this case, a widow was the wife of a faithful prophet. He was not indicted in any way except for the fact that at the time of his death he was deeply in debt. Failure to take care of his home first was possibly his only offense. His wife came to his spiritual father, Elisha, and shared her dilemma. The prophet asked her a series of questions that would benefit us if we answered them for ourselves. *What shall I do for you?* and *What do you have in your house?*

Essentially, the prophet was saying, "Why are you talking to me about this? What do you have in your house to address this crisis?" God, your Heavenly Father, is quite aware of your situation, but has not left you without a remedy. The Prophet gave the widow specific steps to take that at first glance had no direct connection to her financial need. Nevertheless, she did as the prophet directed and ended up debt free and financially stable for the rest of her life. It's about time you used the oil in your house.

Questions for Reflections

1. What's you most pressing need right now?

2. Have you asked the Father for help? What did He instruct you to do?

3. Have you fully obeyed His instructions?

Morning Decree #175
Even Jesus Needed Financial Support

"Now it came to pass, afterward, that He went through every city and village, preaching and bringing the glad tidings of the kingdom of God. And the twelve were with Him, and certain women who had been healed of evil spirits and infirmities— Mary called Magdalene, out of whom had come seven demons, and Joanna the wife of Chuza, Herod's steward, and Susanna, and many others who provided for Him from their substance." Luke 8:1-3

It's a bit hard for me to imagine Jesus, the Son of God and the Word Himself, needing anything from anyone. But according to Scripture, Jesus needed support for His earthly ministry. The support He needed wasn't just for Him but also for His ministry team. In his gospel, Dr. Luke recorded the names of several woman who financed the ministry. These particular women were healed by Jesus and I would imagine wanted others to benefit from His grace as well. By supporting Jesus' ministry, she enabled Him to continue unimpeded by financial needs.

Questions for Reflections

1. Why do you think Jesus subjected Himself to the generosity of others to discharge the duties of His ministry?

2. Do you think Jesus begged them to support His ministry, or do you think there was a willingness on their part?

3. Are you generous toward those ministries have been used by God to bless your life?

Morning Decree #176
How Deep Is Your Love?

"Therefore I say to you, her sins, which are many, are forgiven, for she loved much. But to whom little is forgiven, the same loves little." Luke 7:47

The depth of your love for God is not measured in words only, but in deeds and acts of obedience. When you think of God as an emotion rather than an action, you may think you love God because you feel a particular set of emotions any given day. The Scriptures don't use emotion as the criteria but rather our obedience.

The nameless women in this account demonstrated her love by her radical response to Jesus. Yes, the precious gift used to anoint Him was certainly noteworthy, but Jesus barely noticed it. He commented rather on her motivation. This women's response to Jesus was based upon her understanding of much Jesus has been forgiven her. The depth of a person's love also correlates to their revelation of how much they have been forgiven. When you realize the depth of sin in which you were found by Jesus, your love for Jesus will be shameless and fathomless.

Questions for Reflections

1. Do you ever reflect on where you were when Jesus found you?

2. Are you aware of your ongoing need for Jesus as Savior?

3. In what ways (and how often) do you show appreciation to Jesus for forgiving you of your sins?

Morning Decree #177
The Speaking Gift

"You did not anoint My head with oil, but this woman has anointed My feet with fragrant oil. Therefore I say to you, her sins, which are many, are forgiven, for she loved much. But to whom little is forgiven, the same loves little." Luke 7:46-47

I've come to realize that what I give to God's work on the earth and how I give it speaks louder than my proclamations of love. As the adage goes, "Actions speak louder than words" which is quite poignant because actions, which should emanate from your purest motives, reveals your heart. This nameless woman is not recorded to have said a single word to Jesus. She let her gift speak for her.

When you only allow the time of year or a specific date to dictate when and what you give to God or others, you miss many opportunities to say "love You" in the most moving of ways. Your gift is an extension of love. It's not a thing, it's you. Whether it's as big gift, or small gift, whether it's bought or homemade, your gift is speaking something to God. The question is, "What do you hope to convey to God by your gift?

Questions for Reflections

1. When is the last time you gave a gift that really conveyed your heart to God?

2. What is the most meaningful gift you've ever given
for the work of the Kingdom of God?

3. Why was it so meaningful to you?

Morning Decree #178
Everyone Has Something

"Now may He who supplies seed to the sower, and bread for food, supply and multiply the seed you have sown and increase the fruits of your righteousness . . ."
2 Corinthians 9:10

What you perceive to be significant often determines how you treat it. It's all about perspective. This is very important when it comes to viewing what you have to give or sow toward the Kingdom of God. How your life goes has a lot to do with what you invest and where you invest it. While this definitely applies to money matters, it's equally true when it comes to how you use your time, talents, and opportunities.

How you perceive what you "have" will dictate how you utilize it. Often you can ignore a penny lying in the street because it has very little value to you. However, the $100 bill is comprised of 10,000 pennies! And if a person were to collect thousands of pennies, over time they would have hundreds of dollars. This is a simple example to illustrate a powerful truth. What you perceive as insignificant *is* insignificant to you. However, if you change your perception of a thing, you would realize that it might just be the seed of the breakthrough you've been seeking all along.

Questions for Reflections

1. What do you presently have in your possession
that you perceive as being insignificant?

2. What do you have—time, talents, opportunity—that if you
viewed them differently, could position you better for the future?

3. What do you have now that is a seed to plant in the Kingdom of God?

Morning Decree #179
Stop Trying to Figure It Out?

"The wind blows where it wishes, and you hear the sound of it, but cannot tell where it comes from and where it goes. So is everyone who is born of the Spirit." John 3:8

The human mind is at work all the time. It never stops, not even for a second. Even when you sleep, the mind is trying to solve at night what it couldn't resolve during the day. This is painfully true when it comes to trying to figure out how God is going to answer a prayer or resolve some nagging issue in your life. Worry, anxiety, and fear are born out of a imagination that won't turn itself off. Your job, when it comes to the things of the spirit, is to have faith in God—not figure God out.

Faith and obedience are the lanes in which you must remain during the periods of waiting on prayer answers. How it happens is God's job; trust is your job. You can't figure out the ways of God any more than you can understand how God puts a heartbeat in a womb. You know it occurs, you just can't figure out how. Certain things are God's domain. Let God do His job and you do yours. Have faith in God.

Questions for Reflections

1. Describe your role in faith versus God's role?

2. How can you demonstrate you are trusting God versus playing God?

3. How would your overall mood change if you trusted God concerning your life?

Morning Decree #180
It's Your Move

"But this Man, after He had offered one sacrifice for sins forever, sat down at the right hand of God, from that time waiting till His enemies are made His footstool."
Hebrews 10:12-13

If I had a dollar for every time someone said to me, "I'm waiting on God," I'd be wealthy. The Bible teaches that Jesus is seated. To be seated means to have completed the task assigned. Jesus did all He needed to do on your behalf. He's seated now at the right hand of the Father. He's the one doing the waiting now.

You have been given assignments; assignments in the plural. You have things you need to do that determine your future as well as countless billions. Too often you may be praying when you should be working. You are waiting when you should be deeply engaged performing the last task assigned to you. One major corporation uses this phrase with it's retail employees, "if you have time to lean, you have time to clean." In other words, if you have nothing to do, there is always something to do—like clean!

Your breakthrough is connected to your obedience. Your blessing is released through your actions. The miracle you need for your family is tied to your next move and it's your move. In fact, it's been your move. It's way past time for you to take decisive action. It's your move now.

Questions for Reflections

1. What have you been waiting on the Lord to do that you now realize there is still more for you to do?

2. Reading the Gospels, describe at least three miracles that occurred only *after* actions were taken by the person needing the miracle.

3. What move(s) do you need to make?

Morning Decree #181
The End Can Be
Your New Beginning

"In the beginning God (prepared, formed, fashioned, and) created the heavens and the earth. The earth was without form and an empty waste, and darkness was upon the face of the very great deep. The Spirit of God was moving (hovering, brooding) over the face of the waters." Genesis 1:1, AMP

Usually, the beginning of something new comes after the end of the thing it is replacing. New beginnings are exciting on one hand, but if it means having to start all over again, our tendency is to avoid it. After all, who wants to start all over, having invested time, money, and tears into something like a relationship or business. However, sometimes starting over again is exactly what is necessary.

Take God—the Creator of all—for instance. When we first see Him in action in the book of Genesis, He is creating but as a re-creation. Genesis 1:1-3 tells a story of God creating a world, only to see that world is empty, dark, and void of life or light. That doesn't sound much like something on par with God's style. Something happened between verses one and two; what we aren't sure. What is clear is that He decided on re-creation from scratch and the result was a new planet that reflected His glory.

Starting over again from scratch takes courage, vision, and determination. It's not only do-able but necessary at different times and for different reasons. Take courage and just begin. The same God who started you will finish what He started in you. In the end, you will think it was the original plan all along.

Questions for Reflections

1. Describe a time when everything went wrong and you had to start over again.

2. What was the hardest part about beginning again?

3. Was starting over as difficult as you thought it would be?

Morning Decree #182
If Is a Big Word

"If My people, who are called by My name, shall humble themselves, pray, seek, crave, and require of necessity My face and turn from their wicked ways, then will I hear from heaven, forgive their sin, and heal their land." 2 Chronicles 7:14

If there was ever a time for followers of Jesus to pray and fast for their loved ones, it is now—like today. One only needs to casually look at the spiritual, physical, financial, and emotional condition of those who we love to realize their desperate need for a genuine touch from Jesus. Problems include sickness, diseases, infirmity, divorce and marital dysfunction; addictions of all kinds; sexual confusion and perversions. There are spiritual delusion and deception, emotional instability, anxieties, hardened hearts,

We see sudden and premature deaths, poverty and lack, unbelief, violence and abuses, rebellion against authority. I could go on and on (and so could you) listing the types of challenges many are facing both in the Church and outside. The truth is that unless we pray with fasting and demonstrate a life of devotion to Jesus as Lord of our lives, and the lives of those we love, it will only go from bad to worse.

Fasting is an act of love, a spiritual discipline that invokes God's power to come to bear on the things that matter to us. The most profound impact of fasting is on our ability to believe God's Word. Don't let your family live in conditions of bondage and then miss Heaven because of your unwillingness to fast and pray. Let's seek God on behalf of others and ourselves. Let's show our love for others through sacrifice.

Questions for Reflections

1. Do you know who it was that fasted and prayed for you to come to know Jesus?

2. What sacrifices are you willing to make on behalf of others to experience the same Jesus you are enjoying today?

3. Have you personally benefited from fasting and praying? In what ways?

Morning Decree #183
Intentional Intensity Required

"And violent men seize it by force [as a precious prize—a share in the heavenly kingdom is sought with most ardent zeal and intense exertion]."
Matthew 11:12b, AMP

I've been ridiculed at times for being too intense. I'm not sure what is meant by that criticism, but one thing I'm sure of is that nothing happens unless you make it happen. In other words, a decisive act on your part is required to get the job done. Whether it's a new habit you want to develop or a different career you want to pursue—whatever your prayer aim is—it will, on some level, demand intentionality.

All too often, believer's take prayer as the ultimate act needed to achieve their goals. They say, "I'll prayer about it." But the truth is, not even Jesus just prayed about things. His prayer time seemed to be when and where He received the instructions that were necessary to accomplish the will of the Father. Whereas, believer's often stop with prayer. Prayer should be the starting point. It's the place where instructions are given, grace received, and vision clarified.

By all means pray, but do something after you get up from your knees. Go after it hard, with intensity and fervency. Commit your energy to the task at hand. Some doors need to be kicked down. Obedience is the kick often lacking when it comes to getting what we pray for. Be willing and obedient as the prophet Isaiah said in Isaiah 1:18. Prayer makes you willing, but then you must add the obedience factor.

Questions for Reflections

1. What is the purpose of prayer?

2. What role does obedience play in answering prayers?

3. Consider keeping a record of your prayer requests, instructions, and answered prayers.

Morning Decree #184
You Get What You Expect

"For this reason, I am telling you, whatever you ask for in prayer, believe (trust and be confident) that it is granted to you, and you will [get it]." Mark 11:24, AMP

What we expect is often what we end up with. When it comes to spiritual matters, however, things can and often do appear bleaker before they get better. For example, you begin to pray for the deliverance of a loved one and they seemingly go full throttle into degradation rather than coming to the light. Or you renew your commitment to financial freedom, only to have a sudden financial emergency that threatens to set you back. You make a decisive step toward getting your health in order and discover you suddenly need medication to treat a previously undiagnosed problem. Breathtaking but not in a good way.

It's in these moments when you need to remember your goal and get your mind off the storm of the day. Failure to make this shift usually signals defeat or, at a minimum, unnecessary delay. This is a faith thing, a journey. It's really not about the temporary circumstances because they will change. You need to persevere. Keep doing what's right, at the right time, for the right reasons, and in the right way. God honors faith. The sun will rise again as will you. No quitting allowed.

Questions for Reflections

1. Why is expectation essential in your faith walk?

2. Why do you think believer's often just say, "whatever the Lord wants" rather than expecting an answer according to their prayers?

3. What role does disappointment play in decreasing expectations? What is the best response to disappointments?

Morning Decree #185
Don't Forget to Say Thank You

"Do not fret or have any anxiety about anything, but in every circumstance and in everything, by prayer and petition (definite requests), with thanksgiving, continue to make your wants known to God." Philippians 4:6, AMP

I've found myself lately praying from a desperate emotional place. When I really need something to change in my life or in the life of a loved one, my tendency is to go all out. The Apostle Paul, writing from a jail cell, reminds you of your need to pray. He admonishes you not to be anxious about anything. The word *anything* means, according to Dictionary.com: "in any degree; to any extent; in any way; at all." I like that definition. The challenge for me is how not to be anxious about x, y, or z.

The Scriptures instruct us to pray, and to make specific petitions. Many times, however, even after following that prescription, I'm still a bit anxious. What I've discovered, with the help of the Holy Spirit, is that giving thanks in advance of the answer arriving helps me maintain the right attitude of faith.

Questions for Reflections

1. What are the three things you seem to worry about the most?

2. What's your go-to medication when you start to worry (food, alcohol, sleep, etc.)?

3. What do think will be your greatest challenge in learning to be thankful?

Morning Decree #186
A Sacrifice that Matters

"But King David said to Araunah, 'No, but I will buy it from you for a price. I will not offer burnt offerings to the Lord my God of that which costs me nothing.' So David bought the threshing floor and the oxen for fifty shekels of silver." 2 Samuel 24:24

I often say that if what you give to God or do for God doesn't mean much to you, it probably won't mean much to God either. Fasting doesn't have to be extreme to matter to God, but for it to register in Heaven, it has be a sacrifice at least to you. An impactful fast should cost you a few things:

1. Time. It should cost you time in prayer as you seek the Lord.
2. Comfort. A true fast will create a certain degree of discomfort, both physically and spiritually.
3. Companionship. Fasting, while some occurs corporately, requires a person to be committed to prayer. You may feel alone.

Let me encourage you make your day of fasting count! Challenge yourself to go deeper by praying a bit longer, focusing more on the needs of others. Chronicle the seemingly insignificant convictions the Holy Spirit shows you. Repent and make the changes.

Questions for Reflections

1. What seems to be the predominant emotion you feel as you fast (other than hunger)?

2. How does fasting affect your relationships?

3. Other than food, what are your strongest desires when you fast?

Morning Decree #187
On What Is Your Faith Based?

"So when God desired to show more convincingly to the heirs of the promise the unchangeable character of his purpose, he guaranteed it with an oath, so that by two unchangeable things, in which it is impossible for God to lie." Hebrews 6:17-18

Faith is the lifeline of the followers of Jesus. As the Scripture reads, without faith it is impossible to please God (see Hebrews 11:6). The Bible also states, in no less than three other places, that the "just shall live by faith" (Habakkuk 2:4; Romans 1:16; Galatians 3:11).

Biblical faith is more than a theological point of study or a mental exercise. Faith is the currency required in order to transact spiritual business. Faith is to your spiritual life what money is to a consumer purchase. Faith is what moves God on your behalf. Faith is something that can be lost, stolen, minimized, or increased. While we are all given a measure of faith, what you do with it to cause it to grow or decrease is your responsibility. Faith is so critical to success or failure in life that it's something the devil himself tries to steal right out of your heart.

To have what I call rock-solid faith that is unmovable or unshakable takes something more than mere mental agreement with the Scriptures. God knew that and did the one thing that could make this type of faith possible—He made a Covenant, a Blood Covenant, with us.

Questions for Reflections

1. What does it mean when someone says, "I swear on my family that what I'm saying is true"?

2. Have you ever made a promise to someone but they didn't believe you?

3. What's the main reason for your distrust of certain people in your past?

Morning Decree #188
The Blood Covenant

"For as many as are the promises of God, they all find their Yes [answer] in Him [Christ]. For this reason, we also utter the Amen (so be it) to God through Him [in His Person and by His agency] to the glory of God." 2 Corinthians 1:20, AMP

The Bible is full of promises and blessings that are ours, as sons and daughters of God. However, often they are so far-out and beyond our imagination that it's hard for us to believe that they will one day become ours. Just like Abraham, who was promised a son by God Himself, could not even conceive how God was going to make that miracle happen, given his and Sarah's age and stage in life.

God knows we are naturally predisposed to doubt. Our inability to grasp the impossible or to see the invisible is a human limitation common to all. God understood Abraham's plight and did the thing that would help him keep the faith.

Making a Blood Covenant with Abraham, enabled him to grasp the revelation that God had no intention of changing His mind. The Blood Covenant ritual was understood and reverenced by ancient cultures. Abraham knew this so God knew Abraham would get the picture. The power of the Blood Covenant, understood by Abraham, meant that God would make good on His promise no matter what. His faith was secured by the irrevocability of the Blood Covenant.

Questions for Reflections

1. Describe how the Blood Covenant creates confidence.

2. Why does it seem easier to doubt than to believe what God has said in His Word?

3. How can you develop a deeper faith?

Morning Decree #189
One Thing God Cannot Do

"Accordingly, God also, in His desire to show more convincingly and beyond doubt to those who were to inherit the promise the unchangeableness of His purpose and plan, intervened (mediated) with an oath." Hebrews 6:17, AMP

The imagination of humanity is limitless, but our ability to imagine an unseen God manifesting a miracle for us is often difficult to grasp. As Abram, whose name was later changed to Abraham as a result of the covenant between Him and God, discovered, it was impossible for Him to remain at peace while awaiting the realization of the promised child, Isaac.

Our faith has to be in something other than shear strength of mind. This is especially hard when the circumstances surrounding your prayer request are not favorable. Abraham and Sarah were both old in age; past the age of bearing children as we are told in the Scriptures. The possibility of having a child at their stage in life was non-existent. It was not negative thinking. It was a proper assessment of the facts. However, a Blood-Covenant-based faith can change the facts.

What are you to do if you were ever attacked in your body by a disease for which there was no obvious cure? On what do you base your faith that the healing you seek will overcome the sickness trying to destroy you? Without a revelation that God *cannot* lie, because to lie means He would be breaking the Covenant, it can be difficult to remain in faith until the answer comes. That's precisely why God established a covenant to give us a reminder of His intention to fulfill His end of the deal.

Questions for Reflections

1. How did God prove He has no intention of changing His mind about what He promised?

2. What are some techniques to help you remember the promises God made to you?

3. When you take communion in church, do you reflect on the Blood Covenant? If no, why not?

Morning Decree #190
Do You Have Faith in the Blood of Christ?

"For Abraham, human reason for hope being gone, hoped in faith that he should become the father of many nations, as he had been promised, So [numberless] shall your descendants be." Romans 4:18, AMP

Blood believers are those who bases their trust on the Blood Covenant, not on their ability to believe or to imagine. Blood believers are aware of the facts of their case, but recognize that the outcome is not dependent on favorable conditions but on the God who keeps His Word. Interestingly, not even God expected Abraham to simply take Him at His Word, which is why He "cut" or made the Covenant. Being a blood believer is synonymous with true faith.

It's vital we embrace "blood theology" because the ability to believe God is based on it. Just reading the Bible, or listening to someone say, "You better believe the Word," won't help you much when you're faced with very difficult problems, a situation that requires supernatural intervention like a critical health problem. Understanding the integrity of God as revealed by His making a Blood Covenant is what will give you hope when there is simply no reason to hope. To fail to keep His end of the Covenant is not even a possibility. If there is ever a failure, it's not on God's end—He is the God who keeps covenant.

This is why it's so critical for you to have a practical knowledge and revelation of the Blood Covenant. For by it, you too can receive the promised miracles you desire. He is a God who keeps Covenant.

Questions for Reflections

1. What problems are you currently facing for which supernatural help is required?

2. Name a situation during which you felt totally helpless to address?

3. What examples from the Scriptures do you recall where the victory came through Covenant-based prayers?

Morning Decree #191
There's Something about the Blood

"Know, recognize, and understand therefore that the Lord your God, He is God, the faithful God, Who keeps covenant and steadfast love and mercy with those who love Him and keep His commandments, to a thousand generations." Deuteronomy 7:9

The Blood Covenant is a binding agreement between two or more parties that cannot be broken without penalty of injury or death. I am intentionally restating this definition to cement it in your thinking. A Blood Covenant is not a contract, it's a Covenant. It's solemn and sacred and must be revered. The foundational purpose of establishing a Blood Covenant relationship in the first place is to end any question in the minds of the parties involved whether or not there is a real intention to honor it's terms.

It's like the difference between testifying and doing so under oath. If you lie during testimony but are not under oath, you're not branded as a liar from a legal perspective. On the other hand, when you are testifying under oath, being considered a liar is the least of your problems. In a court of law, a person who lies under oath can be sent to prison!

Likewise, when a person enters in to a Blood Covenant relationship and then fails to keep the terms of the Covenant, a severe penalty will be imposed. God obviously knew that when He revealed Himself to Abraham as a Covenant-making God. He knew that Abraham would be more settled in between the promise and the birth.

If you need more assurance of God's intention to fulfill His promises, you only need to remember Jesus and the blood He shed, which is the Blood of the New Covenant.

Questions for Reflections

1. Why is it important to remember the crucifixion?

2. What should happen to our faith when we reflect on the holy blood of Jesus?

3. How does the Blood Covenant prove that God cannot lie?

Morning Decree #192
A Blood Relative

"So, the men turned from there and went toward Sodom, but Abraham still stood before the Lord." Genesis 18:22

Relationships matter. As the saying goes, it's not what you know, it's who you know. Abraham was in covenant with the Lord God. He had a relationship with God that was based upon blood. It was not a bloodline-type relationship, however, but rather something even more intimate than that.

Abraham was a friend of God, according to the Scripture. More importantly, Abraham was in covenant with Him. When God was fed up with the sins of Sodom and Gomorrah, He decided to destroy it and everybody in it. Before He let loose on that place, He wanted to get the opinion of His Covenant Partner, Abraham.

Abraham wasn't God's favorite for no reason. Abraham was God's Covenant Partner on the earth. Abraham took full advantage of this blood-based relationship to intercede on behalf of that place and the righteous people who might be living there. It was because of the covenant relationship he had that Abraham felt he could change God's mind. The purpose of the Blood Covenant cut with Abraham was not just for him and his generation, but for us as well.

Questions for Reflections

1. On what basis do you have a right to pray to the Father?

2. What's the single most important aspect of your relationship to God as your Father?

3. What's the difference between a stranger asking you for something and a blood relative, like one of your children for instance?

Morning Decree # 193
Blood Confidence

"So, the men turned from there and went toward Sodom, but Abraham still stood before the Lord. Then Abraham drew near and said, 'Will you indeed sweep away the righteous with the wicked?'" Genesis 18:22-23

There is a human-based confidence that could be bolstered by proper nurturing from others or through past successes. But the confidence that comes from understanding the Blood Covenant is not based on earthly logic but rather on the integrity of God.

A Blood Covenant relationship is one that by definition is a two-way, nothing-held-back agreement. It means that everything I have belongs to my Covenant partner. And in my case, all my wife needs to do is ask and she will receive. In the case of Abraham and God, God did not want to make such a devasting move on Sodom without sharing it with Abraham. And Abraham, armed with the confidence that comes only from a Blood Covenant, thought very little of the fact that he was negotiating with the Creator.

Sodom and Gomorrah was a place that was slated for destruction. It's sin was so vile that God could not allow it to remain. Yet for Abraham's sake and that of His nephew Lot, God decided to hear the plea of His Covenant partner. The decision to destroy the city stood because Abraham stopped negotiating.

Questions for Reflections

1. What is your confidence built upon when it comes to your prayer of petition?

2. Are you bold in prayer? If so, on what basis do you approach the God of all the Earth?

3. How can you increase your boldness in prayer?

Morning Decree #194
How Low Can You Go?

"Then he said, 'Oh let not the Lord be angry, and I will speak again but this once. Suppose ten are found there?' He answered, 'For the sake of ten I will not destroy it.' And the Lord went his way, when he had finished speaking to Abraham, and Abraham returned to his place." Genesis 18:32-33

When I read the account in Genesis 18, I am struck by Abraham's confidence and boldness toward God. Sodom and Gomorrah were guilty as charged. God is holy, and cannot let this go unpunished, yet because of Abraham's intercession, remarkably God was willing to change His plan.

Abraham negotiated with God to reduce the requirement of fifty to ten righteous people in the city before God would destroy it. Abraham perhaps thought there had to be at least ten people in the city who were righteous. God agreed if there were at least ten, He would not destroy the city. Sadly, He couldn't find ten righteous. One can only assume, had Abraham continued negotiations down to one righteous person, God would have honored his request to spare the city.

This is a lesson for us to remember. Be specific and let God decide how much is too much, or as in this case, too few. Abraham could have gone lower. Perhaps in your case you could ask for more for yourself. Embrace the confidence that comes through the Blood of the New Covenant, which is in the blood of Jesus. Don't quit until you get what you've been asking for.

Questions for Reflections

1. Recall a time when you gave up, only later to realize if you had stayed with it, you would have come out a winner?

2. What are some of the reasons you quit too soon?

3. In what ways can you learn to stay in the fight a little longer?

Morning Decree #195
My Inheritance, Your Inheritance

"And if we are [His] children, then we are [His] heirs also: heirs of God and fellow heirs with Christ [sharing His inheritance with Him]; only we must share His suffering if we are to share His glory." Romans 8:17, AMP

The loss of a loved one can be very difficult emotionally and financially. Having a last will and testament in place is absolutely critical to avoid unnecessary drama and to guarantee a smooth transition of property to the surviving parties. But just as we have the opportunity to ensure that our house is in order prior to death, we have this same opportunity spiritually as well.

The Word of God is the last will and testament of the Lord Jesus Christ. The promises contained therein were made available to those who are named in His Will. If you have accepted Jesus Christ for the pardoning of your sins, thus being "born of God," you are in His will. Your name, according to the Scriptures, is written in the Lamb's Book of Life (see Revelation 13:8). Keep it there.

When Jesus ascended to Heaven, He presented His own blood as proof-positive that He died. As a result of His death, His will was then activated. In other words, the blessings of God are now available to those who are the legitimate heirs of God. Whether your earthly family has you in their will is of little consequence when you realize that you are an heir of God and a co-heir with Jesus Christ Himself.

Questions for Reflections

1. Have you ever received an inheritance from someone?

2. If so, how did it make you feel knowing that someone cared enough to include you?

3. Have you read the last will and testament of the Lord Jesus Christ?

Morning Decree #196
Remember Him

"And when He had given thanks, He broke [it] and said, 'Take, eat. This is My body, which is broken for you. Do this to call Me [affectionately] to remembrance.'"
1 Corinthians 11:24, AMP

To remember someone who has died is often an important step in the "moving on" process. Jesus asked His followers to do exactly that—to remember Him. However, when I read that Scriptures, I don't see the idea of just remembering Jesus' life or even of His death. I see remembering as re-assembling the suffering that Jesus endured for the entire world.

Each element, every single aspect of the crucifixion, is important to "Re-Member" because they carry significance. For instance, to intentionally call to mind the fact of Jesus receiving thirty-nine lashes represents healing, among other things. There are many meaningful acts to which Jesus submitted that empower us every day and must be deliberately recalled. Every time we take Communion, it will do us well to remember Jesus by Re-Membering His sacrifice.

Questions for Reflections

1. What do you think about each time you take Holy Communion?
2. What aspect of the sufferings of Jesus affect you the most?
3. Have you ever been healed while taking Communion?

Morning Decree #197
When I'm Weak, I'm Strong

" . . . for My strength and power are made perfect (fulfilled and completed) and show themselves most effective in [your] weakness." 2 Corinthians 12:9, AMP

The above statement seems like a contradiction in terms. How can someone be strong when they are weak? This can be best understood as we accept that in the Kingdom of God things are done in reverse order. In order to increase, you must give away stuff. You must love your enemies rather than hate them. It all seems unrealistic.

The Apostle Paul's statement speaks to the fact that the more we rely upon our own human strength, the less we will experience God's grace. He discovered a secret that would be helpful to us to embrace. God's strength is most evident when you acknowledge your weakness.

Questions for Reflections

1. Name a moment when you felt utterly helpless to fix a personal problem?

2. Why is it that although we say "I trust God," we behave as though the outcome is totally dependent upon us?

3. In what ways can you demonstrate you're relying on the grace of God more than your personal grit?

Morning Decree #198
All or Nothing

"'Now, therefore,' says the Lord, 'turn to Me with all your heart, with fasting, with weeping, and with mourning.'" Joel 2:12

Fasting is a God-ordained response to a crisis. I personally believe the Father expects this from us when we are in need of supernatural intervention. The prophets of old would call a nation to their knees in prayer, strengthened by fasting. Fasting was used to demonstrate the depth of sorrow for one's sins. It was also employed when seeking direction from God and deliverance from enemies. There is such power in fasting unto God that hell itself will try to prevent you from developing this important spiritual discipline.

As you know, when you fast, you are dethroning your flesh, your will, and your appetites for something greater. Self denial isn't fun, but it's necessary. Perhaps the most important benefit of fasting is that it increases your ability to believe for miracles!

Questions for Reflections

1. When is the last time you deliberately and intentionally "fasted and prayed"? What was the reason?

2. Why is fasting generally difficult for most people to do?

3. Why do you think fasting builds faith?

Morning Decree #199
Is This What God Really Wants from Us?

"Is such a fast as yours what I have chosen, a day for a man to humble himself with sorrow in his soul? [Is true fasting merely mechanical?] Is it only to bow down his head like a bulrush and to spread sackcloth and ashes under him [to indicate a condition of heart that he does not have]? Will you call this a fast and an acceptable day to the Lord?" Isaiah 58:5, AMP

When fasting for spiritual purposes, keep in mind that your prayers are being heard on high. Recognize that, although you may not see the immediate fruit of your sacrifice, in due season you will reap the benefits—guaranteed.

Spend as much time in prayer and contemplation as possible when fasting. Trust that with each hunger pang and every decision, something of eternal value is taking place. Repent as the Holy Spirit reveals to you areas of sin, things which are displeasing or unproductive in the sight of God. Your family, for whom you are fasting and praying, is dependent upon your commitment. God has and will continue to honor such sacrifice.

Questions for Reflections

1. What ways have your "appetites" controlled your life?

2. How has lack of control negatively affected you health, finances, and relationships?

3. What could you accomplish if you exercised more discipline?

Morning Decree #200
The Proper Response to Craziness

"Do not, therefore, fling away your fearless confidence, for it carries a great and glorious compensation of reward. For you have need of steadfast patience and endurance, so that you may perform and fully accomplish the will of God, and thus receive and carry away [and enjoy to the full] what is promised."
Hebrews 10:35-36, AMP

The sudden onset of sickness, or the "out of nowhere" call from your spouse saying I want a divorce, or getting fired from a job. These are just a few of the realities that some are facing. And when the "crazies" starts happening, your tendency is to question "why me" and wonder where God is in the midst of it all. We lean toward giving up, talking negatively, and returning to self-medication.

This may not be your story today or even yesterday, but when you are serious about following the Lord, endeavoring to seek His will, "craziness" predictably shows up, This is not the time to relax your grip on faith. It's the wrong time to throw in the proverbial towel. Don't stop giving, break your fast, or quit doing a dozen other critical spiritually appropriate things!

Don't let craziness stop your praise or your efforts to push on. Declare your faith in God regardless of the circumstances. Call out to Jesus even more. Expect even bolder miracles. Believe despite seeing evidence to the contrary.

Questions for Reflections

1. What "craziness" made you question, "Where is God?"

2. How did you respond?

3. What can you do to better navigate those crazy moments?

Morning Decree #201
Believers Don't Quit: You're a Believer

"And when he was come into the house, His disciples asked him privately, 'Why could not we cast him out?' And he said unto them, 'This kind can come forth by nothing, but by prayer and fasting.'" Mark 9:28-29

Jesus' response to the question, "Why couldn't we cast out that devil" was that this kind comes out but through fasting and prayer. What is often overlooked is that prayer and fasting are not for or against devils, for fasting changes the one who is fasting. Fasting purges and detoxes from carnality.

The disciples lacked required faith to cast out that particular demon and it required Jesus-level of faith to get the job done. Basically, this kind of faith is a result of detoxing from unbelief and is what drives out our demons, sicknesses, fear, and the like.

Your fasting is working a deeper deliverance from unbelief and ungodliness in your own soul. If you want to be among those who work the works of Jesus, fasting and prayer must be a lifestyle, not just an event.

Questions for Reflections

1. When have you realized that you quit too soon?

2. Why do you think you gave up too early?

3. How do you think fasting will help this tendency?

Morning Decree #202
Superheroes

"For if you keep silent at this time, relief and deliverance shall arise for the Jews from elsewhere, but you and your father's house will perish. And who knows but that you have come to the kingdom for such a time as this and for this very occasion?"
Esther 4:14

We love our superheroes. We love to hear their stories of heroic bravery. But everyone of us has an opportunity to be a hero in the life of another—especially our families. I don't think true heroes wake up thinking, "I'm going to be a hero today," and neither should we.

However, when you consciously fast and pray for someone else, you are acting "superhero-like." Accepting the fact that you may be the one and only person who is taking on that responsibility. It's a noble, superhero-like thing. Your sacrifice may very well be the difference between their living in peace or in torment, sickness, or addiction, and freedom.

Questions for Reflections

1. Do you know who it was (on earth) who sacrificed the most for you to know the Lord?

2. What kind of sacrifices did they make?

3. Have you decided to be someone's silent superhero?

Morning Decree #203
Turn It Up!

"So that your fasting may not be noticed by men but by your Father, Who sees in secret; and your Father, will reward you in the open." Matthew 6:18

Set your faith like you would a thermostat. When you fast, it's not the same as simply modifying a diet or going without food. Fasting is an opportunity to focus your prayers in faith. In other words, when fasting you are stating that what you are praying for is more important than your wants and fleshly desires.

Difficult times require a greater intensity. This is especially true when it comes to your spiritual life. Because faith is easy to talk about, many are unaware of what it takes to live a life of faith. Fasting, among other outcomes, helps eliminate unbelief from your spiritual life. As you know, faith is the currency required to operate supernaturally.

Increase your spiritual intensity by fasting regularly with a pre-determined prayer agenda. Fasting works. Prayer and fasting are an unbeatable combination when done in faith. You get what you expect. You don't get what you don't expect. Turn up your faith-actions and you will receive your faith expectations.

Questions for Reflections

1. Rate your spiritual intensity on a scale from 1 to 10, with 10 being the most intense.

2. How could you better improve your intensity from a spiritual perspective?

3. Do you have a set fasting and prayer plan? If so, what is it?

Morning Decree #204
Your Faith Focus

"Not by might, nor by power, but by my Spirit, saith Jehovah of hosts."
Zechariah 4:6, Darby Bible

"Do not fret or have any anxiety about anything, but in every circumstance and in everything, by prayer and petition (definite requests), with thanksgiving, continue to make your wants known to God." Philippians 4:6, AMP

"... having done all [the crisis demands], to stand [firmly in your place]. Stand therefore [hold your ground]." Ephesians 6:13-14, AMP

I'm reminded that there are many matters requiring prayerful resolutions things like comfort and peace in the midst of loss, the healing of mind or body, financial crisis, the need for reconciliation of an estranged relationship, and so forth.

The above three passages were brought to my mind by the Holy Spirit. They are sterling reminders of where your focus must remain, and where your faith must rest. There are, of course, many other poignant verses that may apply to your situation. Knowing that victory is a product of His Spirit, as you participate with prayer, petitions, and thanksgivings, you will gain the courage and confidence to stand.

Questions for Reflections

1. What is your most dominant emotional response when faced with uncertainty?

2. Why does it seem to take so much work to think positively in the midst of turmoil?

3. What can you do to more quickly make the switch from worry to worship?

Morning Decree #205
Your Sacrifice Matters

"For God is not unrighteous to forget or overlook your labor and the love which you have shown for His name's sake in ministering to the needs of the saints (His own consecrated people), as you still do." Hebrews 6:10

Sometimes it seems that what you do for others doesn't make a difference. Your financial giving, your midnight prayer vigils, your silence when you could have said things out of pain, the sharing of your time and possessions even when you don't have enough for yourself—nothing you have done for others goes unnoticed by God. Nothing. God is the most excellent accountant.

As you make sacrifices for others today, remember that your sacrifice is recorded in Heaven. God hears, sees, and knows your needs and wants. Because of those countless sacrifices, there are rewards that will manifest in your life. The Law of Sowing and Reaping applies to your "intangible" sacrifices as well. Trust God. He's got you are covered. Keep doing good for others because it's the right thing to do. God will honor it.

Questions for Reflections

1. Have you ever felt forgotten by others, despite your massive amount of sacrifice?

2. How did their lack of appreciation affect your attitude and motivation?

3. How will focusing on God as your rewarder impact your overall motivation to serve others?

Morning Decree #206
Don't Forget to Say Thanks

"Do not fret or have any anxiety about anything, but in every circumstance and in everything, by prayer and petition (definite requests), with thanksgiving, continue to make your wants known to God." Philippians 4:6, AMP

When I really need something to change in my life or in the life of a loved one, my tendency is to go all out. I've found myself lately praying from a desperate emotional place. Are you in a difficult period in your life? If you are, listen to what the Word of God said you should do. The Apostle Paul, writing from a jail cell in Philippians 4:6 reminds us of our need to pray. He admonishes us not to be anxious concerning *anything*. The word *anything* means, according to Dictionary.com, "in any degree; to any extent; in any way; at all." So according to this Philippines 4:6, there i's absolutely nothing that should be a cause for you to remain in an agitated state of mind.

The challenge for me then is how *not* to be anxious. The Scriptures instruct us to pray, and to make specific petitions. But many times, even following that prescription, I'm still a bit anxious. What I've discovered, with the help of the Holy Spirit, is that I failed to give thanks after I pray, let alone while I'm waiting on the answer to manifest.

It's not that God needs to hear us say thank you, although it's the polite thing to do. There is something mysterious about giving thanks that settles our heart; knowing that God, our heavenly Father, has heard our prayers. So after you pray, give thanks for the answer *before* it arrives. It will invoke a peace that defies explanation. Didn't your parents teach you this? I know mine did. Thank you, Mom.

Questions for Reflections

1. How do you feel when you do some basic courtesy for someone but they neglect to say thank you?

2. Do you feel inclined to do more or less for an ungrateful person?

3. How do you feel when someone expresses their gratitude for a kindness you expressed?

Morning Decree #207
"If" Is a Really Big Word

"If My people, who are called by My name, shall humble themselves, pray, seek, crave, and require of necessity My face and turn from their wicked ways, then will I hear from heaven, forgive their sin, and heal their land." 2 Chronicles 7:14

If there was ever a time for followers of Jesus to pray with fasting for their loved ones it is now—today. One only needs to casually look at the spiritual, physical, financial, and emotional condition of those whom we love to realize their desperate need for a genuine touch from Jesus. Problems include:

Sickness, Diseases, Infirmity Divorce and Martial dysfunction, Addictions of all kinds, Sexual Confusion & Perversions, Spiritual delusion and deception, Emotional instability, Anxieties, Hardened Hearted, Sudden and Premature Deaths, Poverty and Lack, Unbelief, Violence and abuses, Rebellion against authority, etc.

I could go on and on (and so could you), in listing the types of challenges many are facing both in the Church and outside. The Truth is that unless we pray with fasting and demonstrate a life of devotion to Jesus as Lord of our lives, the lives of those we love will not be helped very much by our preaching at them.

Fasting is an act of love, a spiritual discipline that invokes God's power to come to bear on the things that matter to us. Don't let your family live in conditions of bondage and then miss Heaven for failure to pray and fast. Seek God on behalf of others and yourself. Show your love for others through sacrifice.

Questions for Reflections

1. What are the three most challenging family issues you are facing right now?

2. Have you regularly fasted and prayed concerning those matters? If so, how often?

3. Have you looked in the "mirror" to determine how you may better position yourself to become more effective in prayer?

Morning Decree #208
Intentional Intensity Required

"And violent men seize it by force [as a precious prize—ashore in the heavenly kingdom is sought with most ardent zeal and intense exertion]."
Matthew 11:12b, AMP

I've been ridiculed at times for being too intense. I'm not sure what was meant by that criticism, but one thing I'm sure of is that "nothing happens unless you make it happen." In other words, a decisive act on your part is required to get the job done. Whether it's a new habit you want to develop or a different career you want to pursue, whatever your prayer aim is, it will, on some level, demand intentionality.

All too often, believer's take prayer as the ultimate act needed to achieve their goals. They say, "I'll prayer about it." The truth is that not even Jesus just prayed about things. His prayer time seemed to be when and where He received the instructions necessary to accomplish the will of the Father, whereas believer's often stop with prayer. Prayer is the starting point. It's the place where instructions are given, grace received, and visions clarified.

By all means pray, but do something after you get up from your knees. Go after "it" hard, with intensity and fervency. Commit your energy to the task at hand. Some doors need to be kicked down. Obedience is the key, often lacking when it comes to getting what we pray for. Be willing and obedient as the prophet Isaiah said in Isaiah 1:18. Prayer makes you willing, but you have to add the obedience factor.

Questions for Reflections

1. What issues are you facing that seems to require more "elbow grease"?

2. What makes you stop when pursuing the difficult issues in prayer?

3. Can you remember a challenge that you pushed through by prayer and obedience and it turned out as you had hoped?

Morning Decree #209
Focus on the Faith-Fight

"Therefore, we do not become discouraged (utterly spiritless, exhausted, and wearied out through fear). Though our outer man is [progressively] decaying and wasting away, yet our inner self is being [progressively] renewed day after day." "For our light and momentary affliction (this slight distress of the passing hour) is ever more and more abundantly preparing and producing and achieving for us an eternal weight of glory [beyond all measure, excessively surpassing all comparisons and all calculations, a vast and transcendent glory and blessedness never to cease]."
2 Corinthians 4:16-17

What we often expect is what we end up with. When it comes to spiritual matters, however, things can and often do look bleaker before they get better. For example, you begin to pray for the deliverance of a loved one and they seemingly go full throttle into degradation rather than coming to the light. Or you renew your commitment to financial freedom, only to have a sudden financial emergency that threatens to set you back.

Or you make a decisive step toward getting your health in order and discover you need medication to treat a previously undiagnosed problem. All that is breathtaking but not in a good way. It's in these moments when you need to remember the goal and get your mind off the storm of the day! Failure to make this shift usually signals defeat or, at a minimum, unnecessary delays.

Questions for Reflections

1. How will focusing on your faith help you in the long run?

2. What kind of distractions most often seem to derail your progress?

3. What three things could you do to safeguard yourself from being discouraged?

Morning Decree #210
Handling Disappointments

"And David was greatly distressed; for the people spake of stoning him, because the soul of all the people was grieved, every man for his sons and for his daughters: but David encouraged himself in the Lord his God." 1 Samuel 30:6

Many times, it's not what happened that causes the most damage, it's how the problem is addressed. Problems will come. That's a cold, hard fact of living. However, just because things happen doesn't mean they have to destroy you. Jesus said in the world you will have tribulation, but be of good cheer for I have overcome the world (see John 16:33). Don't let your heart be so troubled that you give up in response to the real problems going on in your world. Rather, determine to handle them with the wisdom that comes from God after it is forged in prayer.

The warrior King David, when overwhelmed with crushing realities, determined to seek God's will concerning all matters. Our answer, regardless of the problem, will always be best addressed after pursuing God's heart. How you handle what you're going through will determine how long and how well you go through it. Don't give up on God, for He won't give up on you. Here are six helpful ideas:

1. Be honest about how you feel.
2. Realize others may be feeling the same way.
3. You're not alone.
4. Take responsibility of your emotional and physical state of being.
5. Seek God's will.
6. Obey the instructions.

Questions for Reflections

1. Which one of those six ideas is toughest for you to implement?
2. Do you pray for wisdom and believe you have received it without doubting, as James instructed you to do?
3. What are the instructions from God's Word to handle inevitable disappointments?

Morning Decree #211
The Proper Response to Craziness

"Do not, therefore, fling away your fearless confidence, for it carries a great and glorious compensation of reward. For you have need of steadfast patience and endurance, so that you may perform and fully accomplish the will of God, and thus receive and carry away [and enjoy to the full] what is promised."
Hebrews 10:35-36, AMP

The sudden onset of sickness; the "out of nowhere" call saying your spouse wants a divorce; the I got fired from a job for "no cause;" the car accident that totaled your only means to get to work; people quitting on you though you never gave up on them. These are just a few of the realities that some are facing right now. And when the "crazies" start happening, our tendency is to question why and wonder where God is in the midst of all of it! We lean toward giving up, talking negatively, or returning to self-medication.

This may not be your story today or even yesterday, but when you are serious about following the Lord, endeavoring to seek His will, craziness predictably shows up.

That is not the time to relax your grip on faith. It's the wrong time to throw in the proverbial towel, or to stop giving, or to break your fast, or quit doing a dozen other critical spiritual right things.

Don't let craziness stop your praise or your push. Declare your faith in God regardless of the circumstances. Don't back down, but rather call out to Jesus even more. Give more in faith, expecting even bigger miracles. Believe despite seeing evidence to the contrary.

Questions for Reflections

1. What craziness has occurred in your life that tried to derail your plans?

2. What is your default reaction to sudden upsets?

3. What are three things you can do to rebound after setbacks?

Morning Decree #212
Confidence Counts

"And this is the confidence (the assurance, the privilege of boldness) which we have in Him: [we are sure] that if we ask anything (make any request) according to His will (in agreement with His own plan), He listens to and hears us. And if (since) we [positively] know that He listens to us in whatever we ask, we also know [with settled and absolute knowledge] that we have [granted us as our present possessions] the requests made of Him." 1 John 5:14-15, AMP

Seeking God by fasting convicts me of the truth that nothing really matters except doing God's will. All the specific prayer requests I have (and there are many) can be summed up into a single prayer: Your will, Oh God, be done!

Times of deep consecration always bring me to the realization that what I really need and want is to live out God's will for my life. Nothing more, nothing less, nothing else will do. For me, it takes fasting to get me back to what is most important.

But knowing God's will and praying accordingly are where boldness and confidence comes from. Actually, one of the reasons so many people fail to receive answers to their prayers is because they do not pray based upon God's will. He is not obligated to answer any request, no matter how sincerely it is offered, if it is not according to His will. God's will is God's Word. Know His Word and you will by default know His will for your life.

Questions for Reflections

1. Why do you think knowing God's will increases you confidence?

2. Can people know God's will in every area of their lives? If so, how?

3. How will confidence improve your prayer life?

Morning Decree #213
What Do I Do Now?

"'Now, therefore,' says the Lord, 'Turn to Me with all your heart, with fasting, with weeping, and with mourning.'" Joel 2:12

Fasting is a God-ordained response to crisis. The Father expects this from us when we are in need of supernatural intervention. The prophets of old would call a nation to their knees in prayer, strengthened by fasting. Fasting was used to demonstrate the depth of sorrow for one's sins. It was also employed when seeking direction from God or deliverance from enemies.

There is such power in fasting unto God that hell itself will try to prevent you from developing this important spiritual discipline. As you know, when you fast, you are dethroning your flesh, your will, and your appetites for something greater. Self-denial isn't fun, but necessary.

Keep in mind that your prayers are being heard on High. Recognize that, although you may not see the immediate fruit of your sacrifice, in due season you will reap the benefits—guaranteed.

Spend as much time in prayer and contemplation as possible. Trust that with each hunger pain and every decision, something of eternal value is taking place. Repent as the Holy Spirit reveals to you areas of sin—things which are displeasing or unproductive in the sight of God.

Questions for Reflections

1. What is the hardest thing you face when you start fasting for spiritual reasons?

2. How often do you fast?

3. Have you ever put yourself on a fast?
What were the circumstances that made you fast?

Morning Decree #214
Are You Satisfied?

"Then I proclaimed a fast there, at the river Ahava, that we might humble ourselves before our God to seek from Him a straight and right way for us, our little ones, and all our possessions." Ezra 8:21, AMP

The theologian John Piper stated,

> The absence of fasting is the measure of our contentment with the absence of Christ. If we don't feel strong desires for the manifestation of the glory of God, it is not because we have drunk deeply and are satisfied. It is because we have nibbled so long at the table of the world. Our soul is stuffed with small things, and there is no room for the great.

Allow me to challenge you to keep the main things in your spiritual sightline. Aren't there situations in your life that are more important than having breakfast and lunch today? Are you troubled in your mind about something? Fast and pray. Are you weak in your faith? Fast and pray. Are you struggling with sin in your life? Fast and pray. Are you lacking a fire and love for God's Word? Fast and pray. If you can't seem to hear and discern God's will. Fast and pray. Are you living your best life? Well, you get the idea by now. Until you are hungrier for God's will to be done more than you want to be comfortable, you will neither be comfortable nor in His will.

Questions for Reflections

1. If you could change one thing about your life right now, what would it be?

2. Do you believe God wants that thing for you as well?

3. Will you commit to prayer and fasting about that matter?

Morning Decree #215
The Deception is More Deceptive Than You Thought

"You are of your father, the devil, and it is your will to practice the lusts and gratify the desires [which are characteristic] of your father. He was a murderer from the beginning and does not stand in the truth, because there is no truth in him. When he speaks a falsehood, he speaks what is natural to him, for he is a liar [himself] and the father of lies and of all that is false." John 8:44, AMP

Do you realize you are God's idea? Regardless of the circumstances around your birth, you were God's idea. You are a product of His imagination. He wanted children, a creature that could experience His love, His glory, and His beauty. Life and the things that have happened to you can change how you view yourself and others. You think things like, "I'm a mistake, an accident?" or "I don't have any real reason to live" or "I'm useless." You may have never said those exact words, but something similar has trafficked through most human minds, probably even yours.

This deception has caused untold, incalculable damage and pain, confusion beyond description, misery, poverty, sickness, premature death, aimlessness, purposelessness, wars, murders, suicides, perversions of all kinds—the list is endless. And because Satan himself cannot attack God, he attacks what God loves the most, which is you.

One of the most important things you will ever do is both to discover God's love for you as demonstrated in the sacrificial death of Jesus Christ as well as your purpose for living. When you began to embrace those two all important things, you will bloom like a flower in Spring.

Questions for Reflections

1. What the most common negative self-talk with which you struggle?

2. Do you remember when you first learned to combat those thoughts?

3. What are five ways you can defeat negative thinking?

Morning Decree #216
The Lie You Believe Becomes the Truth You Live

"...because there is no truth in him. When he speaks a falsehood, he speaks what is natural to him, for he is a liar [himself] and the father of lies and of all that is false."
John 8:44, AMP

The reason why "church" doesn't work for some is because they haven't realized that they have been deceived. Truly the greatest deception is when you don't know you are deceived. It's like being blind, but you don't know it—darkness is natural to you. The devil's ultimate plan is to blind you and have you believe that blindness is the natural order of things. In order for you to be restored to the original plan for your life, you must recognize you have been bamboozled.

The very word *devil* means *deceiver*. His whole game he plays us with is based on smoke and mirrors, lies and deception. Even when the devil has the facts right about you, he doesn't tell you that the truth can change the facts. Then any lie you believe becomes your truth. That lie, which is then your truth, is what you will experience in your life. Therefore, the best way to expose each lie you have believed is to seek truth, the truth that is only found in Jesus Christ.

Questions for Reflections

1. What truth about yourself have you discovered since coming to know Jesus as Lord?

2. How has not knowing the truth affected your past life?

3. What can you do going forward to guard against the subtle lies of the enemy and this fallen world?

Morning Decree #217
Don't Believe Everything You Hear

"In this [union and communion with Him] love is brought to completion and attains perfection with us, that we may have confidence for the day of judgment [with assurance and boldness to face Him], because as He is, so are we in this world."
1 John 4:17, AMP

The relationship Jesus has with the Father is the same relationship we have with the Father at this very moment. Jesus had no sense of guilt or condemnation, likewise we should have no sense of guilt or condemnation. The work, ministries, and miracles Jesus did on Earth are the same miracles we are commissioned to do—no less, and actually more.

This reality only happens when there is a revelation of your true identity. Your true identity is not in your culture, ethnicity, gender, or nationality. Rather, your true self can only be found in your understanding of who our Father and big Brother are. Just as Jesus and the Father are one, you are to be just like Jesus! You were created in the likeness and image of the Godhead. It's only because of sin and it's corruptive nature that you have ceased being like your original parents.

Questions for Reflections

1. Who on earth do you identify with the most?

2. What part of that person do you see in your own being?

3. In what ways do you want to be like Jesus?

Morning Decree #218
Identification (ID)

"So God created man in his own image, in the image of God he created him; male and female he created them." Genesis 1:27

Getting stopped by the police is never a pleasant experience, even when you know you are innocent of any offense. Often, one of the first questions asked is, "May I see your identification please." It sounds like a request, but it's really not. One of the reasons of asking for "ID" is for the police to know with whom they are dealing. Based upon your ID, they surmise what they can expect from you.

Your ID is important, but knowing who you are in Christ is most important. I'm not talking about the one that is in your pocket, but the real you, the ID you received from God when you were born again. We human beings are the only creatures that have to learn to be who they are born to be. Other creatures instinctively live out their nature. We have a new nature in Christ Jesus, but it's something we have to learn about and discipline ourselves to follow the new nature, not the old one.

Questions for Reflections

1. Who do you think you are? How do you know who you are?

2. From where do we get our identification clues?

3. Are you living out the ID with which you were born or the ID you received as a child of God?

Morning Decree #219
To Whom Do You Identify?

"For those whom He foreknew [of whom He was aware and loved beforehand], He also destined from the beginning [foreordaining them] to be molded into the image of His Son [and share inwardly His likeness], that He might become the firstborn among many brethren." Romans 8:29, AMP

What Christ experienced, He did on our behalf. As a father, many generations are within me, as a seed. Therefore whatever I do, wherever I go, whatever I become, by the very fact that they are within me, they are doing what I am doing, going where I am going, and becoming whatever I become. This is even more profoundly true in Christ. We were chosen in Him (Christ) before the foundation of the world (see Ephesians 1:4). He blessed us in Christ with every spiritual blessing in heavenly places (see Ephesians 1:3).

Consequently, to access your best self, you must unwrap the gift of Jesus, for it's in Christ that you discover all the blessings of life. He's the one you are becoming. He's the image, the role model, the standard. If you pursue the knowledge of God in Christ Jesus, you will never suffer an identity crisis. You are to be like your elder Brother, the Lord Jesus Christ. This isn't an imitation only, but rather learning to yield to the reality of His nature being yours.

Questions for Reflections

1. To whom do you Identify with the most?

2. Why? In what ways are you like that person?

3. In what ways do you see yourself identifying with Christ Jesus?

Morning Decree #220
Crucified with Christ

"I have been crucified with Christ [in Him I have shared His crucifixion]; it is no longer I who live, but Christ (the Messiah) lives in me; and the life I now live in the body I live by faith in (by adherence to and reliance on and complete trust in) the Son of God, Who loved me and gave Himself up for me." Galatians 2:20, AMP

Not only was Christ crucified, but because we were in Him at the time, we were crucified also. The disgrace and shame He endured, He did for us, with us, as us. The body of sin (Jesus became sin for us), the old nature, would be completely destroyed. The sinful Adamic nature—the nature that has sin in it, sickness in it, death in it, failure in it—was crucified, nailed to the Cross. *We were crucified with Christ.*

To grasp this by revelation will be the difference between living in glorious victory or wallowing life's problems. The truth that Jesus lived and died for us is more than a theological talking point. It is rather a mystery of all mysteries. It is the very truth that the deceiver wants to keep from you.

Questions for Reflections

1. What does the common phrase "like father, like son" mean to you?

2. What do you expect from a child who is like his or her father?"

3. Why do you think it's difficult to see that you can live like Jesus did?

Morning Decree #221
Our Sin Is His Sin

"For our sake He made Christ [virtually] to be sin Who knew no sin, so that in and through Him we might become [endued with, viewed as being in, and examples of] the righteousness of God [what we ought to be, approved and acceptable and in right relationship with Him, by His goodness]." 2 Corinthians 5:21, AMP

Jesus sinless, but became sin personified with our sin. Christ Jesus became our sin-bearer, our scapegoat (see Leviticus 16:2; 2 Corinthians 5:21; Isaiah 53:3-5). Our sin separates us from our Father. By becoming sin for us, taking the judgement that was due us, Jesus took away our sin, removing the only barrier between us and our Father's love.

Realizing that Jesus Christ took your sin by becoming sin-personified is the most mind-boggling truth to try and grasp. The ramification of this truth impacts both here and now, and the hereafter. Many can hold the idea that Jesus took our sin and therefore we now have access to heaven, but to embrace the truth that, right this very second, we are without sin because of what Jesus did and became on our behalf is more difficult to do. Nevertheless, it's the truth. God the Father deals with you based on the finished redemptive work of Christ. It's a done deal and consequently, sin cannot dominate you without your permission and submission.

Questions for Reflections

1. How does being conscious of personal sin affect your prayer life?

2. Do you feel more or less confident in your relationship with God when you are sin-conscious?

3. Why is it hard to accept the truth that Jesus took away your sins and therefore you are no longer guilty of committing them?

Morning Decree #222
Your Sickness is His Sickness

"He personally bore our sins in His [own] body on the tree [as on an altar and offered Himself on it], that we might die (cease to exist) to sin and live to righteousness. By His wounds you have been healed." 1 Peter 2:24, AMP

The same Jesus who took your sin, also took your sickness. In essence, Jesus became sickness and then all your sins and sicknesses were laid upon Him. If there was never sin, there would never have been sickness, for sickness entered the human experience and bloodline through the doorway of sin, which was opened by Adam. When Jesus took your sin on His body, and His body was crucified, He took sickness with Him and killed it, too.

Sin and sickness are spiritual conditions which manifest in the physical body. You along with your diseases were nailed to the cross when Jesus was crucified. The body of sin and sickness was destroyed and your spirit was born again. The new recreated born again spirit now within you is part of the divine nature (see 2 Peter 1:4). Sickness was the result and penalty of sin. Jesus took your penalty, so Satan has no legal right to put diseases on you.

Laws of physics declare that two things cannot exist in the same place at the same time. This is also true spiritually. Since Jesus took your sins and carried your sicknesses on His own body, neither sin or sickness have a legal right to reside in your life. To not know this truth is the reason why both of these conditions continue to reign in the life of the children of God.

Questions for Reflections

1. How can you build your faith in order to receive healing in your life?

2. What is the "natural" produced from? For example, from where does an apple come?

3. What happens to an apple tree if you kill the root? What will happen to sickness, which is the fruit of original sin, if you kill the sin-seed?

Morning Decree #223
The Truth and Fruit Connection

"For which is easier: to say, 'Your sins are forgiven and the penalty remitted,' or to say, 'Get up and walk?' But in order that you may know that the Son of Man has authority on earth to forgive sins and remit the penalty,' He then said to the paralyzed man, 'Get up! Pick up your sleeping pad and go to your own house.'" Matthew 9:5-6

Understanding the connection between sin and sickness is easier when you think about the connection between seed and fruit. Take an orange for example. It is the natural byproduct of a planted orange seed. No one plants a seed of corn expecting an apple to magically appear. Sin is the seed for all sickness, disease, and death. This is true even if a person hasn't personally sinned. All maladies on earth can be traced back to an original sin. A farmer who no longer desires to harvest corn but prefers oranges will stop planting corn seeds, and then plant oranges. This same principle is true for you. You will reap what you sow.

Jesus handled the root cause of the man's ailment in today's passage by declaring the forgiveness of his sins. Once that was clear, the healing of this nameless man's body was a natural byproduct. As you intentionally call to mind the truth that Jesus Christ took and paid the penalty for your sins, healing will be quickly coming to your life.

Questions for Reflections

1. Have you ever planted a seed in a home garden or pot? What did you expect to grow?

2. Did you have any doubt that the type of seed you planted would produce that type of fruit or flower?

3. What would you conclude, if you planted a sunflower seed, but grew a cucumber?

Morning Decree #224
The Same As Jesus

"In this [union and communion with Him] love is brought to completion and attains perfection with us, that we may have confidence for the day of judgment [with assurance and boldness to face Him], because as He is, so are we in this world."
1 John 4:17, AMP

When Jesus died on the Cross, He died to the power of sin. Sin cannot dictate to the dead so when Jesus died, the power of sin became a non-factor. This is why you are commanded to consider ourselves dead to sin. Just as Jesus died to sin, representing us, so now sin no longer has any power to affect your life just like it has no affect on His life either.

Identifying with Jesus in all aspects is crucial if you are going to walk and enjoy the abundant life. Jesus, just like Adam, was the representative for the entire human race. You had no choice but to identify with Adam because you are born a human being. Consequently, whatever is in Adam's bloodline of sin naturally became part of your life in some way. Likewise, when you identify with Christ, you receive by birth what is yours because you were born of the same Spirit as Christ.

When Christ took your sin and carried it to the grave in death, just as the power of sin no longer has effect on Jesus in any way, so sin should have no effect on you. Just as Jesus is, so are you in this world.

Questions for Reflections

1. What is the reaction of a dead person to pain, criticism, or loss?

2. How is it still possible to be bound by a sinful habit, even though through Jesus you died to sin?

3. What should your response be to temptation based on what Jesus did for you through His death?

Morning Decree #225
Buried Dead

"We were buried therefore with Him by baptism into death, so that just as Christ was raised from the dead by the glorious [power] of the Father, so we too might [habitually] live and behave in newness of life." Romans 6:4, AMP

Identification with Jesus is the key if you are to experience the wonders of redemption. Religion teaches us to come to church, do this or don't do that. While there are undoubtedly things we need to do and not do, religion is behavior modification while identifying with Christ is becoming an entirely new being.

When Jesus was buried, He took the body (His Body) that was made sin and it was placed in a tomb because it was dead. The burial, which obviously followed His death on the cross, was the moment we recognize when our old person was put to rest. Graves are for the dead. The lives of those in the grave have ended, at least as far as their activity on earth is concerned. When Jesus, our representative and substitute, was buried, it signaled the end of our living our lives as we wish on earth. Jesus didn't come to fix our life, rather Jesus came to *become* our life.

Questions for Reflections

1. Why is dying to self so difficult for you?

2. What does denying yourself specifically mean to you?

3. How will living for Christ change your behavior today?

Morning Decree #226
Been There, Done That

"For even as Jonah was three days and three nights in the belly of the sea monster, so will the Son of Man be three days and three nights in the heart of the earth."
Matthew 12:40

There is a judgment coming to all. It's spiritual delusion to think that your sins are insignificant happenings of which God is unaware. The Bible plainly teaches that "the wages of sin is death" (Romans 6:23). That's the bad news. The good news is that Jesus Christ suffered the penalty for your sin. God judged your sin through Jesus! What amazing love. What amazing grace—the innocent paying the penalty for the guilty. Not only did Jesus die on your behalf, He went to hell in your place as well.

Jesus' body was buried in a tomb, His spirit went to hell for three days and three nights, until the claims of justice were met. He paid the penalty for our sins. He was our substitute in Hell.

Why go to hell when you don't have to? Why live in hellish defeat now, when Jesus Christ suffered, bled, died and was buried for you? As far as God is concerned, you've already been to hell in Christ. There is no need to go there again and for all eternity.

Questions for Reflections

1. Have you ever thought that you got away with it, whatever the it is?

2. What should your response be to the truth that Jesus paid the price for your sins?

3. How can you demonstrate gratefulness for Jesus' sacrifice?

Morning Decree #227
It's Either Him or You

"Now the centurion, having seen what had taken place, recognized God and thanked and praised Him, and said, 'Indeed, without question, this Man was upright (just and innocent)!'" Luke 23:47, AMP

The great mystery of the substitutionary work of Jesus is the riddle for the ages. The truth that a man represented all of humanity is truly behind comprehension. Jesus Christ, the Son of God and the Son of Man, lived, died, and performed miracles as a man. He then bore the sins of the entire world—past, present and future. How amazing is that!

Jesus suffered the totality of human suffering. The innocent, sinless One took on all the ailments, illnesses, and human pain. It takes God-sized love to do that; Jesus loves you just that much. Jesus Christ suffered as you, for you, and in your place. He did this fully conscious of the weight and yet went through a literal hell to secure your place in heaven.

The opportunity before you is either to accept and trust that since Jesus did this for you, and as you, so that you don't have to go through it again or to choose to take your chances and suffer through life on your own. Trusting in Jesus is far better. It's either Him or you, but it can't be both. Choose to trust in the finished work of Christ.

Questions for Reflections

1. Is it fair for two people to suffer the penalty for a sin committed by only one of them? Why or why not?

2. What should the "innocent" party do since someone has already suffered the penalty for the offense?

3. Are you confessing that Jesus paid it all when faced with the sufferings this world offers?

Morning Decree #228
That's Not the End of the Story

"He is not here; He has risen, as He said [He would do].
Come, see the place where He lay." Matthew 28:6, AMP

If Jesus' ministry ended with Him being buried in a borrowed tomb, then how tragic would His death had been. However, Jesus' story doesn't end with a grave. *He arose.* The victory wasn't in His dying, it was in His resurrection. So often we cry over what Jesus suffered, and spend much time in contemplation at the tomb. But even as Mary found out, the tomb was empty. Jesus' story didn't end in tragedy, but rather in His triumph over death, hell, and the grave.

Your story doesn't have to end in tragedy either. There is a resurrection after the death you are presently experiencing in your life. It's a resurrection of your dreams, visions, goals, and promises from God. God's plan for your life wasn't to end in a sad drama or a comedy, but rather a picture of utter and complete victory.

As you catch the revelation of identification with Jesus Christ, just as you were with Him in His crucifixion, death, burial, and resurrection, your story isn't over. Quite frankly, it's just beginning.

Questions for Reflections

1. Recall a time when you thought it was all over for you or your situation?

2. How do you think knowing that Jesus' story didn't end with His burial can impact your life today?

3. How will you view your struggle knowing that there is still the possibility of a triumphant outcome?

Morning Decree #229
More Than a Resurrection

"And if we are [His] children, then we are [His] heirs also: heirs of God and fellow heirs with Christ [sharing His inheritance with Him]; only we must share His suffering if we are to share His glory." Romans 8:17, AMP

Identification with Christ is the ultimate revelation once a person receives Him as Lord, understanding that what Jesus did, He accomplished as us, with us and for us. Or to make it very personal—for you, as you, and with you. This identification doesn't end with Jesus only being your Sin-Bearer. The benefit package of God toward you is exhaustive and complete, with nothing missing.

When Jesus was raised from the dead, we were raised as well. To think of Him being raised but not healed or restored would make Jesus a zombie-like creature. No, that' has not what happened. When Jesus was raised from the dead, He regained His former glory, especially after His Ascension. The power of sin was obliterated, healing and health restored, provision including wealth made available again, and, most importantly, unbroken communication with the Father was once again unhindered by sin.

Questions for Reflections

1. If you were an heir to a fortune, but you were estranged from your family for years, what should you expect once your relationship and legal standing were restored?

2. Would you think like an employee or a blood-heir?

3. How should you, knowing that you have been restored back to good graces of the Father through Jesus Christ, now behave?

Morning Decree #230
Cancelled

"Having cancelled and blotted out and wiped away the handwriting of the note (bond) with its legal decrees and demands which was in force and stood against us (hostile to us). This [note with its regulations, decrees, and demands] He set aside and cleared completely out of our way by nailing it to [His] cross."
Colossians 2:14, AMP

     I don't think many of us like to hear the word cancelled, unless it's something we didn't want to happen in the first place. When it comes to our past life of sin, the word *cancelled* has a new and important meaning.

     Our sins, which play like a never-ending movie, were cancelled through the death of Jesus Christ on the cross. Our sins stood against us having a relationship with our God in heaven. Until Jesus came along and died on our behalf, taking our sins with Him, our sins stood as a witness against us. The deception we were all under at one point was that we can erase our bad by doing good. The truth is even our good often falls short of God's standards, not to mention that our good doesn't cancel the bad. All of us from the pulpit to the parking lot have sinned and need our sins to be eradicated." All have sinned and fallen short of the glory of God" (Romans 3:23-24).

Questions for Reflections

1. Can you recall a particular sin that you hope never shows up in your eternal playlist?

2. How would you react if you knew all of your financial obligations were cancelled?

3. What should your daily response be if you knew that, just like your bills could be cancelled, your sins *are* cancelled in Christ Jesus?

Morning Decree #231
It's Right to Be Right

"For if because of one man's trespass (lapse, offense) death reigned through that one, much more surely will those who receive [God's] overflowing grace (unmerited favor) and the free gift of righteousness [putting them into right standing with Himself] reign as kings in life through the one-Man Jesus Christ (the Messiah, the Anointed One)." Romans 5:17, AMP

In today's world, you really do need a good credit score. Your score is a universally accepted criteria that determines your worthiness to be given a loan. In other words, based upon your score, merchants decide whether or not to let you take their product, live in their apartment, or drive their car without having to pay for it all upfront. Rarely understood, however, is that God also uses a credit score criteria which determines your ability to receive His grace or promises. The good news is that the credit score used is not yours, but the one belonging to Christ Jesus Himself.

Righteousness is the ultimate standard or credit score, but this righteousness is Jesus' not yours. Your ability to transact with Heaven is never based upon your good deeds. While good deeds are important, they are never what makes it possible to approach God in prayer. Regardless of how good you are, how much you fast and pray, or give and sacrifice, but ultimately, it's only based upon the gift of righteousness that makes prayer work.

Questions for Reflections

1. When do you feel more acceptable to God? When you are doing everything right or when you are doing wrong things?

2. How much do feelings of righteousness affects your confidence?

3. How will knowing about Christ's righteousness make you more confident in prayer?

Morning Decree #232
Righteousness

"For our sake He made Christ [virtually] to be sin Who knew no sin, so that in and through Him we might become [endued with, viewed as being in, and examples of] the righteousness of God [what we ought to be, approved and acceptable and in right relationship with Him, by His goodness]." 2 Corinthians 5:21, AMP

Righteousness is a subject that is prominent in the *Morning Decrees* because it is the key to success. You were made righteous through the sacrificial death of Jesus Christ. Your righteousness is based 100% upon what Jesus did. Your good acts are in response to the amazing gift of His righteousness. It is a gift received, not a gift earned. As you grow in the revelation of the knowledge of righteousness, your prayer life will take on a new confidence. Instead of retreating from God's presence, you will run to it, for you know that success is granted because of Christ, and Christ alone.

When you are feeling unworthy, your tendency is to shy away from God and the things of God, including prayer, worship, fellowship with others, and sharing your faith. Having a working knowledge of righteousness will draw you toward God. What an amazing gift.

Questions for Reflections

1. Why is it difficult at times to receive rather than to work for the gifts of God?

2. Do you feel you have to earn God's goodness?

3. Where did you think you picked up the thinking of earning rather than receiving?

Morning Decree #233
Just Receive

"For if because of one man's trespass (lapse, offense) death reigned through that one, "... much more surely will those who receive [God's] overflowing grace (unmerited favor) and the free gift of righteousness [putting them into right standing with Himself] reign as kings in life through the one Man Jesus Christ (the Messiah, the Anointed One)." Romans 5:17, AMP

One of the most difficult things for a believer to do is to receive that which was not earned. We exist in such a performance-based society requiring us to do something to get something. That's appropriate in most situations, but when it comes to the blessings of God, it's drastically different. What qualifies us is God's righteousness as revealed in Jesus Christ. Accepting the fact that on your best days, you are never going to be good enough, holy enough, worthy enough, dissipates the pressure to perform. Your trust is in what Jesus accomplished for you.

Regrettably, failure to embrace the fact that righteousness is a gift will cause many to confuse their righteous behavior with the righteousness that comes by Jesus Christ. The two don't mix any more than oil and water do. There is a place for personal righteous deeds, however, but those deeds will never be the reason why you receive the blessings of God.

Questions for Reflections

1. Can you recall a time when you received something you didn't expect and for which you didn't work?

2. When was the last time you did something significant for someone you were not obligated to do?

3. Why did you do it? And how did it make you feel?

Morning Decree #234
Team Effort

"For those whom He foreknew [of whom He was aware and loved beforehand], He also destined from the beginning [foreordaining them] to be molded into the image of His Son [and share inwardly His likeness], that He might become the firstborn among many brethren." Romans 8:29, AMP

Did you know that if your team wins a championship, let's say the Super Bowl, even if you don't play in the game itself, you still get a credit for the victory? You get the championship ring, bonus check, and can rightfully forever call yourself a Super Bowl Champion. It seems too good to be true, yet it is.

The above truth is even more profound when you understand that Jesus' victory over the devil is your victory as well, making you not one degree less a conqueror than He is. The miracle of identification includes this all-too-important principle: Jesus' victory over death, hell, and the grave is your victory over death, hell, and the grave. All the powers of the devil, which Jesus seemingly effortlessly subdued, are also part of your dominion. Perhaps that's why the Apostle Paul spoke of "the good fight of faith" because any fight that you know you won before it even starts is a good fight.

What Jesus achieved, acquired, and overcame are the same things you can achieve, acquire, and overcome. Jesus had zero failure in His mission. You are to walk in the same level of victory. Why would Jesus say you are to do the greater works than He did if you were destined to fail at every turn?

Questions for Reflections

1. In what areas of your life are you fighting to win?

2. In what ways can you relate to Jesus' victory over devils and haters?

3. How can you see yourself as Jesus sees you?

Morning Decree #235
Diamonds are Everywhere

"Though thy beginning was small, yet thy latter end should greatly increase."
Job 8:7, KJV

What makes diamonds so valuable is the fact that they are rare. What's often not considered is the time it takes for a diamond to become a diamond or the fact that they are created in deep, dark places encrusted with dirt.

I'm not encouraging you to drop everything and start digging in the dirt to find a diamond. The diamonds that are everywhere are people. The diamonds are you. You are the piece of carbon that is deep in the heart of a dirty, hidden place experiencing great pressure. You are the diamond-in-the making that is unnoticed at this point in time.

Recognize that God didn't give you a life that is less than the value of someone else'. Your circumstances may be resemble where diamonds are found covered by tons of rock and dirt, but just like a diamond, you are still precious and valuable. As soon as you realize you are a diamond, you will rise above the pressure, the obstacles, and the dark seasons.

Questions for Reflections

1. Do you see yourself as a diamond? Why or why not?

2. What can you do to embrace your value despite the mountain of life's dirt on top of you right now?

3. Can you see the diamond potential in others?

Morning Decree #236
It Ain't Gonna to Be Pretty, but It's Necessary

"I assure you, most solemnly I tell you, Unless a grain of wheat falls into the earth and dies, it remains [just one grain; it never becomes more but lives] by itself alone. But if it dies, it produces many others and yields a rich harvest." John 12:24, AMP

The process of change, growth, development whether within an individual life or an organization like a church usually isn't easy or pretty. The process can be a bit messy and much more difficult than originally thought. Like the refining of a precious metal such as gold before it's placed in store to be sold, it has undergone intense heat, shaping, and buffing. We don't think much about the process, we just want the finished product.

The same unpleasant process would be jewelry must endure is the same for your spiritual life and development. There's heating, there's reshaping, and there's polishing. No one arrives ready for "display" but must submit to a process, one that lasts one's entire life. The process of perfection involves multiple trips to the potter's wheel and furnace. It's where your edges are smoothed out, your cracks are fixed, and your shine is brightened. Without such a process, your true beauty would never be seen. You would be dull, uninviting, and in no way reflective of the work of the Master.

Questions for Reflections

1. Looking back, can you remember a season in your life that was full of unpleasant experiences but yet caused you to discover valuable personal characteristics?

2. How did you feel as you were going through the process?

3. What spiritual resources did you rely on to help you make the most of the situations?

Morning Decree #237
Embrace the Process

"Trembling and astonished he asked, 'Lord, what do You desire me to do?' The Lord said to him, 'But arise and go into the city, and you will be told what you must do.'"
Acts 9:6

I like the finished product. When the goal is completed, the weight has been lost or the home built. Few people enjoy the process. You can embrace it, however, recognizing that, "I must go through this to get to my goal." When you look at your goals, understanding the amount of work it will take to accomplish them, it is sometimes possible to quit before you even get started. This is because you fail to embrace the process as normal.

Growing up, my siblings and I were not allowed to go out and play before finishing our chores. Cutting the grass, cleaning rooms, vacuuming, and so forth all needed to be completed to our parents' standard, otherwise play time never came. The chores got done a lot faster with less angst when we embraced the process.

To receive the promises of God, embracing the reality that there will be a process you must navigate is essential. Even when God promised Moses and His people a "land that flowed with milk and honey", there were still walled cities, giants, and deserts to overcome. Not knowing or remembering there will be something worthwhile once you overcome leads to unnecessary disappointments and inability to endure the process.

Questions for Reflections

1. What are some projects you need to complete but are neglecting because of the process required to get them done?

2. What "process-type things" do you dislike doing the most?

3. What are some practical ways you can learn to embrace your process?

Morning Decree #238
Guaranteed Outcomes

"Do not be deceived and deluded and misled; God will not allow Himself to be sneered at (scorned, disdained, or mocked by mere pretensions or professions, or by His precepts being set aside.) [He inevitably deludes himself who attempts to delude God.] For whatever a man sows, that and that only is what he will reap."
Galatians 6:7, AMP

Have you ever heard the statement, "The only guarantees in life are death and taxes?" I have heard it many times. The truth is that the one thing you can really count on is the spiritual law that everything reproduces after its own kind. This biblical law simply reveals that a corn seed will produce corn 100% of the time. It's foolish to think that anything other than a stalk of corn is going to grow from the kernel of corn.

This law has far-reaching implications, way past simple agriculture. The truth that seeds produce according to their type applies also to your spiritual, physical, and economic lives. What you sow is what you are going to reap. The one caveat is that what is harvested is exponentially greater than the seed sown.

Nevertheless, corn seeds produce corn, apple seeds produce apples. When you intentionally sow let's say money into the Kingdom of God, there is a guaranteed outcome, based upon the heart condition in which the money was given along with the amount. The system is divinely pre-determined to work on your behalf. If you sow it, you can with absolute certainly expect a harvest of more money along with what money cannot buy.

Questions for Reflections

1. Why do Christians struggle so much with giving or sowing?

2. Why do you think God set it up that the more we give, the more we receive?

3. Are you receiving the return from your financial seeds you desire?

Morning Decree #239
Decide Before You Do It

"Let each one [give] as he has made up his own mind and purposed in his heart, not reluctantly or sorrowfully or under compulsion, for God loves (He takes pleasure in, prizes above other things, and is unwilling to abandon or to do without) a cheerful (joyous, "prompt to do it") giver [whose heart is in his giving]."
2 Corinthians 9:7, AMP

It sounds pretty basic doesn't it? Before you do something like plant a garden, you need to decide what you want to grow and how large a garden you want to plant. This simple concept is rarely considered when sowing financial or other types of spiritual seeds. When sowing, many times you just give a portion of what you have, hoping that something good will come from your sacrifice. While that's not totally out of order, perhaps the most efficient way is to determine how much of a harvest you need, and then sow seeds accordingly.

No farmer simply selects to plant seeds without first having determined, the amount of seed needed to achieve the desired harvest. Additionally, the kind of seed is also predetermined. Since God uses the agriculture metaphor to express spiritual realities, it's not a stretch to realize that when it comes to your sowing of financial resources, we should also predetermine the size and kind of harvest you need or desire. You will only get what you expect if you sow with intentionality and wisdom. Wise sowers determine these matters beforehand. Decide before you do it!

Questions for Reflections

1. Describe the type of harvest you need to receive this year?

2. Based on the type of harvest, have you sown that kind of seed?

3. How much and where have you planted those seeds?

Morning Decree #240
Only If You Want To

"Let each one [give] as he has made up his own mind and purposed in his heart, not reluctantly or sorrowfully or under compulsion, for God loves (He takes pleasure in, prizes above other things, and is unwilling to abandon or to do without) a cheerful (joyous, "prompt to do it") giver [whose heart is in his giving]."
2 Corinthians 9:7, AMP

When it comes to sowing seeds beyond tithing, it's a personal decision between you and the Holy Spirit. If you feel pressured by someone or even by yourself to give, rather than giving because you want to, it will be better for you to just keep and not give it. Giving is a heart issue, not a financial one. God looks at your heart, your motivation.

Your giving should be based upon your desire to give and the need or request presented to you. The need may be let's say $1,000, but you feel to give only $10. You may even have the $1,000, but you feel that $10 is all you should give. It's better to give the $10 and experience the joy and blessing of God than to give the larger amount and not receive the commendation of God.

The opposite also holds true. If you know you should give the $1,000 and then you gave only $999, your gift will bless the recipient, but you on the other hand have not pleased God. Do what's in your heart to do, and in the absence of a clear directive from the Lord, do what you can that gives you peace and joy.

Questions for Reflections

1. Describe a time when you gave either more than you should and less than you were led to give?

2. How did you feel in both situations? How did you feel when you did exactly what you thought you should have done?

3. Do you have a giving plan?

Morning Decree #241
How Much Do You Want?

[Remember] this: he who sows sparingly and grudgingly will also reap sparingly and grudgingly, and he who sows generously [that blessings may come to someone] will also reap generously and with blessings." 2 Corinthians 9:6, AMP

Farmers determine the minimum amount they require from their harvest. They decide this long before planting season because they will need to acquire the land and the seed necessary to get what they need. If they want to plant 40 acres of tomatoes, they need 40 acres of land, and enough seed to cover the entire acreage. This calculation isn't made the day of planting or even during planting, but months and sometimes years before.

If you sow abundantly, you will reap abundantly. If you sow sparingly, you will reap sparingly. This law is one of the most vital, for it puts back under your control the amount of harvest you receive. Sowing and reaping from a biblical perspective is as predictable as planting seeds in a family garden. The more you plant, the more you will reap. The less you plant, the less you will reap.

Therefore, when you give financial seeds, based upon your available resources decide how much harvest you want to receive before you plant. The amount, in comparison to others, may not seem to be a lot. The ultimate judge who determines whether you sowing is considered abundant, is God. Don't compare what you do to others. Just do what's in your heart and within your capability. God sees, knows, and will multiply your harvest for you accordingly.

Questions for Reflections

1. What are some of the harvests you need in your life in the next twelve months?

2. What resources do you think you'll need to acquire in order to meet your harvest goal?

3. Where will you sow your seeds? Why in that ministry?

Morning Decree #242
God Counts What's Left

"For if the [eager] readiness to give is there, then it is acceptable and welcomed in proportion to what a person has, not according to what he does not have. I don't know about you, but I've been in a number of services when I didn't have what was asked for during the offering, or even what I would like to give. I felt so defeated. Then I realized that God was judging my giving based on what I have, not what I don't have. He knows better even the bank what I can give and should give. He knows my desire to give more, but don't have the resources to match." 2 Corinthians 8:12, AMP

There are times when you just don't have the money that you want in order to give. I've been in many church meetings where I didn't have the "asked for amount." I felt defeated, less than and condemned. It wasn't that the minister was making me feel that way, but rather my own incorrect thinking. It wasn't until I realized that God really didn't care about how much I gave, but rather my heart or intention as I decided to give any amount. My pride at times caused me to either give more than I could afford or not give for fear of embarrassment. In either case, I missed out on the blessing.

Consequently, I've learned to listen to God within my own circumstances. According to the Scriptures, God will neither require something of you that you have no ability to deliver nor would He hold you accountable. Instead, God gives you "credit" for your intention, in this case, rather than what you actually put in the offering plate. Giving is a heart matter, not a math matter.

Questions for Reflections

1. Can you recall a time when you felt God was asking something of you that you knew you had no way of doing or giving?

2. When did you realize it wasn't God after all?

3. Why is it important to have the right heart when it comes to doing anything in Jesus' name?

Morning Decree #243
Take Charge of Your Own Garden

"And God blessed them and said to them, 'Be fruitful, multiply, and fill the earth, and subdue it [using all its vast resources in the service of God and man]; and have dominion over the fish of the sea, the birds of the air, and over every living creature that moves upon the earth.'" Genesis 1:28, AMP

Understanding the awesome responsibility you have to determine what your future will look like is critical. While God's sovereignty is without question, His influence is limited. This limitation, however, is by choice. He has given much leeway to His creation. From the beginning of creation, humans were given the responsibility to take care of their environment. This is still true today.

You have the wonderful opportunity to determine what type of garden grows in your life. Through the seeds your sow, or don't sow, you determine the fruit you enjoy. This doesn't by any stretch of the imagination factor God out, but rather it is a demonstration of God's decision to make you the chief steward.

Decide today by choosing the right seeds, efforts, actions, or words with which you will need to harvest in your life. The seeds you plant are under your complete control. What you speak is a seed, what you do is a seed, even how you think is a seed. As much like a cliché as it sounds, "sow it to grow it" is nevertheless as true today as it has been since the beginning of time.

Questions for Reflections

1. Have you ever noticed weeds growing in a garden and wondered how they got there? What did you conclude as possible answers?

2. Who ultimately decides what kind of garden grows in your (backyard) garden?

3. How can you change the type of plants your grow?

Morning Decree #244
Plant This to Harvest That

"And God said, 'See, I have given you every plant yielding seed that is on the face of all the land and every tree with seed in its fruit; you shall have them for food.'"
Genesis 1:29

The Law of Seedtime and Harvest are in full effect (see Genesis 8:22). This law is working, just like gravity, regardless of one's geographic location, socioeconomic status, or gender. The universal Law of Seedtime and Harvest cares nothing about your race, nationality, or religious views. Essentially, if you sow pumpkin seeds, you will grow pumpkins. It's just that simple.

As you navigate your day with enthusiasm, do so with the full knowledge that everything, absolutely everything, is a seed. Every action has a seed-like impact. What you do will produce a predictable outcome over time. If you act carelessly with your time, for instance, you will reap the fruit of poverty. If you fail to sow energy by way of proper and appropriate exercise, you will produce a health profile that is considered unhealthy.

If you want something, you must sow that kind of seed. If you want more energy, you must plant exercise seeds. If you want this, whatever your "this" is, you must sow that type of seed. Everything is a seed.

Questions for Reflections

1. Describe an area of your life as a garden. What are you growing in that area that you didn't plan to grow?

2. What actions did you plant to grow that fruit in your life?

3. What type of fruit do you want more of in your life? What seeds do you need to sow?

Morning Decree #245
A Pinch Here, A Pinch There

"Any branch in Me that does not bear fruit [that stops bearing] He cuts away (trims off, takes away); and He cleanses and repeatedly prunes every branch that continues to bear fruit, to make it bear more and richer and more excellent fruit." John 15:2

Pruning is necessary for more growth. This is true of plants and people. The cutting away of dead branches is essential to further the development of healthy plants and saints. To ignore the pruning process is not an act of mercy but of neglect; a dereliction of duty.

Clipping the dead, non-productive branches allows a plant to bloom to its potential. Jesus mentioned that growth, in a spiritual sense, is directly tied to the degree of pruning to which a disciple is submitted. Your desire to be more effective must include periods and seasons of pruning or chastening. It is during those periods that the most important facets of development actually occur. Therefore, instead of avoiding the pruning process, seek it out. Look for opportunities to stretch and grow.

Questions for Reflections

1. What "pruning" experience are you avoiding?

2. In what area(s) are you failing to see new growth?

3. What should you do to ensure that you experience timely prunings?

Morning Decree #246
Pain Precedes Progress

"If you live in Me [abide vitally united to Me] and My words remain in you and continue to live in your hearts, ask whatever you will, and it shall be done for you."
John 15:7, AMP

I'm not talking about pain that requires medical attention or prescription medications. Instead, I am referring to the pain that often follows physical exercise and the pain that accompanies making a difficult, emotionally charged decision. Pain should be expected, anticipated, and embraced. It's the avoidance of this kind of pain that results in stunted growth.

Making hard choices, like breaking away from an unhealthy relationship, or choosing to be alone because of your personal convictions, can be painful. This pain is temporary, especially when you consider the prolonged dysfunction that accompanies failure to make the tough decision.

Embrace your situation knowing that even though it's painful now, the resulting progress is ultimately worth every minute of emotional or physical discomfort. Doing the best thing is always the right thing, though it feels like the wrong thing to do in the moment. Progress is awaiting you.

Questions for Reflections

1. Name three moments when you balked at making the best decision because you didn't want to embrace the pain that would follow?

2. Looking back, would you make a different decision today? Why?

3. What advice would you give someone who is facing difficult decisions for their life?

Morning Decree #247
Exercise Is Required

"For physical training is of some value (useful for a little), but godliness (spiritual training) is useful and of value in everything and in every way, for it holds promise for the present life and also for the life which is to come." 1 Timothy 4:8, AMP

The Bible does not say that physical exercise is unnecessary. It simply asserts that it's not the most important factor. The point of this devotional, however, is that just as in the case the physical exercise, spiritual disciplines are necessary for optimum health.

What are the spiritual disciplines that you regularly practice? My most productive workout sessions at the gym are those that I both consistently do and plan beforehand. I don't base my workout routines on my feelings on a specific morning because most mornings, I simply don't feel like working out. I commence the trainings regardless of how I feel due to the fact it is part of my personal discipline.

Your spiritual life is more important than your physique. It takes serious planning and determination to properly develop spiritually. The idea behind being a disciple is that of disciplined practices. To grow in Christ is more than knowing Scriptures or even agreeing with them. To develop properly requires the daily practice of certain key disciplines.

Questions for Reflections

1. What are the spiritual disciplines you practice daily?

2. Why do you feel the need to employ these practices?

3. What are your strongest disciplines? What are the areas in which you struggle the most?

Morning Decree #248
Committed or Churched?

"Then Jesus said to His disciples, 'If anyone desires to be My disciple, let him deny himself [disregard, lose sight of, and forget himself and his own interests] and take up his cross and follow Me [cleave steadfastly to Me, conform wholly to My example in living and, if need be, in dying, also].'" Matthew 16:24, AMP

There's a big difference between being committed to Christ and being a good church member. Every pastor appreciates it when their members follow the rules per se, but following Jesus' way is the goal. Being a good member has it's challenges, but following Jesus requires total commitment, no retreat, and going all in. This story really is one of commitment.

There's a fable of a farmer who was in financial trouble. The farm animals got wind of the problem and called a meeting. In the meeting, each animal offered to help in some way. The chickens said, "We'll give some eggs." The sheep said, "We'll give some wool." However, when the pig was asked if he would give some bacon, he responded by saying, "Eggs are a commitment, wool is a commitment, but bacon is total devotion."

That's my version of the story, and I hope you get the point. Devotion is beyond church or farm membership. It's the point of no return. Our Lord Jesus Christ was devoted to saving us by giving His life as a ransom. It's not even close to being a fair transaction. He died for us by crucifixion and now we live for Him. No matter how you look at it, we got the greater end of the deal.

Questions for Reflections

1. How would you describe your relationship with the Lord: committed or membership?

2. If you are committed, can you point to a moment when your commitment to Christ really cost you something?

3. How do you maintain this level of commitment?

Morning Decree #249
Don't Forget to Be Thankful

"And let the peace of Christ rule in your hearts, to which indeed you were called in one body. And be thankful." Colossians 3:15

Lists are helpful for sure but when that list is only about what you want or need to get and does not include reasons to be thankful, it's not much better than making a list for Santa Claus. It's always advantageous to write a list of the things for which you are thankful. It's hard to stay down in the dumps when you realize all the good things in your life. I know there are tough times, seasons, and events that can be hard to deal with. There are things that make us mad, sad, and even depressed. However, even in the midst of these periods, remembering the many blessings of God in your life is the perfect exercise.

By intentionally calling to mind the many ways in which God has redeemed you, answered your prayers, and helped you and those you love, you will increase your faith ten-fold. There's even scientific research that says being thankful has a direct impact on your health, both mind and body. With increased faith, you can fight the battles you're facing at this very moment. Regrettably, it seems so much easier to complain about what's wrong with your life rather than praise God for what is right. Practice being thankful.

Questions for Reflections

1. Name three things that come to mind when you think of being thankful.

2. When is the last time you actually verbally thanked God for those things, or anything for that matter?

3. How do you feel when someone remembers and expresses thanks for what you did for them without asking for something more?

Morning Decree #250
Actions Are More Articulate Than Words

"These people draw near Me with their mouths and honor Me with their lips, but their hearts hold off and are far away from Me." Matthew 15:8

What you spend your time and money on indicates to what or whom you are devoted. That's a hard statement but difficult to dispute. A person can expound on their love or desire for something, but without corresponding actions, their words carry little weight.

Honoring the Lord requires demonstrated devotion. It requires actions that support the confessions of faith. The phrase "talk is cheap" conveys the idea that it costs nothing to say something, while to have the courage to live out those convictions is an entirely different matter.

If your devotion to God, or anything else for that matter, doesn't require some sacrifice from you, then you should ask yourself, "Am I truly devoted?" What's interesting is when you devote ourselves to God, you are the biggest beneficiary of your sacrifice. You cannot lose in the long-run by being devoted to Christ in the long run.

Questions for Reflections

1. What does being devoted mean to you?

2. How do you demonstrate your devotion to your loved ones? To Jesus?

3. Whose devotion do you admire? Perhaps someone you have never met? Why do you admire them?

Morning Decree #251
Your Next Move Matters More

"Never return evil for evil or insult for insult (scolding, tongue-lashing, berating), but on the contrary blessing [praying for their welfare, happiness, and protection, and truly pitying and loving them]. For now know that to this you have been called, that you may yourselves inherit a blessing [from God—that you may obtain a blessing as heirs, bringing welfare and happiness and protection]." 1 Peter 3:9, AMP

Injury, insult, and disappointments can happen to anyone. What you do or how you respond to them that determines if they have a lasting impact. Just like a physical injury that is improperly treated and infection sets in, the invisible injuries, if not treated promptly and properly, will lead to more devastation.

Your devotion to Christ is one way of remaining focused despite the inevitable disappointments and discouraging things that may happen. Remain steadfast to do what Jesus has assigned for you to do in life. Surely then you will overcome the issues, hills, and valleys.

As a devoted follower of Jesus, your response to the issues of life should be based upon His teachings and His Spirit. This will ensure the best possible outcome. Remain focused on the Author and Finisher of your faith.

Questions for Reflections

1. What are the three things that seem to quickly derail you from you goals the?

2. What can you do to minimize the "being off" time?

3. How can your devotional life help you recover more quickly?

Morning Decree #252
Defeating the 'D' Word

"Looking away [from all that will distract] to Jesus, Who is the Leader and the Source of our faith [giving the first incentive for our belief] and is also its Finisher [bringing it to maturity and perfection]. He, for the joy [of obtaining the prize] that was set before Him, endured the cross, despising and ignoring the shame, and is now seated at the right hand of the throne of God." Hebrews 12:2, AMP

The temptation to become discouraged is a common attack. As a matter of fact, it's so common that most people expect it, treating it as a normal occurrence. Actually, discouragement is not normal. Nowhere in the Bible does it say, "Welcome your discouragement for I, the Lord your God, have sent it to you." Nevertheless, it did grip many of the heroes of our faith. When it shows up, the question becomes, "How do you defeat it?"

Developing your ability to remain focused on the promises of God is one important key to fend off the waves of discouragement. Failure to remain fixed on the Author of your faith is the single most common reason for prolonged seasons of discouragement.

Studying the life of Jesus is a seminar in how to overcome things that would try to overwhelm you. He remained focused on the joy that was set before Him. His perspective helped Him overcome the momentary issues. Pursuing your dream will pull you out of your nightmare.

Questions for Reflections

1. Where does your mind go when you are discouraged?

2. How can a clear and compelling vision support you in times of discouragement?

3. What spiritual resources should you employ to work through the temptation to be discouraged?

Morning Decree #253
Go Through It to Get to It

"Yes, though I walk through the [deep, sunless] valley of the shadow of death, I will fear or dread no evil, for You are with me; Your rod [to protect] and Your staff [to guide], they comfort me." Psalms 23:4, AMP

Jesus' words before his departure were, "In the world, you shall have tribulation. But be of good cheer; I have overcome the world" (John 16:33). Those words have a far-reaching impact and importance as you work through the issues of life as you face the. inevitable challenges, tests, and trials common to all.

Challenges arise from doing both the "right things" and the "wrong things." There are even some challenges you are confronted with as a result of your faith in Christ Jesus. The Lord Jesus in His wisdom chose to let you know in advance what to expect, and through faith in Him, you can overcome those problems.

Sometimes, when bad things are happening, you may tend to feel like it's "all my fault." Also, when you think it's your fault, you lack confidence in God's grace to see you through. However, even though you may be suffering as the result of your actions, His grace is yet available to help you through. Therefore, the next time you're faced with life's tests, make the changes needed to eliminate future issues and receive God's grace to give you what it is you need to get through it.

Questions for Reflections

1. When you're going through difficult times, what is the first thought that comes to your mind?

2. What are some of the Scriptural things you can do to get through what you're going through?

3. How did Jesus overcome the world for you?

Morning Decree #254
You Got It

"For everyone who has been born of God overcomes the world. And this is the victory that has overcome the world—our faith." 1 John 5:4

Jesus said sometimes we would face troubles in our lives. He also told His followers to be of good cheer because He has overcome the world. Now, how are we supposed to overcome the problems we face every day?

As the Scriptural lesson reads, "And this is the victory that has overcome the world—our faith" (1 John 5:4). It takes faith to overcome life's difficulties. Faith is vital because it is the knowledge that as you act according to the Word of God, which is faith, things will work out for your good. Faith is more than just believing in God. Faith is acting on the belief that God will make a way for you to overcome the uncertainties of life. Faith is active trust in God's Word. Faith has nothing to do with how you feel or your circumstances. Faith moves things based upon the Word of God. You have what you need for victory when you have faith.

Questions for Reflections

1. Do you trust your ability to handle the situation or rely on your faith in Him?

2. Feelings are real, so how do you handle your feelings when faced with challenging situations?

3. What can you do to keep your faith strong during troubling times?

Morning Decree #255
Thank Him for the Right Thing

"The thief comes only in order to steal and kill and destroy. I came that they may have and enjoy life, and have it in abundance (to the full, till it overflows)."
John 10:10, AMP

"Be ye thankful" is a word to live by. We should cultivate a heart of thanksgiving, but regrettably, some have been taught that we should give thanks for *everything* that happens to us. While it's important to give God thanks in the midst of something like a tragedy, we don't thank God for the tragedy. Why? Because that tragedy came to destroy your faith in God. It came to rob you and otherwise wreck your life. But the most important reason why you don't thank God for anything that robs you of life is that it came from the devil. A follower of Jesus doesn't thank the devil for *anything*. God is a great God. The devil is a bad devil.

Tragedies, sickness, premature death—to name a few troubling things—are the kind of events for which we don't thank God. The God of the Bible as revealed in Jesus Christ is not a God who kills children or puts diseases on the innocent. Jesus stated in no uncertain terms that His mission was to provide an abundant life for us—thank God for this.

Questions for Reflections

1. What are you thankful for today? List at least five things.

2. How does gratefulness affect your energy levels?

3. How do you think begin thankful will increase your faith?

Morning Decree #256
Feel It but Do It Anyway

"But overhearing what they said, Jesus said to the ruler of the synagogue, 'Do not fear, only believe.'" Mark 5:36

I don't think you can go through life without feeling the emotion of fear. It's how your mind reacts or responds to certain external stimulation. It's designed to do that. So, if you're waiting to take that next step in life until you're fearless, you will never make the move.

Feel the fear—recognize what it is—then do the thing you are supposed to do regardless of how you feel. Sometimes I just drag my fears with me until they fall off like stages of a rocket entering outer space after a launch.

Fear is one indicator that you're alive and that you have something that's important to you that you don't want to lose. Fear is an indicator, it's not a determinator. Just because I'm afraid, doesn't exempt me from the task at hand. Fear is something that can be controlled and certainly should never be the determining factor in my going forward. Fear is an emotion, not my God.

Questions for Reflections

1. What is the number one thing of which you're afraid?

2. In what ways has it affected you?

3. If you continue to live life based on your fears, what do you think you will lose in the future?

Morning Decree #257
More than Conquerors

"No, in all these things we are more than conquerors through him who loved us."
Romans 8:37

Nike, the billion-dollar sports company, coined the phrase, "just do it." What's not widely known is that the word *nike* has its origins in the Greek Language and is found in the New Testament. In Romans 8, it says, "We are more than conquerors." The word *conquerors* is *nike*. Therefore, Christ's substitutionary death causes us to be more than *nike* which means more than victorious. Being in the will of God positions us to win. Still, it requires that we know who we are in Christ and to whom we belong from a spiritual standpoint.

Too often, we view ourselves through the lens of our circumstances and conclude that we are victims. It's about time we saw ourselves in the light of God's perspective and begin to declare, " I am more than a conqueror through Jesus Christ."

Questions for Reflections

1. What's the number one hindrance to your goals?

2. Why have you not pursued your dreams to this point?

3. What support do you need to go forward?

Morning Decree #258
Watch Where You're Going

"And the Lord answered me and said, 'Write the vision and engrave it so plainly upon tablets that everyone who passes may [be able to] read [it easily and quickly] as he hastens by.'" Habakkuk 2:2, AMP

As a child, I often heard my mother utter these words, "Watch where you're going." This was her way of getting my attention that I was about to drop a plate or trip over a toy because I was focused on something else at the time.

This parental admonition is something that is still relevant for me today, but with a little different emphasis on the word *watch*. To *watch* where you're going in light of Habakkuk 2:2, you are to visualize where it is you want to go. Your responsibility is to have a vision, which is "a pictorial representation of a future destination" clear in your mind. The failure to have a clear, easily visualized plan is the main reason for the lack of productivity. What's your vision?

Questions for Reflections

1. What's your vision for your financial, physical, or spiritual future?

2. What's the value of writing your vision down in clear terms?

3. What happens when your vision isn't clear?

Morning Decree #259
Fail Lately?

"For the righteous falls seven times and rises again." Proverbs 24:16

Failing at something isn't the worst thing that happens to a person unless they fail to do one very important thing. That important thing is to try again. According to the Scriptures, even a good man falls—but falling must be married to getting up, otherwise failing or falling is final.

Your failure doesn't have to be final. It needs not be the last chapter in the book of your life. There is not one highly successful person who hasn't had to overcome failure. Some fail at a business endeavor or fail to gain admission into a particular college. Some fail to maintain a healthy body or a vibrant marriage. Whatever your failure was or is, don't let it be the reason for not trying again. Failure isn't fatal nor is it final—unless you let it be. Get up. Refocus. Start again.

Questions for Reflections

1. What has been the biggest failure you've experienced in your life?

2. How did you feel when it occurred and what did you do about it?

3. What advice would you give the younger you pertaining to overcoming personal failure?

Morning Decree #260
Flatlined

"David was greatly distressed, for the men spoke of stoning him because the souls of them all were bitterly grieved, each man for his sons and daughters. But David encouraged and strengthened himself in the Lord his God." 1 Samuel 30:6

Life isn't lived in a straight line. As a matter of fact, when someone has their heart checked and a printout of their heartbeat is analyzed, a straight or flat line means they are dead! Hills and valleys are appropriate both in electrocardiograms and in life itself. Flatlines are not acceptable.

Being willing and ready to adjust to the terrain of life is an important key to success. There will be days, weeks, and even long months that require constant adjustments and course corrections. To expect any other reality isn't real but delusional. The rain will fall on the wise and just along with the unwise and unjust, and the sun will shine on both as well. There will be days when you feel like you're winning, and other days when the score tells you a different story. Understanding that this is part of the course while being willing to make the necessary adjustments as required ensures that your breakthrough is inevitable.

Questions for Reflections

1. On a scale of 1 to 10, 10 being the most flexible, and 1 being the least, how would you rate yourself on your flexibility when faced with setbacks?

2. What are the types of setbacks that really do set you back emotionally?

3. How would you advise another person who is facing those same kinds of setbacks to overcome them?

Morning Decree #261
If You're not Changing,
You're Not Growing: You're Dying

"When I was a child, I talked like a child, I thought like a child, I reasoned like a child; now that I have become a man, I am done with childish ways and have put them aside." 1 Corinthians 13:11

Every living thing is also changing. Though these changes are not usually visible to the naked eye, change nevertheless is happening. If it's not happening, something is wrong, and death will occur in just a matter of time.

Our spiritual life is no different than an acorn. An acorn is the seed that produces a mighty oak tree. For that oak tree to manifest, the acorn must experience both death and growth. The acorn undergoes decay, so that what's locked in the inner part can develop and emerge.

This is equally true for you and me to grow in that the matured "oak" of our nature is housed in the shell of immaturity. As we change, certain ways of thinking also change or are intentionally discarded. Without change, which often means growth, we are mainly childish, and largely ineffective.

Questions for Reflections

1. Why do we seem to resist change?

2. What areas of your spiritual life are begging for change but you have resisted it?

3. What are some practical steps you can take now
to embrace change and growth in your life?

Morning Decree #262
Uncomfortable

"All chastening seemeth for the present to be not joyous but grievous; yet afterward it yieldeth peaceable fruit unto them that have been exercised thereby, even the fruit of righteousness." Hebrews 12:11

Every now and again, I actually sing on key. It might be in the shower or in an elevator where the acoustics seem to be just right. When I do experience those magical moments, I feel uncomfortable. It literally sounds foreign to my ears. What I've learned from this is that being off key has become normal and comfortable, whereas singing on key is abnormal to my ears and therefore makes me feel uncomfortable.

Our life's rituals and habits have normalized subnormal behavior. We are now okay with certain things because it's what we are used to. It's what we see around us, on social media, and even within our family. Since everybody is doing it, doesn't have it, or has never experienced something different, then "I'm okay too." The subnormal becomes normal and normal becomes abnormal.

Sadly, this is the how it is for way too many of us. Subnormality, which is not a biblical standard, is now normal. In order to attain the ancient paths, however, we will have to live with being uncomfortable for a period of time. Be uncomfortable, and let it become the new normal as you shake off subnormality to become biblically normal.

Questions for Reflections

1. What have you normalized in your life that at one time you thought otherwise about it?

2. What are you doing because it's more comfortable to do or easier than what you know you need to do?

3. Name one thing you are willing to become uncomfortable with going forward?

Morning Decree #263
Be Careful How You Hear

"And He said to them, 'Be careful what you are hearing. The measure [of thought and study] you give [to the truth you hear] will be the measure [of virtue and knowledge] that comes back to you—and more [besides] will be given to you who hear.'"
Mark 4:24, AMP

What you heard may be different from what was said. Even the best communicators can't control what their audience hears because hearing is more than auditory ability. it's also a function of how you process information.

How you process the information you hear or even read is largely affected by your ability to concentrate. If you approach hearing or reading the Word of God with the intention of learning something, you are more likely going to pick up a new thought or better understand what is being shared. However, if you are engaged in a Bible study while on your phone texting, or otherwise treating the moment with no particular special emphasis, you will find yourself missing out on what is the intention of the lesson. What you hear and how you hear, determine how you grow or develop spiritually, emotionally, and relationally.

Questions for Reflections

1. Have you ever been accused of saying something you know you didn't say because of how the person perceived your comments?

2. What does the term "selective hearing" mean to you?

3. Have you ever had a case of "selective hearing?"

Morning Decree #264
Talk to Yourself About It

"Being born again, not of corruptible seed, but of incorruptible, by the word of God, which liveth and abideth forever." 1 Peter 1:23, KJV

Self-talk is often a negative habit that undermines even your best of intentions. The internal words you speak to yourself about yourself is what ruins your day. I liken self-talk to the operating system in a laptop. If the laptop has a bug in the operating system, regardless of how silver and shiny the case may be or how intricate the programs are, that bug will bog down the computer. That is how it is with negative self-talk. If you find yourself telling yourself in your head that your ugly, you're going to fail, or you're dumb, no matter how much education or other external support you have, your internal operating system will own the day. Really it will own your life.

You must learn to discipline yourself to only say what is true about yourself as dictated by your Creator. He's the one who determines truth, not your experience, family, circumstances, or culture. What has God already declared about you? Speak that and only that.

Questions for Reflections

1. Are you aware of how much and how often you talk to yourself?

2. Is your self-talk positive or negative, or both?

3. How do you think you can begin to improve your self-talk?

Morning Decree #265
Keep Your Receipts

"Now faith is the assurance (the confirmation, the title deed) of the things [we] hope for, being the proof of things [we] do not see and the conviction of their reality [faith perceiving as real fact what is not revealed to the senses]." Hebrews 11:1, AMP

I've found the things that really matter require true faith—a faith that doesn't quit until the manifestation of the promise is realized. Too many times, I've quit before the answer came or the breakthrough showed up, only to later realize I was closer to the goal than I thought. Biblical faith demands that you place all your trust in the power of the Word of God for you to become what the Word says you are designed to do instead of what your natural senses tell you.

Faith is the substance, the thing for which you are praying. It's not just the currency upon which the divine transaction is based, it's the actual the thing you are seeking. This means that when you arrive at faith for a particular prayer request, you have received it, and are then just waiting on delivery. The example of a postal delivery notification illustrates this point well.

Nowadays when you purchase a product online, you can receive a notice when your product has been shipped to your address. That is to serve as confirmation that your parcel has been paid for and is on it's way. Your job at this point is simply to make room for it when it arrives. You no longer wonder if you'll get it because you know it's yours already. Keep the faith. It's your receipt.

Questions for Reflections

1. What was the last order you placed online? How was the experience?

2. Describe your confidence level knowing that the order was placed and shipped?

3. When is the last time you prayed, knowing it was a matter of time before the manifestation—and you felt at peace?

Morning Decree #266
Do, Don't Just Believe

"So also faith, if it does not have works (deeds and actions of obedience to back it up), by itself is destitute of power (inoperative, dead)." James 2:17, AMP

Faith is more than believing that something is true. Faith always requires some action on your behalf. That action may have been asking, or giving, or forgiving, or praying, or knocking. There's always a corresponding action that accompanies biblical faith. You don't need to prove your faith to anyone, but your faith should be on display. That's not to show off, but since faith is an action word, you should show others you are able to identify the appropriate faith action.

One mistake many often make is thinking that since they prayed about it, nothing else is needed. When you read the Scriptures, you quickly see there is often something you still need to do to activate the miracle. Biblically speaking, faith is not a noun but a verb—that is, faith is action. To receive the things your heart desires, what actions are you willing to take to see the promises of God manifest in your life? What effort are you willing to put forth? In order words, are you willing to put your back into it?

Even where redemption is concerned, though it was the Father's plan, it still requires something more than desire. It needed a sacrifice. Jesus was that sacrifice. Jesus literally gave His back for us. So, for you and me to receive the untold riches of His sacrifice, we have to do and not just believe.

Questions for Reflections

1. What actions are you taking out of obedience according to your faith?

2. Is there a difference between believing God and obeying God?

3. Can you recall a time when you didn't follow through with an action even though you made the appropriate prayers?

Morning Decree #267
Add Your Touch

"And beside this, giving all diligence, add to your faith virtue;
and to virtue knowledge . . ." 2 Peter 1:5

Sloppy, indifferent, and careless Christianity is the order of the day it would seem. The idea of thinking about God, or belonging to a church, seems to be the extent of the devotion many have in their spiritual life. The Bible reveals the correct and only way to spiritual maturity and effectiveness.

There is a required work ethic that you must embrace if you are going to emulate Jesus in your generation. I'm not talking about working for your salvation, but instead working on yourself to reflect the character, nature, and faith of Jesus Himself.

You must be diligent with the intent to develop fruit that bespeaks of your relationship with God through Jesus Christ. This requires prayer, studying, accountability, and know-how. It demands patience and humility as well. Don't be fooled by the instant-this-and-instant-hat mantras. Being a disciple requires sustained discipline. Prayer alone won't get the brass ring. You must do your part—your touch is needed.

Questions for Reflections

1. Do you have a strong work ethic regarding your occupation?

2. What areas in your spiritual life do you know are weak because of lack of effort on your part?

3. How do you think the lack of focus on those areas has affected your life to date?

Morning Decree #268
What You Need Is Faith

"I tell you, He will defend and protect and avenge them speedily. However, when the Son of Man comes, will He find [persistence in] faith on the earth?" Luke 8:18, AMP

I'm talking about faith. Money answers problems, but money isn't the problem or the answer, faith Is! When you have faith, you get the things you need and want. If you believe that money is what will get it for you, you will quickly find that there are many things for which money is useless to acquire.

I truly believe everyone should be rich, but what I do not subscribe to is the idea that money is the answer. Faith is your money. As a matter of fact, you can't get faith with money, but you can get both money and faith with faith.

Understanding and developing biblical faith is of the utmost importance. Jesus said regarding the time of His return, "Will the Son of Man find faith?". If Jesus is looking for faith upon His return, that indicates faith is very important. He didn't say He was looking for the how much money you have, though having the means to acquire, to buy, sell, and pay for things is important. There is nothing more important than having a faith for which Jesus is looking. Take time to develop your faith life, and the other things will come along as well.

Questions for Reflections

1. Name five things that money can't buy no matter how much a person has?

2. Why do you think Jesus said you can't serve God and money at the same time?

3. What are biblical ways to build your faith in times like these?

Morning Decree #269
Your Private Parts Are Showing

"So that your deeds of charity may be in secret; and your Father Who sees in secret will reward you openly." Matthew 6:4

What comes to mind when you read the title of this decree? I'm not talking about your private parts, but rather the reality that what you do in private eventually shows up in your public life. Whether it's what you eat, what you spend your money on, or what you do in the dark, eventually and predictably, what you do in private will manifest at some point in our life.

This, however, isn't always negative. Many of the celebrities who are idolized spend years in private developing their skills to one day be an overnight success. Sometimes decades are spent in obscurity before the world stage is their playground. So, whatever is showing up in your life for others to see is a direct manifestation of what's been going on in your private world. If you want to change what is seen, change what is unseen.

Questions for Reflections

1. Name a celebrity you've heard about who spent years hidden before becoming a global sensation.

2. Call to mind an example where someone was living a double life but eventually got busted.

3. What habits, good or bad, are you presently engaged in that are showing up in our life in some way?

Morning Decree #270
One-Eyed Success

"But the Lord replied to her by saying, 'Martha, Martha, you are anxious and troubled about many things.'" Luke 10:41

This is not about science-fiction. Instead, I am saying that the most fruitful people are those who are simply focused on their work, goals, or dreams. You can't serve two gods Jesus said. If you think you can, you are wrong for you will love one and hate the other. It takes a directed focus, like a laser beam, to accomplish really important things over time.

If you don't like your life, the way it has shaped up over the years, could it be because of the things that took your attention away from the really important stuff? Many of us fail not for lack of effort, but because we spread our efforts like we are scattering seeds. We grew things, but not enough of this or that. Therefore, we are frustrated, disillusioned and discouraged.

The way to turn things around in your spiritual life is to make Jesus Christ the most important things in your life, honoring His life and Word. It's out of this commitment that your priorities are adjusted and you become refocused. Many, maybe even you, are busy with so many things—good things. Ultimately, you're not progressing, effective, or satisfied. Refocus. Discover the main thing, which happens to be a person, the Lord Jesus Christ, and become a one-eyed or singly focused success.

Questions for Reflections

1. Did you ever experience working hard throughout your day only to feel you didn't accomplish much?

2. In your mind, is there a difference between being busy and being productive?

3. How would describe the difference? Do you see yourself as busy or productive?

Morning Decree #271
Inside Out

"And may the God of peace Himself sanctify you through and through [separate you from profane things, make you pure and wholly consecrated to God]; and may your spirit and soul and body be preserved sound and complete [and found] blameless at the coming of our Lord Jesus Christ (the Messiah)." 1 Thessalonians 5:23

You are not what you see in the mirror neither are you what others see. You are not even what you think. You are a spirit, with a soul that lives in a body. According to the Holy Writ, you are a tri-part being—spirit, soul, and body. The world puts that list in reverse order— body, soul, and spirit. Their emphasis is on the physicality of people—what they look like. God's focus, as should ours, is on the spirit of a person.

God is a Spirit, and we were created in His likeness and image. It stands to reason, God as our creator created us to be like Him so therefore we are spirit. Our spirit and our soul, which is comprised of our mind, will, emotions, and intellect are tantamount to the operating software that run our computer. Both our spirit and soul are eternal—meaning they will live forever.

Your body, however, will return to dust eventually. That deems eternal things more important than temporal things. Focus on your spirit–person. Make your spiritual health your top priority.

Questions for Reflections

1. Why is the spirit of a person more important than their body?

2. In what ways could you 'feed' your spirit in positive ways?

3. Why is there more emphasis on the physical characteristics of a person rather than their inner qualities?

Morning Decree #272
Soul Power

"And be constantly renewed in the spirit of your mind [having a fresh mental and spiritual attitude]." Ephesians 4:23, AMP

The power of the mind is underestimated and not fully understood. Some research says the average person uses less than 10% of their mind. Think of all that has been created and accomplished with less than 10% usage! Humans are tri–part beings: spirit, soul, and body. The Spirit which must be born again is the real person, but this spirit has a soul, which is made up of the mind, will, intellect, and emotions. It's the soul that makes us human beings, but unlike the spirit, the soul must be renewed or transformed; essentially, we need to be reconfigured in our thinking.

The renewal of the mind is the most important activity that a follower of Jesus Christ is tasked with doing. Without learning to think differently, you will continue to do what you were doing before being born again. The soul is the operating system of the body. It is the computer program that determines the outcomes and calculations of life. If the program is corrupted, bugged, or otherwise in error, your life will be full of poor and unwise decisions. Tragically, the unrenewed soul will struggle and constantly be frustrated as it attempts to serve the Lord with an old, faulty operating system.

Questions for Reflections

1. In what ways do you think your mind needs to change?

2. Can you recall times when the way you think has gotten you in big trouble?

3. What activities can you do to encourage the transformation of your mind?

Morning Decree #273
Two Against One

"O unhappy and pitiable and wretched man that I am! Who will release and deliver me from [the shackles of] this body of death?" Romans 7:24

Two against one isn't fair. All things being equal, if you are outnumbered two to one, you will lose. When it comes to your spiritual life, the two-against-one odds are also in effect. Because we are comprised of three parts—spirit, soul, and body—the two against one principle works as well. For example, a person can be born again (spirit), but if their soul and body have not been aligned with their spirit, their spirit will not dominate. Their soul and body will run their world.

True growth comes as you develop your soul (mind) and discipline your body. Without renewing your mind and disciplining your physical body, your spirit—though born again—will not help you here on Earth. The greatest power and benefit in your spiritual life comes when you are in alignment—spirit, soul, and body.

Questions for Reflections

1. Have you ever been outnumbered before?

2. How did you feel? What did you do about it?

3. What lessons did you learn about how to avoid being outnumbered in the future?

Morning Decree #274
Life

" . . . the reason the Son of God was made manifest (visible) was to undo (destroy, loosen, and dissolve) the works the devil [has done]." 1 John 3:8

The verb *to save* in the Bible means more than escaping from the tormenting fires of Hell. While eternal life is one of the benefits of being saved, it's only one aspect. The Greek word translated *to save* is *sozo*. It includes eternal life but also includes other truths that are necessary here on Earth now. Jesus came to make an abundant life available to all who would call Him Lord. Neither sickness, premature death, poverty, nor a confused mind are what I would call living an abundant life.

Jesus came to save the whole world. This salvation through Christ is comprehensive; encompassing the whole person. *Sozo* carries the benefits of prosperity, peace, deliverance from temporal evil, and healing. Eternal life is only one-fifth of the blessing of salvation. Granted, eternal life is a really big deal. However, before you go to Heaven, you will need healing, financial prosperity, deliverance, and peace within your soul.

Questions for Reflections

1. What is the main reason you've heard about why Jesus Christ came in the first place?

2. How will knowing that Jesus came to provide an abundant life for you change your expectations?

3. What areas of being saved (eternal life, healing, prosperity, peace, deliverance) have you yet to experience?

Morning Decree #275
Good Luggage Holds More Stuff

"For which is easier: to say, Your sins are forgiven and the penalty remitted, or to say, Get up and walk? But in order that you may know that the Son of Man has authority on Earth to forgive sins and remit the penalty, He then said to the paralyzed man, Get up! Pick up your sleeping pad and go to your own house." Matthew 9:5-6

  I recently received a really expensive piece of luggage, a beautiful and thoughtful gift. Not only was it beautifully crafted, but it was also large enough to contain seven days of clothing. My new piece of luggage reminds me of what Jesus did for us by living and dying as our sacrifice.

  Many within the Church world see Jesus as only taking away our sins. Indeed, Jesus did come to take away our sins. However, what is rarely seen is that Jesus also carried our pains and sicknesses as well. Part of our redemption through His blood includes healing. As a matter of truth, Jesus' sacrificial death dealt with sin, the root cause of every malady, sickness, disease, and the like. Our redemption through Christ is like my big suitcase. It has room for everything I need to live free from bondage and enjoy the abundant life.

Questions for Reflections

1. Did you know that Jesus, with one sacrificial act, took both your sin *and* sickness?

2. Why do you think Jesus took your sins, but not your sicknesses?

3. Is it possible to receive the forgiveness of sins, but not the healing?

Morning Decree #276
Have You Received Forgiveness?

"Who forgives [every one of] all your iniquities, Who heals [each one of] all your diseases." Psalm 103:3, AMP

"Take courage, son; your sins are forgiven and the penalty remitted." Matthew 9:2

Failure to understand that sin and sickness are connected could be one of the reasons some people don't receive their healing. As shared previously, sickness is a result of sin. It's not always "our sin" but because we live in a world affected by sin, sickness gets a grip on many. And because sickness is in the bag of sin, once sin is taken out of the equation, sickness goes with it. This is always true but not often realized because few seem to know that sickness is from the tree of sin. Kill the tree, the fruit dies as well.

Receiving forgiveness is critical to receiving healing. When you embrace the truth that the two—sin and sickness—are connected, you can more easily receive your healing. If you knew that sickness had no right to hang around your life, just like sin, you would not put up with it. Those who embrace a theology of suffering think that suffering with sickness is holy. Sickness robs and kills. Sin does the same. Why would Jesus only come to deal with sin, but leave sickness unchecked? He wouldn't. He didn't. Receive forgiveness for all your sins and while you're at it, receive your healing as well.

Questions for Reflections

1. Did you know that sickness comes from the roots of sin?

2. Why does it seem harder to believe that sickness is part of our redemption from sin?

3. Have you received forgiveness of your sin *and* deliverance from sickness?

Morning Decree #277
It's Your Life

"The beginning of Wisdom is: get Wisdom (skillful and godly Wisdom)! [For skillful and godly Wisdom is the principal thing.] And with all you have gotten, get understanding (discernment, comprehension, and interpretation)."
Proverbs 4:7, AMP

Your life, such as it is, is a result of decisions. These decisions, sometimes made unconsciously, are the elements that constructed your life, and because it's your life, it's personal. Your problems and challenges may involve other people, but at the end of the day—it's your life.

It's critical that you take full responsibility for your life starting now. Regardless of what happened and who might be to blame, the unavoidable fact is that you are the one responsible for your life. Accept that this is a personal matter. Embrace it. When you take responsibility for your life, you will be more conscientious when making decisions so as to make the wisest choices possible. There is one way I know of to be on the best possible path and that is by asking God for wisdom. Start with getting wisdom.

Questions for Reflections

1. What's happened in your life for which you have a tendency to blame others?

2. Have you taken responsibility for your life?

3. What actions would you take to change your life knowing that "if it's going to be, it's up to me"?

Morning Decree #278
Still Healing

"And, behold, there came a leper and worshipped Him, saying, 'Lord, if thou wilt, thou canst make me clean.' And Jesus put forth His hand, and touched him, saying, 'I will; be thou clean. And immediately his leprosy was cleansed.'" Matthew 8:2-3, KJV

"Is it God's will to heal me?" is the question most people ask when they are faced with a painful, debilitating physical or emotional problem. We see what Jesus did in the Bible and occasionally we may hear of someone, usually a stranger getting miraculously healed. When it comes to our personal issues, however, we wonder, "Is it God's will to heal me?"

The best way to approach this question is to ask another question: What did Jesus come to do and is it still valid today? If Jesus came to heal and is still healing today, then it's a pretty good chance, it is His will to heal just as Jesus healed the lepers of His day. Scripture says, "Jesus Christ is the same yesterday, today and forever" (Hebrews 13:8), so if His heart was to heal yesterday, then it is His heart to heal today.

Questions for Reflections

1. How sure are you that it's God's will to heal people?

2. Are you 100% sure that it's God's will to heal you, too?

3. What Scriptures do you base your above responses?

Morning Decree #279
Heal the Sick

"Heal the sick, cleanse the lepers, raise the dead, cast out devils: freely ye have received, freely give." Matthew 10:8, KJV

I recently challenged a group of ministers *not* to pray for the sick, but rather to *heal* the sick. The response was priceless. They immediately responded, "We can't do that; it's Jesus who heals." While that is technically correct, the reality is Jesus expects us to do what He did. He didn't just pray for the sick, He healed the sick. Our assignment is to do what Jesus Christ did. We are to represent Him to this world.

Jesus modeled the will of the Father. He also did what was on the heart of the Father. He also said only what He heard the Father say. Therefore, since Jesus healed people and instructed His followers to do the same, it then must be the will of the Father to do the same in our generation. How wonderful will it be for followers of Jesus to manifest the good news to a hurting humanity.

Questions for Reflections

1. When is the last time you saw someone healed miraculously?

2. Have you ever been the instrument of healing in someone's life?

3. Do you believe you can be used to perform miracles in Jesus' name?

Morning Decree #280
Obey Your Way

"And said unto him, 'Go, wash in the pool of Siloam' (which is by interpretation, Sent.) He went his way therefore, and washed, and came seeing." John 9:7, KJV

There's a reason why Jesus said, "Follow me." We neither hear much about following Jesus nor what that means. The key to discover who Jesus really is requires a relentlessly following Jesus—His words, His actions, His thoughts, His instructions.

In the verse above, the key that unlocked the miracle healing for the blind man is found in what the blind man did. What he did was more important than what Jesus did. Why? Because until the blind man followed the command of Jesus to "go wash," no miracle was going to take place. After he did as required, a miracle occurred. He obeyed his way to his miracle. We can do the same.

Questions for Reflections

1. Is there a difference between being a Christian and being a follower of Christ?

2. What instructions have you followed that turned out to be valuable to your life?

3. How important is it to follow instructions?

Morning Decree #281
Children Only

"But to as many as did receive and welcome Him, He gave the authority (power, privilege, right) to become the children of God, that is, to those who believe in (adhere to, trust in, and rely on) His name—Who owe their birth neither to bloods nor to the will of the flesh [that of physical impulse] nor to the will of man [that of a natural father], but to God. [They are born of God!]." John 1:12-13, AMP

Not everyone is a child of God, despite the prevailing thinking in society today. Usually, what is meant is that all human beings are God's children. While this may sound good and even reassuring, the Bible doesn't support this claim. There is a difference between a child of God and God's creation. God created all people, for only God can create life. However, a child of God is different. They are given privilege, not by natural birth, but spiritual rebirth.

According to the Bible, only those human beings who receive Jesus as their Christ are children of God. Family members have privileges and access to the blessings of the family, so knowing and living as a child of God is very important. Not everyone is child of God.

Questions for Reflections

1. Are you a child of God based upon the Biblical requirements?

2. What benefits can you think of that a child has that just a "kid" down the street might enjoy?

3. Once becoming a child of God, can you lose your status as a son or daughter?

Morning Decree #282
Where Do You Come From?

"Jesus answered him, 'I assure you, most solemnly I tell you, that unless a person is born again (anew, from above), he cannot ever see (know, be acquainted with, and experience) the kingdom of God.'" John 3:3, AMP

Being a child of God is a spiritual thing. From a purely biological perspective, a child takes on the DNA of both parents, but the father contributes the blood! It is also true from a spiritual perspective. It is the seed (sperm) that is the Word of God that recreates a person's human spirit. This miracle as described in the Bible is being born again or born from above.

When a person receives the Word of God, the miracle of inner transformation occurs. It's when a spiritual conception takes place making one a child of God, who Himself is the seed/word giver. It is a great mystery, but those who have had such an experience will confirm it is the best and most important decision they have ever made.

Questions for Reflections

1. Are you born again? If so, how do you know?

2. What does being born again mean to you?

3. What characteristics of your parents do you demonstrate the most?

Morning Decree #283
Second Chance

"Marvel not [do not be surprised, astonished] at My telling you, you must all be born anew (from above)." John 3:7, AMP

Isn't believing in Jesus enough? Doesn't going to a Christian church count for something? These are common questions that many good, well-intentioned people ask. However, the answer is something that is not so readily accepted because religion teaches us to simply believe. The problem is that believing in the reality of Jesus is not uncommon or just something only Christians do. There are other religious groups that believe in the historical fact of Jesus. That, however, is not enough.

Since we all have sinned, our spirit—the real us—is corrupted. We need to be born a second time. Of course, this isn't a physical rebirthing but rather a spiritual one. Everyone, regardless of age, race, gender, or societal status, must be born a second time to be a child of God. That's not my opinion; it's what Jesus said and the Bible teaches. You must be born again.

Questions for Reflections

1. Do you believe you have sinned and therefore need to be born again?

2. Is there any kind or amount of good deeds that can make up for your sins?

3. Can you save yourself or do you need a Savior?

Morning Decree #284
Are You Authorized?

"Behold! I have given you authority and power to trample upon serpents and scorpions, and [physical and mental strength and ability] over all the power that the enemy [possesses]; and nothing shall in any way harm you." Luke 10:17-19, AMP

The ability to use power is different from the right or authorization to use power. As the youngest of four, I was always the one my parents would send to get my siblings for dinner or the one to tell them to clean up their room. However, when I would say, "Time for dinner," my siblings would look at me as if I had two heads and ignore me. However, when I'd say, "Mommy said, it's time for dinner," the older siblings would obey my words. The difference was they knew I had the authority to tell them what to do because of whom I was representing.

Recognize that you have authority because you are a child of God given the right to use the name of Jesus. That name is even more powerful than saying "Mommy said"—if you can believe that. You are authorized.

Questions for Reflections

1. In your own words, describe the difference between power and authority.

2. Name at least two people (professions) that exercise authority over people.

3. What does it mean to be a delegated authority?

Morning Decree #285
You Have the Authority

"And Jesus summoned to Him His twelve disciples and gave them power and authority over unclean spirits, to drive them out, and to cure all kinds of disease and all kinds of weakness and infirmity." Matthew 10:1

Authority is for a specific purpose. Having authority—the right to use power—is of no value unless it is directed for godly purposes. Jesus gave His disciples, which includes you and me, authority over demons and unclean spirits. However, it would be tragic for the disciples of Jesus to have all that authority and merely sit in the pews of the synagogue. As ludicrous as that seems, that is exactly what happens every week in most churches.

We have power and authority, but we are not using it for the common good. Most Christians sit and observe problems and issues, but few understand they have the authority and responsibility to do something about them. It's time, really far past the time, to use the authority given to us by Jesus Christ.

Questions for Reflections

1. Why do you think most Christians are bored with their spiritual life?

2. Can you think of people who need to be touched by God in their body, mind, or family?

3. What is your role in helping others?

Morning Decree #286
What Are You Making?

"Go then and make disciples of all the nations." Matthew 28:19-20

Christianity is a "do" thing, not just a "believe" thing. Jesus commanded His disciples to go and make—not just come and sit. Going to Church is extremely important. Nevertheless, coming to church is not the end, but it's the launch pad for ministry inside and outside the building.

Jesus said to go then and make disciples. That's a pretty specific command. Sadly, we don't think of making disciples as our responsibility. It's not the pastor's job or the church's job — it's *all* of our responsibility. Just praying for people to receive Jesus is not enough. The goal is to make disciplined learners become followers of Jesus. Let's do what Jesus commanded us to do.

Questions for Reflections

1. Have you ever prayed with someone to receive Jesus Christ as their Lord?

2. Do you consider yourself a disciple?

3. Are you personally discipling someone? If not, why?

Morning Decree #287
What Did You Get for Christmas?

"Now about the spiritual gifts (the special endowments of supernatural energy), brethren, I do not want you to be misinformed . . . But to each one is given the manifestation of the [Holy] Spirit [the evidence, the spiritual illumination of the Spirit] for good and profit." 1 Corinthians 12:1, 7

Christmas, by definition, speaks to the worship of Christ. The holiday is symbolized typically by the giving and receiving of gifts. While there is much to comment on regarding the commercialism of Christmas, the gift we should focus on is the present the Holy Spirit has given us to help others.

The stated purpose of the gifts of (from) the Spirit is to help others. They are the supernatural endowments that are never earned or bought. Rather the gifts are learned and freely given for the benefit of humanity. The real problem, however, is that many are unaware the Holy Spirit has gifted them. As a matter of fact, everyone who is a true follower of Jesus Christ has been gifted. That means you, me, and the person in the pew right next to you. You are in the presence of many gifts. What's your gift(s)?

Questions for Reflections

1. What qualifies you to receive a Gift of the Spirit?

2. What happens when people don't know they are gifted by God?

3. How has your life been affected by not knowing what your gifts.

Morning Decree #288
You Are Gifted

"Now there are distinctive varieties and distributions of endowments (gifts, extraordinary powers distinguishing certain Christians, due to the power of divine grace operating in their souls by the Holy Spirit) and they vary, but the [Holy] Spirit remains the same." 1 Corinthians 12:4, AMP

Getting up early on Christmas morning is a tradition in many households. It's when the family rushes to the holy site called the Christmas tree, because under that tree are *gifts*! Based on the size or shape of the package, you may try to determine what's inside, which is a magical exercise. However, without the benefit of x-ray vision, the only way to know the contents inside the box is to open it.

The same is true as to how we can determine our spiritual gift(s). We have to open the box. In this case, the box is a book called the Bible. As we study the gifts, how they function, and what the specific purpose is for each of the individual gifts are how we can know what gift(s) we have.

Questions for Reflections

1. With what gifts do you think you have been endowed?

2. Do you know what types of gifts are available from the Holy Spirit?

3. What have you done to understand your gift(s) and how to utilize it (them) best?

Morning Decree #289
No Such Thing as Good Enough

"Since all have sinned and are falling short of the honor and glory which God bestows and receives." Romans 3:23

A gift by definition is something given, not something earned or bought. The idea that God gives us something we don't deserve is still hard for many to accept. This thought is probably due to the fact that we live in a performance–based society. In other words, your value to a company is based on your performance, or how well you perform is based on your job description.

However, when it comes to the gifts of the Spirit, they are never earned. They can't get earned. The Holy Spirit can't be bribed or manipulated. The Holy Spirit decides what gifts you need based on the assignments predestined for you to have. When you think you qualify for a particular gift because of some ability you have, you are devaluing the gift and are sure to misuse or abuse it eventually. It's a gift, not a reward.

Questions for Reflections

1. Name at least three areas in which you feel you must perform to be rewarded?

2. Since the gifts of the Holy Spirit are "given" and not earned, what's your responsibility regarding them?

3. How can you develop your gift(s) to be more effective?

Morning Decree #290
Integrity and Godly Character

"For God's gifts and His call are irrevocable. [He never withdraws them when once they are given, and He does not change His mind about those to whom He gives His grace or to whom He sends His call.]" Romans 11:29, AMP

The gifts of God are so precious and vital that they come with a tremendous amount of responsibility. As gifts, they are to be valued, prized, guarded, and appropriately used. God won't take the gift away, but He can decide to cease providing the power source, which is the Holy Spirit. The Holy Spirit does not work with anyone, regardless of how gifted they are, if they persist in ignoring His presence by acting or speaking in ways that are dishonorable. Integrity and godly character are two fundamental requirements to operate in the gifts of the Holy Spirit. Failure to do so is tantamount to having a luxury vehicle without gasoline or electricity to operate it. That said, the cleanness of your hands and heart matter.

Questions for Reflections

1. What gifts do you feel you have been given by God?

2. Have you ever met someone who was gifted by God but was a poor steward of their gift?

3. How can you ensure you will remain honorable as well as gifted?

Morning Decree #291
Manager of God's Stuff

"And if you have not proved faithful in that which belongs to another [whether God or man], who will give you that which is your own [that is, the true riches]?"
Luke 16:12, AMP

Have you ever met someone who just to think a bit more highly of themselves than they should? Usually, that's because the individual has a misunderstanding when it comes to their real role or status. As a follower of Jesus, we should recognize what we have, especially when it comes to the divine enablements, come from God. They are not something we own or earned. We are the containers and vessels, not the gift to the world.

There is a vast difference between owning something and managing it. When you own it, let's say your car (free and clear), you can decide what you are going to do with it. You can give it away, sell it, or do whatever you want with it. However, when you are still making payments, you can't just do what you want with it. The owner —usually a bank or some other finance company—has you bound by a contract. Similarly, this is true when it comes to every area and aspect of your life. You are a manager. You possess gifts of the Holy Spirit. You do not own them. They came from God, and they belong to God. You have the right, privilege, and responsibility to use them for the benefit of all.

Questions for Reflections

1. What's the role of humility when it comes to being used by God?

2. What do you have that didn't come from God, either directly or indirectly?

3. How can you keep in mind yourself that you are a manager and not an owner?

Morning Decree #292
Divine Amazon Prime

"For I passed on to you first of all what I also had received..." 1 Corinthians 15:3

Each week, millions if not billions of letters and parcels get delivered to homes and businesses around the world. The postal service is a finely-tuned machine that ensures your packages arrive at their intended destination. I can't quite imagine what life would be like if such a service did not exist. In a like manner, the gifts of the Spirit which you carry are to work similarly. You are "mail carriers." You are a divine postal service—working for the Kingdom of God, commissioned to deliver gifts to others.

As a carrier of the gifts, it's your responsibility—rain or shine—to deliver what others need and may or may not be expecting. Though you have the gifts, the truth is you only have the gifts to give to someone else. The mail carrier never thinks of him or herself as the owner of the letters, they are the ones to deliver. You should recognize you are not owners of the gifts you carry. Your job is to ensure the packages get delivered as quickly as possible to whom it is addressed and in the condition it left the Giver.

Questions for Reflections

1. Relate an experience in which the mail service you were expecting was below your expectation?

2. Recall a time when you were very blessed by a package you received?

3. How would you feel if you could be the delivery person of a gift that literally could save someone's life?

Morning Decree #293
You Have Something Special

"So then, whatever you desire that others would do to and for you, even so do also to and for them, for this is (sums up) the Law and the Prophets." Matthew 7:12, AMP

Like it or not, somebody (actually many people) are expecting you to show up with the goods. Just like you are awaiting the arrival of goods, good news, or a gift, which most likely will be delivered to you by someone just like you, others are waiting on you. Sometimes, while waiting on your package, you fail to deliver the packages you have for others. Without question, you have "goods" for someone today. You, despite how you're feeling or what's going on in your life, still have a job to do. Do your job! Your rewards will be in doing your job of delivering and serving someone else.

What about me? This question gets asked often when a person has their own needs in mind. However, what the Bible teaches is that by doing for others, it creates a "must show up in my life" effect. In other words, when you despite your own glaring needs do what you can to help someone else, it obligates God to supply what's lacking in your life. The Law of Seedtime and Harvest comes into play here as well. Seed (your gift) into someone else and watch God do that and more for you.

Questions for Reflections

1. Recall a time when you expected something important to be delivered to you but the person failed in getting it to you.

2. What "goods" do you have that could benefit others?

3. Name a time when you didn't feel like "it" but did "it" anyhow and "it" proved to be a significant help to someone else?

Morning Decree #294
The Receiving Line

"But I have prayed especially for you [Peter], that your [own] faith may not fail."
Luke 22:32, AMP

"And He said to them, '[Why are you so fearful?] Where is your faith (your trust, your confidence in Me—in My veracity and My integrity)?'" Luke 8:25, AMP

Being in the publishing business, I send out books and other products daily. Sometimes, the books are returned because the incorrect address made it undeliverable. It is frustrating because it costs time and money to resend it. Regrettably, this is true when it comes to the blessings that have your name on them but cannot be delivered because the address is not right.

A wrong address, in this case, is when you are not in the position of faith. You have a need, made a request, but did not remain in faith until the product got delivered. Maybe, this happened because the request took longer than you expected to arrive or perhaps you didn't believe it would happen in the first place. However, when it comes to the mail—the proper postage and correct address—it will be delivered. Just make sure you're home to sign for the package—both in the natural and spiritual sense.

Faith is not just a belief, but it's a place, a position. God's answers get delivered to specific people at a particular address—Faith Lane.

Questions for Reflections

1. Have you ever missed a delivery to your home?
What did you have to do to get the package?

2. Do you remember a time when you sent a family member a gift,
but it never arrived because you had the wrong address?

3. Since faith is more than a belief system, it's a place.
Are you at the location of faith awaiting the arrival of what you ordered?

Morning Decree #295
Do You Have the Right Amount?

"But if God so clothes the grass of the field, which today is alive and green and tomorrow is tossed into the furnace, will He not much more surely clothe you, O you of little faith?" Matthew 6:30

"Money, money, money" as the song goes, is what makes the world go 'round. Whether or not that's a fact, is open to debate. However, what can't be argued is that you need faith to make transactions in Heaven. Faith is a currency. It's what one must have to do business with God and on behalf of the Kingdom of God. However, if you don't have biblical faith, you can't spend what you don't have.

Many confuse believing the right things with faith. You can't have faith without believing the right things, but you can believe and still not have faith. Belief in today's culture is an intellectual agreement that something exists or is true. However, biblical faith is taking what one believes to be true and expressing it with actions that support it. For instance, a person can believe that a "bed" will support their weight—correct belief. However, faith happens when a person lies down on that bed. Belief won't get you a good night's sleep, but faith will. You demonstrate your faith by your actions in concert with what you believe to be true. If you have faith, then spend it by doing, not by merely believing.

Questions for Reflections

1. Reflect upon a time when you arrived at the checkout counter only to realize you didn't have enough money to pay for what you had in your basket?

2. Whose fault was it that you didn't have sufficient currency to purchase those items?

3. Did the store let you take home those things or did you have to come up with the money?

Morning Decree #296
You Need More to Get More

"The apostles said to the Lord, 'Increase our faith!'" Luke 17:5

Saving money is remarkably difficult for many people. It is especially true when you barely have enough money to meet your current needs. However, it's believed by many economists and pragmatists that having a savings account is critical to overall financial and emotional security. Furthermore, without more than enough in the bank, it's next to impossible to get the things you desire—a parallel truth when it comes to having faith. Although you can never stockpile faith, you certainly can have the amount required to get what you need or want.

Faith is like money. It doesn't discriminate against individuals because of race, gender, or nationality. If you've got it, it will work to "buy" what you need. If you don't have it, you can't use it. Faith is unemotional, and it's not affected by the whims of people or the current cultural malaise. Instead, faith is up for the task—providing you have enough of it. Just like money, faith can increase but it can also decrease. If you have needs, build your faith and then go "buy" what you need.

Questions for Reflections

1. Name a time you wanted something and you saved up for a long time until you were able to purchase it. How did it make you feel?

2. When you were focused on buying that particular item, how did you treat the money you were earning?

3. What did you do to save more money?

Morning Decree #297
Give "It" to Get "It"

"She did as Elijah said. And she and he and her household ate for many days."
1 Kings 17:15

It's counterintuitive to think that the way to get more is to give more. It's just not logical. However, the methods of God often don't make sense to the natural mind. As seen in the above story, the way that this single mother and widow was able to thrive during a drought was in giving what she had. She gave to the prophet, in this case, but the Law of Sowing and Reaping works for everyone, every time.

What you lack is what you need to give away. When a farmer needs a harvest of a particular agricultural product, they sow that seed. It is so simple that you can overthink it. If you need love, then you must give agape love to others. If you need friends, be a better friend to someone else. If you need a favor, do a favor for someone who needs a favor. You have in your present possession something that can be used as a seed to meet your need.

Questions for Reflections

1. Why is it hard for us to give when we have needs?

2. When is the last time you intentionally gave away something expecting a return on your giving?

3. Do you have a giving plan?

Morning Decree #298
Your Credit Score

"Thus Abraham believed in and adhered to and trusted in and relied on God, and it was reckoned and placed to his account and credited as righteousness (as conformity to the divine will in purpose, thought, and action)." Galatians 3:6, AMP

A credit score is used to determine many things, including your ability to buy or acquire loans. Merchants, insurance companies, and several other industries use a credit score to determine if they are willing to do business with you. Little did you know, there is a spiritual credit score you need to be conscious of as well.

This spiritual credit score is what gives you the right to ask the Father for things you need and want. It's a score that determines your worthiness to even be on speaking terms with God. The problem with your rating is that just one "ding" on it completely disqualifies you from any hope of being qualified. God knew this would be the problem and gave you His credit status—it's called Righteousness. Simply put, Jesus became your righteousness. You have access to the Father through Jesus' righteous status. Perfect Credit. It's so glorious, undeserved, and unearned.

Questions for Reflections

1. Do you know your credit score? Has your credit ever negatively affected you in the past?

2. Have you ever felt you weren't good enough to receive a blessing from God?

3. What do you think will be the result when you use Jesus as your credit score in prayer?

Morning Decree #299
The Forgetfulness of God

"If You, Lord, should keep account of and treat [us according to our] sins, O Lord, who could stand?" Psalms 130:3, AMP

Often when I pray, I am flooded with all the things that, in my mind, should disqualify me from getting the blessing I seek. The ideas of being considered unworthy, along with condemnation and guilt—whether self-imposed or through the words of another—make me feel like giving up. However, the thing I need to remember is that my past is not the determining factor of whether or not the Father hears my prayer. Righteousness and faith are what matter.

On your best day, having done everything right, you still do not meet the holy standard that qualifies you to approach a holy God. To think otherwise is self-righteousness and is an exercise in futility. The reason you can approach God in prayer is because of what Jesus Christ accomplished for you. It's not how good you have been or how much money you give to the church nor how much you are willing to suffer for Christ. Through Jesus Christ is how your prayer and relationship with God get solidified. To remember this will give you both peace and comfort when your pray.

Questions for Reflections

1. When you pray are you reminded of why your prayers won't be answered? If so, what in your past does the enemy use to disqualify you?

2. How can you develop more confidence in your prayers in Jesus' Name?

3. Is there anything you think you can do to qualify for access to the Father?

Morning Decree #300
The More You Do,
The Less God Does

"For if because of one man's trespass (lapse, offense) death reigned through that one, much more surely will those who receive [God's] overflowing grace (unmerited favor) and the free gift of righteousness [putting them into right standing with Himself] reign as kings in life through the one Man, Jesus Christ (the Messiah, the Anointed One)." Romans 5:17, AMP

Seemingly, the way of the Kingdom of God is upside down. Give to receive. Forgive to be forgiven. Bless instead of curse your enemies. Strange? The more you try to earn from God, the further you move away from the things you need and want. God's favor is not for sale. God can't be bribed or manipulated, but you can worship Him. However, that isn't a way to get Him to bless you. His blessing is an unearned and undeserved gift.

Righteousness, which means right standing with God, is a gift. A gift by definition is not something for which you can qualify or earn. It can and must be received, but it can't be to settle an account. Yes, you need to pray, fast, give, love, and forgive, along with many other spiritual and practical disciplines, but none of them buy the favor and blessing of God. The gift of being right with God through Jesus Christ is what places you in such a marvelous position.

Questions for Reflections

1. Why is it so hard for many people, maybe even you,
to receive something you know you didn't earn?

2. How would you pray if you were conscious of His Righteousness
rather than the lack of yours?

3. What does it mean for you to be righteousness conscious versus. sin conscious?

Morning Decree #301
Bold Is Indeed Beautiful

"Let us then fearlessly and confidently and boldly draw near to the throne of grace (the throne of God's unmerited favor to us sinners), that we may receive mercy [for our failures] and find grace to help in good time for every need [appropriate help and well-timed help, coming just when we need it]." Hebrews 4:16, AMP

Boldness is necessary when pursuing God. It's important to note, however, that this boldness is not bravado or pride. The boldness that gets things done is effective because of what Jesus Christ accomplished by dying in your place on the Cross.

I see this boldness of approaching God in prayer as similar to what my daughters did (and still) do when they need money from me. Because of their security in knowing that they are my flesh and blood, coupled with the revelation of my love for them, they ask without hesitation! I find it refreshing to know they are secure in the reality of our relationship.

When you fully grasp the truth of Jesus being your mediator with the Father—reconciling you through His blood—you will also have a boldness to approach the throne of God without hesitation or reservation. He has proven that the basis of His love for you is not your works or good deeds. God loves you just because we are written on His heart. Boldness is a beautiful thing.

Questions for Reflections

1. What's the difference between being bold vs. brazen?

2. What stops you from being bold in your prayer requests?

3. How would your confidence in your relationship with God be affected if you understood the reason you have for being bold?

Morning Decree #302
No Casting Allowed

"Do not, therefore, fling away your fearless confidence, for it carries a great and glorious compensation of reward." Hebrews 10:35

When I hear the word casting, I automatically think of fishing. To reach where the fish are when fishing, you have to cast or hurl your fishing line and hook quite a distance away from the boat. While fishing, this is a good thing; but when it comes to your confidence, it's the wrong thing to do.

Confidence is the assurance that what you are doing or where you are headed is correct. It's the quality of being, despite the obstacles, able to maintain focus and direction. However, if you cast away your confidence like a fishing line, you will lose this ever-important quality. Consequently, you will not be able to stay in faith to apprehend or receive the answer to your request. Without confidence, delays become denials. Challenges become hopeless exercises that yield nothing of value to you. Don't throw away your confidence. Hug it and hold it tight—you'll need it to achieve your goals.

Questions for Reflections

1. Why do many people lack confidence?

2. What are some reasons in the past that made you lose confidence?

3. Can you remember a time when you held onto your confidence and you got through the problem you were facing?

Morning Decree #303
Don't Leave Home Without It

"For you have need of steadfast patience and endurance, so that you may perform and fully accomplish the will of God, and thus receive and carry away [and enjoy to the full] what is promised." Hebrews 10:36, AMP

As I told you before, I once received an expensive piece of luggage as a gift. Never would I have solicited such a gift or decided to buy it. It's beautiful and even has my name on it. It's a piece of travel art. However, it's for a definite purpose—to transport stuff I want to carry with me. Confidence is that inner quality that will empower you to carry your goals and dreams with you at all times. Confidence is needed in times and seasons when it looks improbable that you will achieve the dream. Having confidence, however, will cause you to endure the vicissitudes of life more patiently.

Dropping your confidence is like forgetting or losing your luggage. Confidence carries what you need—both patience and endurance—so you can arrive at your intended destination. Hold on to your confidence. Don't allow anything or anyone to drain it out of you because you need it.

Questions for Reflections

1. Can you describe a situation that built your confidence?

2. Who do you have in your life that may be hindering your confidence?

3. What activities strengthen your resolve and which ones weaken it?

Morning Decree #304
Do the Right Thing

"The wicked flee when no man pursues them, but the [uncompromisingly] righteous are bold as a lion." Proverbs 28:1, AMP

Have you ever loaned a friend some money but they seem to have forgotten it was a loan? Moreover, every time you run into them, they can't look you in the eye or try to avoid you altogether? You were once confident in your relationship with this person, but because they did not do the right thing, your confidence in them and the relationship have weakened.

The same is true when it comes to your relationship with God through Jesus Christ. When you are not doing the right things, you usually know it. Also, when you pray or need something from that relationship, you lack the requisite confidence to approach God. This lack of confidence is tied directly to your behavior and not God's rejection.

The truth is, whether you are doing what's right or wrong, there is only one way you can come to the Father and that is through and in the name of Jesus. However, the Holy Spirit convicts your conscience and won't allow you to continue with business as usual with God. You will be timid, reserved, and unsure unless and until you own the truth of your unrighteousness. Conversely, when you are doing as the Word of God demands, you will have zero reservation in coming to God.

Questions for Reflections

1. On a scale of 1–10, 10 being most confident, how would you score your confidence in prayer?

2. What is the main reason for your lack of confidence in approaching God?

3. What is it that you need to do to increase your boldness?

Morning Decree #305
Wanting Is Not Asking

"You do not have, because you do not ask." James 4:2

It's remarkable to think that one reason why you don't have what you want or need may be that you failed to ask for it. Often in prayer, you spend your time talking to God about the problem, sharing all the challenges and complaining about the people involved, instead of asking the Father in Jesus' name for what it is you desire.

Elder James in today's verse reminds you of this simple yet profound reality that you don't have "it" because you didn't ask for "it." Jealousy and envy rise within you when you look at what others are enjoying—perhaps mistakenly thinking that they took or have what belongs to you. The reason for the deficit in your life stems from your failure to ask in faith with the right motives. Could it be you don't have that outstanding need met solely because you failed to ask the Source Himself for it?

Questions for Reflections

1. Are you jealous of someone else?

2. What is it that they have or are doing that you feel you should be doing?

3. Have you asked the Father for what you need and/or want?

Morning Decree #306
What's Really Motivating You?

"[Or] you do ask [God for them] and yet fail to receive, because you ask with wrong purpose and evil, selfish motives. Your intention is [when you get what you desire] to spend it in sensual pleasures." James 4:3, AMP

Motives matter and like motivation can be understood by thinking about what it is that makes you move, take action. By definition, it is the reason for doing a certain thing. However, when it comes to praying, you don't often think about our true motives behind the request in the first place. There's nothing wrong with asking God for something that benefits or blesses you. The problem arises when you are unaware of the real motivation behind your prayers.

Be honest as to why you want that "thing." Without a level of personal awareness, your prayers get blocked. Don't pretend to want that new big house so you can take in homeless people when you don't plan to operate a rooming house. Be transparent with your plans. If you want a big house to enjoy a spacious living space, then say so. God wants you to enjoy life, just be honest with yourself and with God.

Questions for Reflections

1. What is it that you really want and feel bad about wanting it?

2. Do you secretly envy others, even followers of Jesus, for what they have?

3. What's stopping for asking your heavenly Father for those same things?

Morning Decree #307
Why Not You?

"Keep on asking and it will be given you; keep on seeking and you will find; keep on knocking [reverently] and [the door] will be opened to you." Matthew 7:7, AMP

Limitations are a human construct, something that finite human beings have concluded are real and necessary. However, the God of the universe is a limitless, infinite Being. God doesn't put limits on His children in terms of what's possible or acquirable. The only caveat is what they desire will bless and do no harm. However, most believers live with a self–imposed limiting belief system. God the Father did not declare "you shall go this far and no further." We did that to ourselves or allowed society to put those limitations on our thinking.

Who said you couldn't be healed? Who said you couldn't be happy and joyful every day? Who said you couldn't prosper? Consider the source, but I assure you it wasn't your Creator. Who said you couldn't ask for this or that? Who told you only expect rain and no sunshine days?

Questions for Reflections

1. What happened in your life that caused you to downplay your dreams?

2. Can you remember a time in your life where you dreamed bigger, bolder dreams than you do now?

3. What can you do to recapture a limitless mindset?

Morning Decree #308
Stop for No One

"You were running the race nobly. Who has interfered in (hindered and stopped you from) your heeding and following the Truth?" Galatians 5:7, AMP

Everyone is born to soar above life's storms and challenges. It is your destiny to thrive in life, not just survive life. However, stuff happened to you that grounded you even though you were born to fly. People, situations, money challenges, the expectations of others—to name a few—tend to be weights around your ankles that make it nearly impossible to rise above average to exceptional.

Identify what clipped your wings that now keeps you pecking around instead of flying around. What happened to create this *Groundhog Day* movie nightmare that keeps playing in your mind? You are designed to soar and fly. You are designed to live above, not to get tied to the ever-changing winds of life. Flying is more fun than trudging through mud.

Questions for Reflections

1. What was the dream before "life" happened to you?

2. What is your expectation of yourself at this point?

3. What's your real dream—the thing you would do if you had the money, time, and support?

Morning Decree #309
Nightmares or Nighttime Dreams?

"And we shall see what will become of his dreams!" Genesis 37:20

Dreams can be a picture of a future reality. This is even more powerful when the dreams are from God. Just because you have a dream, however, is no guarantee it will become a reality. As a matter of fact, dreams from God are often resisted by Hell itself. Then what was a dream turns into a nightmare, from which we have no hope of waking.

One failure that many believers often make is to allow the inevitable obstacles to distract them from realizing their dream. Many simply give up pursuing their goals, only to end up living a life well below their privilege. Instead, you should recognize anything worth having will require a persistence that doesn't come naturally.

Continue working toward the fulfillment of the dream by accepting the rain and the sun, the support and obstacles, as just part of the process. Determine today that you will live your dream. What comes of your dreams has more to do with how you respond to frustrations along the way than anything else.

Questions for Reflections

1. Describe how you will feel when your dream becomes a reality?

2. What are the issues hindering your dream from coming to pass?

3. How have you allowed the obstacles to stop your pursuit?

Morning Decree #310
Who's Your Helper?

"Now Reuben heard it and he delivered him out of their hands." Genesis 37:21

God has rigged life that no one can reach their full potential without the help of others. Even Jesus Christ had folks who helped with the administration of His ministry, not to mention those who funded the mission. Being aware of your need for others is the first step in accomplishing the dream—whatever it may be.

When God wants to bless someone, He usually brings someone into your life's situation. At the same time, when the devil wants to sabotage someone, he usually uses someone to do his dirty work. It's not always clear, at least not initially, who is on your side. The key is to recognize that there are people who God has assigned to your life—to bless you, to encourage you, to rescue you, and even correct you when you're wrong. Learning how to incorporate them into your dream may be the difference between being frustrated and fulfilled. Thank God for the Reubens who will deliver you out of harm's way.

Questions for Reflections

1. Who has been your go-to person in your past?

2. On a scale of 1 to 10, how open are you to the support of others?

3. Can you recall a time where you failed to recognize
the God-sent people in your life?

Morning Decree #311
Dreams Work

"He becomes poor who works with a slack and idle hand, but the hand of the diligent makes rich." Proverbs 10:4

Dreams are easy to come by, but they take work to make a reality. Many people have a vision and desired goals. The question isn't do you have a dream, but rather what are you doing about it? Contrary to popular belief, dreams—even when they are from the Throne Room of God—require your partnership.

Dreams work when dreamers do their work. When is the last time you scheduled time to work on your dream? What resources are you allocating to support your plan? Who are you meeting with to learn more about how to make your dream a reality? The idea that dreams just happen is a fantasy. If your dream has value to you, then invest the sweat equity necessary to make it happen.

Questions for Reflections

1. What's your dream, your *big* dream?

2. What are the steps you've taken to make your dream a reality?

3. What are three obstacles you're facing to manifest your dream?

Morning Decree #312
Are You Deceiving Yourself?

"But be doers of the Word [obey the message], and not merely listeners to it,
betraying yourselves [into deception by reasoning contrary to the Truth]."
James 1:22, AMP

We erroneously think that being deceived is a spooky magic thing or that only the spiritually weak fall prey to the wiles of the devil. Deception is evil, but to be self-deceived is the worst kind of deception. Nobody wakes up one morning and says, "Today, I'm going to deceive myself." Deception is sneaky; it doesn't announce it's coming. And this is even more evident when it comes to being self-deceived.

Self–deception occurs when you fail to adjust your life according to what the mirror of the Word of God shows you. To think that just seeing the need, problem, or dream is enough for it to become a reality is the essence of deception. Don't allow yourself to be a deceived dreamer by "thinking more than doing."

Questions for Reflections

1. Can you remember a time when you thought something to be true only to find you were deceived?

2. As you reflect on the Word of God, what have you determined needs to change in your life but you have failed to take action?

3. What do you call someone who sees the truth but fails to obey it?

Morning Decree #313
Is Your Foundation Cracking Up?

"So everyone who hears these words of mine and acts upon them [obeying them] will be like a sensible (prudent, practical, wise) man who built his house upon the rock."
Matthew 7:24, AMP

Any builder would agree that the most important part of an edifice is the foundation. But the foundation of the house, unlike the color of the front door or the type of windows, cannot be seen. As a matter of fact, there's really no esthetic value placed on the foundation whatsoever. Nevertheless, more time and sometimes money is spent on getting the foundation laid properly than any other part of the building.

When it comes to our faith, little thought is given to ensure that it's built on right biblical truth. When speaking about their faith, many only have a cursory understanding. Perhaps this is why the majority of people in the United States claim to have Christianity as their faith, but in practice they demonstrate very little evidence to support such a claim. Consequently, when the storms of life blow against their faith, they are not able to weather the storms. Evidence of having the right foundation is seen when the storms passes by.

Questions for Reflections

1. Describe a situation that was so difficult that it tested your faith in God?

2. Explain why the foundation of your faith is based on Jesus Christ?

3. What are the types of storms you've faced that having a sure foundation is vital to victory?

Morning Decree #314
You're Not the Only One

"Whom resist steadfast in the faith, knowing that the same afflictions are accomplished in your brethren that are in the world." 1 Peter 5:9

To believe that as a follower of Jesus, there won't be seasons of difficulty is naive at best. The Bible teaches us that in the world you will have tribulations. The questions then aren't if you will have trouble, but when and what to do before and during the storms. During the storm and after the storm are critical to surviving the hard times.

One of the important keys to getting through hard times is realizing your situation is not unique, nor are you alone. While you are special, your situation is not. In fact, it's actually rather common. Understanding that others have and are going through nearly identical challenges to their faith while overcoming is comforting. Success leaves clues. Finding out what they did to win their faith fight will save you time, energy, and sleepless nights. Others won, why can't you?

Questions for Reflections

1. Why do many people feel alone when they are going through a difficult season?

2. Do you feel no one understands how challenging the problem is you're facing?

3. Would hearing about other people's problems and solutions be helpful to you?

Morning Decree #315
Turn Up the Thermostat

"So that your fasting may not be noticed by men but by your Father, Who sees in secret; and your Father, Who sees in secret will reward you in the open."
Matthew 6:18

When you fast, it's different than simply modifying a diet or going without food. Fasting is an opportunity to focus your prayers in faith. In other words, by fasting, you are stating that what you are praying for is more important than your wants and fleshly desires.

Difficult times require a greater intensity. This is even more true when it comes to your spiritual life. Because faith is easy to talk about, many are unaware of what it takes to live a life of faith. Fasting, among other outcomes, helps eliminate unbelief from your spiritual life. And as you know, faith is the currency that is required to operate supernaturally.

Set your faith like you would a thermostat. Turn up your spiritual intensity by fasting regularly with a pre-determined purpose. Prayer and fasting are an unbeatable combination when done in faith. You get what you expect. You don't get what you don't expect. Turn up the temperature of your faith actions.

Questions for Reflections

1. Rate your spiritual intensity on a scale from 1–10, 10 being the most intense.

2. How can you better improve your intensity using what spiritual disciplines?

3. Do you have a set fasting and prayer plan? If so, what is it?

Morning Decree #316
Three Words from God

"Not by might, nor by power, but by my Spirit, saith Jehovah of hosts."
Zechariah 4:6, KJV

"Do not fret or have any anxiety about anything, but in every circumstance and in everything, by prayer and petition (definite requests), with thanksgiving, continue to make your wants known to God." Philippians 4:6, AMP

"Having done all [the crisis demands], to stand [firmly in your place] ... Stand therefore [hold your ground] ..." Ephesians 6:13-14, AMP

I'm reminded that there are many life matters which require prayerful resolutions–comfort and peace in the midst of loss, the healing of mind and body, financial crisis, the need for reconciliation of estranged relationship, and so on.

The three Scriptures above were brought to my mind by the Holy Spirit and I consider them three "words" from the Lord. They are sterling reminders of where our focus must remain, and where our faith must rest. There are, of course, many other poignant verses that may apply to your situation. It's important to know and remember that victory is a product of His Spirit. That knowledge, along with prayer, petition, and thanksgivings, will enable you to gain the courage and confidence you need to stand in the day of trouble.

Questions for Reflections

1. What is your most dominant emotional response when faced with uncertainty?
2. Why does it seem to take so much work to think positively in the midst of turmoil?
3. What can you do to more quickly make the transition from worry to worship?

Morning Decree #317
What God Can't Forget

"For God is not unrighteous to forget or overlook your labor and the love which you have shown for His name's sake in ministering to the needs of the saints (His own consecrated people), as you still do." Hebrews 6:10, AMP

Sometimes, it seems that what you do for others doesn't make a difference. Your financial giving, your midnight prayer vigils, your silence when you could have said things out of pain, the sharing of your time and possessions, even when you don't have enough for yourself—nothing you have done for others goes unnoticed by God. Nothing. God is the most excellent accountant.

As you make sacrifices for others, remember that your sacrifice is recorded in Heaven. God hears, sees, and knows your needs and wants. In light of those countless sacrifices, there are rewards that will manifest in your life. The Law of Sowing and Reaping applies to your "intangible" sacrifices as well. Trust God. He's God and has you covered. Keep doing good for others because it's the right thing. God will honor it and will never forget.

Questions for Reflections

1. Have you ever felt forgotten by others despite your massive amount of sacrifice?

2. How did their lack of appreciation affect your attitude and motivation?

3. How will focusing on God as your rewarder impact your overall motivation to serve others?

Morning Decree #318
Thank You

"Do not fret or have any anxiety about anything, but in every circumstance and in everything, by prayer and petition (definite requests), with thanksgiving, continue to make your wants known to God." Philippians 4:6, AMP

When I really need something to change in my life or in the life of a loved one, my tendency is to go all out. I've found myself lately praying from a desperate emotional place. Are you in a difficult period in your life? If you are, listen to what the Word of God says you should do. The Apostle Paul, writing Philippians 4:6 from a jail cell, reminds you of your need to pray. He admonishes you not to be anxious concerning *anything*. The word *anything*, according to *Dictionary.com*, means "in any degree; to any extent; in any way at all."

Therefore, according to Philippians 4:6, there's absolutely nothing that should cause for you to remain in an agitated state of mind. The challenge for me then is how *not* to be anxious. The Scripture instructs us to pray and to make specific petitions. But many times, even after following that prescription, I'm still anxious. What I've discovered, with the help of the Holy Spirit, is that I failed to give thanks after I pray—let alone while I'm waiting on the answer to manifest.

It's not that God needs to hear us say thank You, although it's the polite thing to do. There is something about giving thanks that settles our heart knowing that God our Heavenly Father has heard our prayers. So after you pray, give thanks for the answer *before* it arrives. It will invoke a peace that defies explanation. Didn't your parents teach us this? I know mine did. Thank you, Mom!

Questions for Reflections

1. How do you feel when you do some basic courtesy for someone but they forget to say thank you?

2. Do you feel inclined to do more or less for an ungrateful person?

3. How do you feel when someone expresses their gratitude for a kindness you shared?

Morning Decree #319
Permissible Violence

"Violent men seize it by force [as a precious prize—a share in the heavenly kingdom is sought with most ardent zeal and intense exertion]." Matthew 11:12b, AMP

I've been ridiculed at times for being too intense. I'm not sure what was meant by that criticism, but one thing I'm sure of and that is nothing happens unless you make it happen. In other words, a decisive act on your part is required to get the job done. Whether it's a new habit you want to develop or a different career you want to pursue— whatever your prayer aim is—it will on some level demand intentionality.

All too often, Believers take prayer as the ultimate and final act needed to achieve their goals. They say, "I'm praying about it." The truth is that not even Jesus just prayed about things. His prayer time seemed to be when and where He received the instructions necessary to accomplish the will of the Father, whereas believers often stop with prayer. Prayer is the starting point. It's the place where instructions are given, grace received, and vision clarified.

By all means pray, but do *something* after you get up from your knees. Go after it hard with intensity and fervor! Commit your energy to the task at hand. Some doors need to be kicked down. Obedience is the kick many times lacking when it comes to getting what you pray for. Be willing and obedient as the prophet said in Isaiah1:18. Prayer makes you willing, but you have to include "the obedience factor."

Questions for Reflections

1. What issues are you facing that require more "elbow grease"?

2. What makes you stop when pursuing the difficult issues in prayer?

3. Can you remember a challenge you pushed through by prayer and obedience and it turned out as you had hoped?

Morning Decree #320
The Only Fight to Fight

"Therefore, we do not become discouraged (utterly spiritless, exhausted, and wearied out through fear). Though our outer man is [progressively] decaying and wasting away, yet our inner self is being [progressively] renewed day after day." "For our light and momentary affliction (this slight distress of the passing hour) is ever more and more abundantly preparing and producing and achieving for us an eternal weight of glory [beyond all measure, excessively surpassing all comparisons and all calculations, a vast and transcendent glory and blessedness never to cease!]"
2 Corinthians 4:16-17

What we often expect is what we end up with. However, when it comes to spiritual matters, things can and often do look bleaker before they get better. For example, you begin to pray for the deliverance of a loved one and they seemingly go full throttle into degradation rather than coming to the light. Or you renew your commitment to financial freedom, only to have a sudden financial emergency that threatens to set you back. And you make a decisive step toward getting your health in order and discover you have a rare condition you have never had to deal with before. This can be breathtaking, but not in a good way. It's in those moments you need to remember the goal and get your mind off the storm of the day. Failure to make this shift usually signals defeat or at, a minimum unnecessary, delays.

Questions for Reflections

1. How will focusing on your faith help you in the long run?

2. What kind of distractions seem to derail your progress most often?

3. What three things could you do to safeguard yourself from being discouraged?

Morning Decree #321
Disappointments Are Temporary

"And David was greatly distressed; for the people spake of stoning him, because the soul of all the people was grieved, every man for his sons and for his daughters: but David encouraged himself in the Lord his God." 1 Samuel 30:6, KJV

Many times, it's not what happened that causes the most damage, it's how the problem was addressed. Problems will come; that's a hard, cold fact of living. However, just because things happen doesn't mean they have to destroy you. Jesus said, "In the world you will have tribulation, but be of good cheer for I have overcome the world" (John 16:33). Don't let your heart be so troubled that you give up because of the real problems going on in your world. Rather, determine to handle them with the wisdom that comes from God and is forged in prayer.

The warrior King David, when overwhelmed with crushing realities, determined to seek God's will concerning the matters. Your answer, regardless of the problem, will always be best addressed after pursuing God's heart. How you handle what you're going through will determine how long and how well you go through it. Don't give up on God; He won't give up on you.

Here are six helpful ideas:

1. Be honest about how you feel.
2. Realize others may be feeling the same way.
3. You're not alone.
4. Take responsibility of your emotional and physical state of being.
5. Seek God's will.
6. Obey the instructions in the Word of God.

Questions for Reflections

1. When you hear the word *lifestyle*, what comes to mind?

2. How is a lifestyle created?

3. Is following Christ a lifestyle, habit, or hobby?

Morning Decree #322
Overcome the Craziness

"Do not, therefore, fling away your fearless confidence, for it carries a great and glorious compensation of reward. For you have need of steadfast patience and endurance, so that you may perform and fully accomplish the will of God, and thus receive and carry away [and enjoy to the full] what is promised." Hebrews 10:35-36

The sudden onset of sickness; the out of nowhere call saying your sibling is terminally ill; the pink slip at work after you bought a new home; the car accident which totaled your only means to get to work; people disappointing you even though you always tried to be there for them. These are just a few of the realities that some are facing right now. And when these "crazies" start happening, your tendency may be to ask the question "Why me?" or wonder where God is in the midst of it all. When those things happen, you can lean toward giving up, talking negatively, and turning to self–medication.

This may not be your story, today or even yesterday, but when you are serious about following the Lord, endeavoring to seek His will, "craziness" predictably shows up! When it does, that is not the time to relax your grip on faith. It's the wrong time to throw in the proverbial towel, to stop giving, or to break your fast, or quit doing a dozen other critical but crucial spiritual things.

Don't let "craziness" stop your praise or your push! Declare your faith in God regardless of the circumstances. Call out to Jesus even more. Give more in faith, expecting even bolder miracles. Believe to see your breakthrough despite seeing evidence to the contrary.

Questions for Reflections

1. What "craziness" has occurred in your life trying to derail your plans?

2. What is your default reaction to sudden upsets?

3. What are three things you can do to rebound after setbacks?

Morning Decree #323
Confidence Is Not Optional

"And this is the confidence (the assurance, the privilege of boldness) which we have in Him: [we are sure] that if we ask anything (make any request) according to His will (in agreement with His own plan), He listens to and hears us. And if (since) we [positively] know that He listens to us in whatever we ask, we also know [with settled and absolute knowledge] that we have [granted us as our present possessions] the requests made of Him." 1 John 5:14-15

Seeking God by fasting convicts me of the truth that nothing really matters except doing God's will. All the specific prayer requests I have (and there are many) can be summed up into a single prayer: Your will, oh God, be done!

Times of deep consecration always bring me to the realization that what I really need and want is to live out God's will for my life—nothing more, nothing less, nothing else will do. For me, it takes fasting to get me back to what is most important.

Knowing God's will and praying accordingly is the source for boldness and confidence. Actually, one of the reasons so many people fail to receive answers to their prayers is because they do not pray based upon God's will. He is not obligated to answer any request, no matter how sincerely offered, that is not according to His will. God's will is God's Word. Know His Word and you will be default know His will for your life.

Questions for Reflections

1. Why do you think knowing God's will increases your confidence?

2. Can a person know God's will in every area of their life? If so, how?

3. How will confidence improve your prayer life?

Morning Decree #324
Do This Now

"'Now, therefore,' says the Lord, 'turn to Me with all your heart, with fasting, with weeping, and with mourning.'" Joel 2:12

Fasting is a God–ordained response to crisis. I personally believe the Father expects this from us when we need supernatural intervention. The prophets of old would call a nation to their knees in prayer—strengthened by fasting. Fasting was used to demonstrate the depth of sorrow for one's sins. It was also employed when seeking direction from God and deliverance from enemies.

There is such power in fasting unto God that Hell itself will try to prevent you from developing this important spiritual discipline. As you know, when you fast, you are dethroning your flesh, your will, and your appetites for something greater. Self-denial isn't fun, but necessary.

Keep in mind that your prayers are being heard on high. Recognize that, although you may not see the immediate fruit of your sacrifice, in due season you will reap the benefits—guaranteed. Spend as much time in prayer and contemplation as possible. Trust that, with each hunger pang and every decision, something of eternal value is taking place. Repent as the Holy Spirit reveals to you any areas of sin—things which are displeasing or unproductive in the sight of God.

Questions for Reflections

1. What is the hardest thing you face when you start fasting for spiritual reasons?

2. How often do you fast?

3. Have you ever put yourself on a fast?
What were the circumstances that made you fast?

Morning Decree #325
Being Hard-Headed Has Its Place

"And be constantly renewed in the spirit of your mind [having a fresh mental and spiritual attitude] . . ." Ephesians 4:23, AMP

A mindset is an established way of thinking. Much like cement, once a mentality is hardened it is hard to reshape. However, when the Word of God creates a mindset, it provides a consistent framework through which the plan of God can be fulfilled. However, it takes a certain mindset to operate in the realm of the Spirit. The carnal mind, which is a thought process based on the six senses, works against the Spirit-led life. A person who attempts to operate in the Spirit while utilizing the natural/carnal mind will fail miserably.

Mindsets are all based upon a clear and ever-increasing revelation of who Jesus Christ is and what He came to do for us, in us, and through us. Please re-study these and discover the many others that reveal the Living Christ.

Questions for Reflections

1. Do you know anyone you feel is set in their ways?
How do you think that is hindering their growth?

2. In what areas do you think you are stubborn—slow to change?

3. In what ways can you improve your life if you changed the way you think?

Morning Decree #326
The Deception is Real

"You are of your father, the devil, and it is your will to practice the lusts and gratify the desires [which are characteristic] of your father. He was a murderer from the beginning and does not stand in the truth, because there is no truth in him. When he speaks a falsehood, he speaks what is natural to him, for he is a liar [himself] and the father of lies and of all that is false." John 8:44, AMP

Do you realize you were God's idea? Regardless of the circumstances around your birth, you were His idea. You are a product of His imagination. He wanted children, a creation that could experience His love, glory, and beauty. Life and the things that have happened to you have changed how you view yourself and others. You hear a voice whisper in your ear, "I was mistake, an accident" or "I don't have any real reason to live" or "I'm useless." You may have never said those exact words, but something similar has trafficked through most human minds.

This deception has caused untold, incalculable damage and pain, confusion beyond description, poverty, sickness, premature death, aimlessness, purposelessness, wars, murders, suicides, and perversions of all kinds. Because Satan himself cannot attack God, he attacks what God loves the most, which is you.

One of the most important things you will ever do is to discover God's love for you as demonstrated in the sacrificial death of Jesus Christ along with your purpose for living. When you began to embrace those two all-important things, you will bloom like a flower in the springtime.

Questions for Reflections

1. What's the most common negative self-talk with which you struggle?

2. Do you remember when you first had to combat those thoughts?

3. What are five ways you can defeat negative thinking?

Morning Decree #327
The Lie You Believe Becomes the Truth You Live

"Because there is no truth in him. When he speaks a falsehood, he speaks what is natural to him, for he is a liar [himself] and the father of lies and of all that is false."
John 8:44, AMP

The reason why church doesn't work for some is because they haven't realized that they have been deceived. Truly, the greatest deception is when you don't know you're deceived. It's like being blind, but you don't know it—darkness would be natural to you. Satan's ultimate plan is to blind you and have you believe that blindness is the natural order of things. In order for you to be restored to the original plan for your life, you must recognize you have been bamboozled.

The word devil means deceiver. His whole game he plays with you is based on smoke and mirrors, lies and deception. Even when the devil has the facts right about you, he doesn't tell you that the truth can change the facts. Any lie you believe becomes your truth. That lie, which is now your truth, is what you will experience in your life. The best way to expose each lie you have believed is to seek truth—the truth that is only found in Jesus Christ.

Questions for Reflections

1. What truth about yourself have you discovered since coming to know Jesus as Lord?

2. How has not knowing the truth affected your life?

3. What can you do going forward to guard against the subtle lies of the enemy and this fallen world?

Morning Decree #328
Like Him, Not Like That

"In this [union and communion with Him] love is brought to completion and attains perfection with us, that we may have confidence for the day of judgment [with assurance and boldness to face Him], because as He is, so are we in this world."
1 John 4:17, AMP

The relationship Jesus has with the Father is the same relationship we have with the Father at this very moment. Jesus had no sense of guilt or condemnation, likewise we should have no sense of guilt or condemnation. The work, ministries, and miracles Jesus did on Earth are the same miracles we are commissioned to do—no less and actually more.

But this reality only happens when there is a revelation of your true identity. Your true identity is not in your culture, ethnicity, gender, or nationality. Rather, your true self can only be found in your understanding of who your Father and Big Brother are. Jesus and the Father are one; you are to be just like Jesus!

You were created in the likeness and image of the Godhead. It's only because of sin and its corruptive nature that you have ceased being like your original parents.

Questions for Reflections

1. Who on Earth do you self-identify with the most?

2. What about that person do you see in your being?

3. In what ways do you want to be like Jesus?

Morning Decree #329
No Identity Crisis

"For those whom He foreknew [of whom He was aware and loved beforehand], He also destined from the beginning [foreordaining them] to be molded into the image of His Son [and share inwardly His likeness], that He might become the firstborn among many brethren." Romans 8:29

What Christ experienced, He did on your behalf. As a father, many generations are within me as a seed; whatever I do, wherever I go, whatever I become, they (by the very fact that they are within me) are doing what I am doing, going where I am going, and becoming whatever I become. This is even more profoundly true in Christ. You were chosen in Him (Christ) before the foundation of the world (see Ephesians1:4); He blessed us in Christ with every spiritual blessing in heavenly places (see Ephesians 1:3).

So to access your best self, you must unwrap the gift of Jesus because it's in Christ where you discover all the blessings of life. He's the one you are becoming. He's the image, the role model, the standard. If you pursue the knowledge of God in Christ Jesus, you will never suffer an identity crisis. You are to be like your Elder Brother, the Lord Jesus Christ. This isn't about imitating only, but rather learning to yield to the reality of His nature being ours.

Questions for Reflections

1. To whom do you identify with the most?

2. Why? In what ways?

3. In what ways do you see yourself identifying with Christ Jesus?

Morning Decree #330
You Too

"I have been crucified with Christ [in Him I have shared His crucifixion]; it is no longer I who live, but Christ (the Messiah) lives in me; and the life I now live in the body I live by faith in (by adherence to and reliance on and complete trust in) the Son of God, Who loved me and gave Himself up for me." Galatians 2:20

Not only was Christ crucified, but because you were in Him at the time, you were crucified also. The disgrace and shame He endured, He did for you, with you, as you. Jesus became sin for you) so the old nature would be completely destroyed. The sinful nature—Adamic nature, the nature that has sin in it, sickness in it, death in it, failure in it—was crucified, nailed to the Cross. *You were crucified with Christ.*

To grasp this by revelation will be the difference between living in gracious victory and struggling. The truth that Jesus lived and died as you and for you is more than a theological talking point. Rather, it's the mystery of all mysteries. It is the very truth that the deceiver wants to keep from you.

Questions for Reflections

1. What does the common phrase "like father, like son" mean to you?

2. What do you expect from a child who is "like his or her father?"

3. Why do you think it's difficult to see how we can live like Jesus did?

Morning Decree #331
What's Yours Is His

"For our sake He made Christ [virtually] to be sin Who knew no sin, so that in and through Him we might become [endued with, viewed as being in, and examples of] the righteousness of God [what we ought to be, approved and acceptable and in right relationship with Him, by His goodness]." 2 Corinthians 5:21, AMP

Jesus was made sin for your sin. He was sinless but became sin—personified as your sin. Christ Jesus became your sin-bearer, your scapegoat (see Leviticus 16; 2 Corinthians 5:21; Isaiah 53:3-5). Your sin separates you from your Father. By becoming sin for you, taking the judgment was due you, Jesus took away your sin, removing the only barrier between you and your Father's love.

Realizing that Jesus Christ took your sin by becoming sin-personified is the most mind–boggling truth to grasp. The ramifications of this truth have impact both here and now and the hereafter. Many get the idea that Jesus took our sin and therefore we now have access to Heaven. However, to embrace the truth that right this very second you are without sin because of what Jesus did and became on your behalf is more difficult to do. Nevertheless, it's the truth. God the Father deals with you based upon the finished redemptive work of Christ. It's a done deal. Consequently, sin cannot dominate you without your permission and submission.

Questions for Reflections

1. How does being conscious of personal sin affect your prayer life?

2. Do you feel more confident in your relationship with God or less if you are sin-conscious?

3. Why is it hard to accept the truth that Jesus took your sins away and therefore you no longer have them?

Morning Decree #332
He Took That Too

"He personally bore our sins in His [own] body on the tree [as on an altar and offered Himself on it], that we might die (cease to exist) to sin and live to righteousness. By His wounds, you have been healed." 1 Peter 2:24, AMP

The same Jesus that took your sin also took your sickness. Jesus became sickness. All your sins and sicknesses were laid upon Him. If there was never sin, there would never have been sickness, for sickness entered the human spirit and bloodline through the doorway of sin which was opened by Adam. When Jesus took your sin on His body, and His body was crucified, He took sickness with Him and killed it, too.

Sin and sickness are spiritual conditions which manifest in the physical body. You, with your diseases, were nailed to the Cross when Jesus was crucified. The body of sin and sickness was destroyed and your spirit was born again. The newly-recreated, born-again spirit now within you is part of the divine nature (see 2 Peter 1:4). Sickness was the result and penalty of sin. Jesus took your penalty, so Satan has no legal right to put diseases on you.

Laws of physics declare that two things cannot exist in the same place at the same time. This is also true spiritually. Since Jesus took your sins and carried your sicknesses on His own body, so neither sin nor sickness has a legal right to reside in your life. To not know this truth is the reason why both of these maladies continue to reign in the life of the children of God.

Questions for Reflections

1. How can you build your faith in order to receive healing in your life?

2. What is the natural produced from (for example, an apple seed)?

3. What happens to an apple tree if you kill the root? What will happen to sickness, which is the fruit of original sin, if you kill the sin seed?

Morning Decree #333
I CAN DO ALL THINGS

"Not that I am speaking of being in need, for I have learned in whatever situation I am to be content. I know how to be brought low, and I know how to abound. In any and every circumstance, I have learned the secret of facing plenty and hunger, abundance and need. I can do all things through him who strengthens me." Philippians 4:11-13

This is an oft-quoted passage many people would claim is among their "favorites" for times of trouble. It is indeed helpful and I have used it myself many times to be encouraged along the way. Yet, I wonder if we are using and applying it correctly. Don't get me wrong, it is true we can do all things through Christ who gives us strength. But notice the context in which Paul wrote this. It was about finances and he told his readers he had learned to be content in plenty and in lack. He had learned a secret and that was Christ would help him when things were either lean or fat. I can understand Christ's help when our finances are depleted, but why would we need Him in times of plenty? Perhaps it's because sometimes when things are good we can easily forget the One who made them good. Paul had learned the secret of contentment in whatever financial season he was in.

What's more, Paul's statement is one of potential. By that, I mean he wrote he "can" do all things. When you can do something, it means you have the potential but it doesn't mean you choose to do it. If you can do all things in Christ, what are the "all things" you are doing? Is that statement a declaration of reality or potential? I hope it's reality, but don't be lulled into believing you are doing or being something just because you can. After the belief or declaration, there is the doing and that is the most important part where the Lord is concerned.

Questions for Reflections

1. Do you quote and rely on this passage? Is it a statement of reality or potential for you?

2. Have you learned to be content in all kinds of financial seasons? What do you think is the "secret" of such contentment?

3. What do you need to do to move on from being an "I can" believer to an "I do" or "I am" believer?

MORNING DECREES

Morning Decree #334
He Represented You

"In this [union and communion with Him] love is brought to completion and attains perfection with us, that we may have confidence for the day of judgment [with assurance and boldness to face Him], because as He is, so are we in this world."
1 John 4:17, AMP

When Jesus died on the Cross, He died to the power of sin because sin cannot dictate to the dead. Therefore, when Jesus died, the power of sin became a non-factor. This is why you are commanded to consider yourself dead to sin. Just as Jesus died to sin and sin no longer had any power to affect His life, sin has no power to affect our lives either because He was representing you when He died.

Identifying with Jesus in all aspects of His life is crucial to walking in the abundant life. Jesus, just like Adam, was the representative for the entire human race. You had no choice but to identify with Adam because you were born a human. Consequently, whatever is in Adam's bloodline of sin just naturally became part of your life in some way. Likewise, when you identify with Christ, you receive by birth what is yours because you are born of the same Spirit as Christ.

When Christ took your sin to the grave in death, and just as the power of sin no longer has affect on Jesus in any way, sin should have no affect on you. Just as Jesus is, so are you in this world.

Questions for Reflections

1. What is the reaction of a dead person to pain, criticism, or loss?

2. How is it still possible to be bound by a sinful habit even though Jesus died for all sins?

3. What should our response be to temptation and what Jesus did for you through His death?

Morning Decree #335
Dead and Buried

"We were buried therefore with Him by baptism into death, so that just as Christ was raised from the dead by the glorious [power] of the Father, so we too might [habitually] live and behave in newness of life." Romans 6:4, AMP

Identification with Jesus is the key to experiencing the wonders of redemption. It's religion that teaches you to go to church, do this, or don't do that. While there are undoubtedly things you need to do and not do, where Identification with Christ and religion part are concerned, the former is being someone new, and the latter is basic behavior modification.

When Jesus was buried, he took the body (His Body) that was made sin and it was placed in a tomb because it was dead. The burial which obviously followed His death on the Cross was the moment in which you recognize that your old person is put to rest. Graves are for the dead. The lives of those in the grave have ended, at least as far as their activity on Earth is concerned. However, when Jesus, your representative and substitute, was buried, it signaled the end of living your life as you wish on Earth. Jesus didn't come to fix your life, but rather Jesus came to become your life.

Questions for Reflections

1. Why is dying to self so difficult for you?

2. What does denying yourself specifically mean to you?

3. How will living for Christ change your behavior today?

Morning Decree #336
Been There, Done That

"For even as Jonah was three days and three nights in the belly of the sea monster, so will the Son of Man be three days and three nights in the heart of the Earth."
Matthew 12:40

There is a judgment coming to all. It's spiritual delusion to think that your sins are insignificant happenings of which God is unaware. The Bible plainly teaches the wages of sin is death (see Romans 6:23). That's the bad news, but the good news is that Jesus Christ suffered the penalty for our sin. God judged your sin through Jesus. What amazing love and grace—the innocent died for the guilty! Not only did Jesus die on your behalf, He went to Hell in your place as well.

Jesus' body was buried in a tomb. His spirit went to Hell for three days and three nights, until the claims of justice were met. He paid the penalty for your sins. He was your substitute in Hell. Why go to Hell when you don't have to? Why live in hellish defeat now when Jesus Christ suffered, bled, died and was buried for you? Hell, as far as God is concerned, is a place where you've already been in Christ. No need to go there again for all eternity.

Questions for Reflections

1. Have you ever thought that you got away with something?

2. What should your response be to the truth that Jesus paid the price for your sins?

3. How can you demonstrate gratefulness for Jesus' sacrifice?

Morning Decree #337
It's Either Him or You

"Now the centurion, having seen what had taken place, recognized God and thanked and praised Him, and said, 'Indeed, without question, this Man was upright (just and innocent)!'" Luke 23:47

The great mystery of the substitutionary work of Jesus is the riddle of all times. The truth that a man represented all of humanity is truly behind comprehension. Jesus Christ, the Son of God and the Son of Man, lived, died, and did miracles as a man. He then bore the sins of the entire world—past, present, and future. How amazing is that!

Jesus suffered the totality of all human suffering. The innocent, sinless One took on all the ailments, illness, and human pain; it takes God-sized love to do that. Jesus loves you just that much. Jesus the Christ suffered as you, for you, and in your place. He did this fully conscious of the weight and yet went through a literal Hell to secure your place in Heaven.

The opportunity before you is either to accept and trust that since Jesus did this for you as you, you don't have to go through it again or you can choose to take your chances and suffer through life on your own. Trusting in Jesus is far better. It's either Him or you, but it can't be both. Choose to trust in the finished work of Christ.

Questions for Reflections

1. Is it fair for two people to suffer the penalty for a sin committed by only one of them? Why not?

2. What should the innocent party do since someone has already suffered the penalty for the offense?

3. Are you confessing that Jesus paid it all when you're faced with the sufferings this world offers?

Morning Decree #338
It's Not Over

"He is not here; He has risen, as He said [He would do]. Come, see the place where He lay." Matthew 28:6, AMP

If Jesus' ministry ended with Him being buried in a borrowed tomb, then how tragic would His death have been. However, Jesus' story doesn't end with a grave. He arose. The victory wasn't in His dying, it was seen in His resurrection. Often we cry over what Jesus suffered and spend much time in contemplation at the tomb. However, even as Mary found out, the tomb was empty. Jesus' story didn't end in tragedy, but rather in triumph over death, Hell, and the grave.

Your story doesn't have to end tragically either. There is a resurrection after the death you're presently experiencing in your life. It's a resurrection to your dreams, visions, goals, and God's promises. God's plan for your life wasn't to end in a sad drama or a comedy, but a picture of utter and complete victory.

As you catch the revelation of identification with Jesus Christ, just as you were with Him in crucifixion, death, burial, you were and are with Him in resurrection. Your story isn't over—to the contrary, it's just beginning.

Questions for Reflections

1. Recall a time when you thought it was all over for you or your situation?

2. How do you think knowing Jesus' story didn't end with His burial can impact your life today?

3. How will you view your struggle knowing that there is still the possibility of a triumphant outcome?

Morning Decree #339
Resurrection Plus

"And if we are [His] children, then we are [His] heirs also: heirs of God and fellow heirs with Christ [sharing His inheritance with Him]; only we must share His suffering if we are to share His glory." Romans 8:17, AMP

Identification with Christ is the ultimate revelation once you receive Him as Lord. What Jesus did, He accomplished as us, with us, and for us or to make it very personal—for you, as you, and with you. This identification doesn't end with Jesus being your sin–bearer only. The benefit package of God toward you is exhaustive—complete, with nothing missing.

When Jesus was raised from the dead, you were raised as well. However, to think of Him being raised but not healed or restored would make Jesus a zombie-like creature. Of course, that's not what happened. When Jesus was raised from the dead, He regained His former glory, especially after His Ascension. The power of sin was obliterated, healing and health restored, provision (including wealth) was made available again, and most importantly, unbroken communication with the Father was once again unhindered by sin.

Questions for Reflections

1. If you were an heir to a fortune, but were estranged for years, what should you expect once your relationship and legal standing were restored?

2. Would you think like an employee or a blood heir?

3. How should we, knowing that we have been restored back to good graces of the Father through Jesus Christ, now behave?

Morning Decree #340
Put in the Work

"For this very reason, adding your diligence [to the divine promises], employ every effort in exercising your faith to develop virtue (excellence, resolution, Christian energy), and in [exercising] virtue [develop] knowledge (intelligence)..." 2 Peter 1:5

Not only is change uncomfortable, but it also requires real work. It takes a new level of commitment and focus. One of the most important revelations you can receive is that you are under construction by the Lord. Because of sin and the world in which you live, there is a requirement for reconstruction. Failure to recognize this fact is perhaps one of the main reasons why so many Christians do not mature in their faith, relationships, or purpose.

Even Jesus Christ had to mature. Of course, He was sinless. Still, it was required of Him to be raised by His earthly parents, in complete submission to their nurture and oversight. I'm sure there were times He was expected to do something He did not always want to do but He did it anyhow. If Jesus had to put the work in to mature and grow, then I can assure you that you must do the same.

Questions for Reflections

1. Why does change seem to be so difficult for you?

2. What areas do you feel you need to change the most? List at least three.

3. What steps are you willing to take to make the changes you listed above?

Morning Decree #341
His Credit Score, Not Yours

"For if because of one man's trespass (lapse, offense) death reigned through that one, much more surely will those who receive [God's] overflowing grace (unmerited favor) and the free gift of righteousness [putting them into right standing with Himself] reign as kings in life through the one Man Jesus Christ (the Messiah, the Anointed One)." Romans 5:17, AMP

In today's world, you really need good credit. Your credit score is a universally accepted criterion that determines your worthiness to be given a loan. In other words, based upon your score, merchants decide whether or not to let you take their product, live in their apartment, or drive their car without having to pay for it upfront. Rarely understood, however, is that God also uses a credit score criteria which determines your ability to receive.

The good news is that the credit score used is not yours, but the one of Christ Jesus Himself. Righteousness is the ultimate standard, "credit score," but this righteousness belongs to Jesus and is not yours. Your ability to transact with Heaven is never based upon your good deeds. While good deeds are important, they are never what makes it possible to approach God in prayer. Regardless of how good you are, how much you fast and pray, give and sacrifice, ultimately your spiritual credit score is only based upon the gift of righteousness that undergirds your relationship with the Lord.

Questions for Reflections

1. When do you feel more acceptable to God?
When you're doing everything right or when you're doing wrong things?

2. How much do feelings of righteousness affect your confidence?

3. How will knowing about Christ's righteousness make you more confident in prayer?

Morning Decree #342
Put In The Work

"For this very reason, adding your diligence [to the divine promises], employ every effort in exercising your faith to develop virtue (excellence, resolution, Christian energy), and in [exercising] virtue [develop] knowledge (intelligence) . . ."
2 Peter 1:5, AMP

Not only is change uncomfortable, but it also requires real work. It takes a new level of commitment and focus. One of the most important revelations you can receive is that you are under construction by the Lord. Because of sin and the world in which you live, there is a requirement for reconstruction. Failure to recognize this fact is perhaps one of the main reasons why so many Christians do not mature in their faith, relationships, or purpose.

Even Jesus Christ had to mature. Of course, He was sinless. Still, it was required of Him to be raised by His earthly parents, in complete submission to their nurture and oversight. I'm sure there were times He was expected to do something He did not always want to do but He did it anyhow. If Jesus had to put the work in to mature and grow, then I can assure you that you must do the same.

Questions for Reflections

1. Why does change seem to be so difficult for you?

2. What areas do you feel you need to change the most? List at least three.

3. What steps are you willing to take to make the changes you listed above?

Morning Decree #343
Freely Receive

"For if because of one man's trespass (lapse, offense) death reigned through that one, much more surely will those who receive [God's] overflowing grace (unmerited favor) and the free gift of righteousness [putting them into right standing with Himself] reign as kings in life through the one Man Jesus Christ (the Messiah, the Anointed One)." Romans 5:17, AMP

One of the most difficult things for a believer to do is to receive that which was not earned. We exist in a performance-based society that requires us to do something to get something. That's appropriate in most situations; however, when it comes to blessings of God, it's drastic. What qualifies us is God's righteousness as revealed in Jesus Christ—accepting the fact that on our best days we're never going to be good enough, holy enough, worthy enough. Once we accept that fact, the pressure to perform dissipates. Our trust is in what Jesus accomplished for us.

Regrettably, many fail to embrace that righteousness is a gift. They confuse their righteous behavior with the righteousness that comes through and from Jesus Christ. The two don't mix together any more than oil and water. However, there is a place for personal, righteous deeds but those deeds will never be the cause of why you receive the blessings of God. They will be the response to receiving the blessings of God.

Questions for Reflections

1. Can you recall a time when you receive something that you didn't expect and for which you didn't work?

2. When was the last time you did something significant for someone which they did not earn or deserve from you?

3. Why did you do it and how did it make you feel?

Morning Decree #344
Blood Covenant

"So when God desired to show more convincingly to the heirs of the promise the unchangeable character of His purpose, He guaranteed it with an oath, so that by two unchangeable things, in which it is impossible for God to lie, we who have fled for refuge might have strong encouragement to hold fast to the hope set before us."
Hebrews 6:17-18

Faith is the lifeline of the follower of Jesus. As the Scripture reads, without faith it's impossible to please God (see Hebrews 11:6). The Bible says in no less than three other places that the "just shall live by faith" (Habakkuk 2:4, Romans 1:16, Galatians 3:11). Biblical faith is more than a theological point of study or a mental exercise. Faith is the currency required in order to transact spiritual business. Faith is what moves God on your behalf. Faith is something that can be lost, stolen, minimized, or increased. While you are given a measure of faith, what you do with it to cause it to grow or decrease is your responsibility. Faith is so vital to success or failure in life that it's something the devil tries to steal right out of your heart.

God knows that you are naturally predisposed to doubt. Your inability to grasp the impossible and see the invisible is a human weakness common to all. God understood Abram's plight and did the thing that would help him keep the faith.

Making a Blood Covenant with Abram enabled him to grasp the revelation that God had no intention of changing His mind. The Blood Covenant ritual was understood and honored by ancient cultures. Abram knew this. God knew Abram would get the picture. The power of the Blood Covenant, understood by Abram, meant that God would make good on His promise—no matter what. His faith was secured by the irrevocability of the Blood Covenant.

Questions for Reflections

1. Why is faith never blind?

2. What gives a believer confidence during difficult moments?

3. How can you strengthen your faith?

Morning Decree #345
Blood Believers

"The blood shall be for a token or sign to you upon [the doorposts of] the houses where you are, [that] when I see the blood, I will pass over you, and no plague shall be upon you to destroy you when I smite the land of Egypt." Exodus 12:13, AMP

Your faith has to be in something other than shear willpower. This is especially hard to accept when the circumstances surrounding your prayer requests are not favorable. Abram and Sarai were both up there in age—past the age of bearing children we're told in the Scriptures. What are you to do when you are attacked in your body and there's no obvious cure? Yet you know there is a plethora of Scriptures that prove healing is God's will. On what do you base your faith for healing? Without a revelation that God *cannot* lie, it's next to impossible to believe for the manifestation of your healing. If there is ever failure, it's not on God's end. He is the God that keeps covenant.

A Blood Believer is one who bases their trust on the Blood Covenant, not on their ability to believe or to imagine. A Blood Believer is very much aware of the facts of their case, recognizing that the outcome is not dependent on favorable conditions but on the God who keeps His Word. Interestingly, not even God expected Abram to simply take Him at His Word, which is why He "cut" the covenant with him. Being a Blood Believer is synonymous with true faith.

Questions for Reflections

1. On what do you base your faith?

2. When is the last time you trusted God despite the circumstances?
Were you victorious in the end?

3. What things can a believer do to build their faith in the Blood Covenant?

Morning Decree #346
Blood Qualified

"Then Jonathan made a covenant with David, because he loved him as his own life."
1 Samuel 18:3

A Blood Covenant is a binding agreement between two or more parties that cannot be broken without penalty, injury, or death. I continue to restate this definition to ingrain it in your thinking. A Blood Covenant is not a contract; it's a covenant. It's solemn, sacred, and must be revered. The fundamental purpose for establishing a Blood Covenant relationship in the first place is to end any question in the minds of the parties involved whether or not their real intention is to honor its terms.

It's like the difference between testifying and doing so under oath. If you lie during testimony, but are not under oath, you're branded as a liar who cannot be trusted. But when testimony is given under oath, being considered a liar is the least of one's problem. In a court of law, a person who lies under oath can be sent to prison.

When a person enters into a Blood Covenant relationship and then fails to keep the terms of the covenant, a severe penalty will be imposed. The purpose of the Blood Covenant cut with Abram was not just for him and his generation, but for us as well.

Questions for Reflections

1. Can you describe other earthly examples of covenants?

2. Why is it so wrong to break a promise?

3. What does the phrase, "Your word is your bond" mean to you?

Morning Decree #347
Blood Intercession

"So the men turned from there and went toward Sodom, but Abraham still stood before the Lord." Genesis 18:22

Relationships matter. As the saying goes, "*It's* not what you know, it's who you know." Abraham was in covenant with the Lord God. He had a relationship with God that was based upon a binding, blood deal. It was this Blood Covenant that gave Abraham a boldness that otherwise no mortal had a right to expect.

Blood Covenant intercession is never based on one's goodness or righteousness, but rather it's predicated on what was sworn to while standing in blood. It's not emotionally driven or merit–based. God answers our prayers solely based on the covenant that was cut in Jesus' blood. His blood is the blood of the New Covenant. This is why we pray in the name of Jesus. It's in the name of Jesus that our prayers can be offered with an unquestionably and uncommon boldness.

Questions for Reflections

1. Why do you think God should answer your prayers?

2. Is being good a prerequisite for answered prayer?

3. Is Abraham's relationship with the Almighty God more special than yours? If so, why or why not?

Morning Decree #348
Guaranteed

"Do not be deceived and deluded and misled; God will not allow Himself to be sneered at (scorned, disdained, or mocked by mere pretensions or professions, or by His precepts being set aside.) [He inevitably deludes himself who attempts to delude God.] For whatever a man sows, that and that only is what he will reap."
Galatians 6:7, AMP

Have you ever heard the statement, "The only things guaranteed in life are death and taxes?" I have heard it many times. The truth is what you can really count on is the spiritual law that states, "Everything reproduces after its own kind." This biblical law simply reveals that a corn seed will produce corn every time. It's foolish to think that anything other than a stalk of corn is going to grow from a kernel of corn.

This law has far reaching implications beyond simple agriculture. The truth that seeds produce according to their type applies also to your spiritual, physical, and economic life. What you sow is what you are going to reap. The one caveat is that what is harvested is exponentially greater than the seed sown. Nevertheless, corn seeds produce corn, apple seeds produce apples.

When you intentionally sow let's say money into the Kingdom of God, there is a guaranteed outcome, based upon the heart in which the money was given—and the amount. The system is divinely pre-determined to work on your behalf. If you sow it, you can with absolute certainty expect a harvest of more money and/or what money could not buy.

Questions for Reflections

1. Why do Christians struggle so much with giving or sowing?

2. Why do you think God set it up that the more we give, the more we receive?

3. Are you receiving the financial seeds you desire?

JEFFERY A. WILLIAMS

Morning Decree #349
Decide First

"Let each one [give] as he has made up his own mind and purposed in his heart, not reluctantly or sorrowfully or under compulsion, for God loves (He takes pleasure in, prizes above other things, and is unwilling to abandon or to do without) a cheerful (joyous, "prompt to do it") giver [whose heart is in his giving]."
2 Corinthians 9:7, AMP

Before you do something like plant a garden, you need to decide what type and how large of a garden you want to plant. It sounds pretty basic, doesn't it? This simple concept is rarely considered when sowing financial or other types of spiritual seeds.

When sowing, many times we just give a portion of what we have—hoping that something good will come from our sacrifice. While that's not totally out of order, perhaps the most efficient way is to determine how much of a harvest we need and then sow seed, accordingly.

No farmer simply elects to plant seeds without first having determined the amount of seed needed to achieve the desired harvest. Additionally, the kind of seed is also pre-determined. Since God uses the agriculture metaphor to express spiritual realities, it's not a stretch to realize that when it comes to your sowing of financial resources, you should also pre-determine the size and kind of harvest you need or desire. You will only get what you expect if you sow with intentionality and wisdom. Wise sowers determine these matters beforehand. Decide before you do it!

Questions for Reflections

1. Describe the type of harvest you need to receive this year?

2. Based on the type of harvest, have you sown that kind of seed?

3. How much and where have you planted those seeds?

Morning Decree #350
It's 100% Up to You

"Let each one [give] as he has made up his own mind and purposed in his heart, not reluctantly or sorrowfully or under compulsion, for God loves (He takes pleasure in, prizes above other things, and is unwilling to abandon or to do without) a cheerful (joyous, "prompt to do it") giver [whose heart is in His giving]."
2 Corinthians 9:7, AMP

When it comes to sowing financial seeds beyond tithing, it's a personal decision. Giving is a decision between you and the Holy Spirit. If you feel pressured by someone or even by yourself to give—rather than giving because you want to—it's better for you just to keep it. Giving is a heart issue, not a financial one.

Your giving should be based upon your desire to give and the need or request presented to you. The need may be $1,000, but you feel like giving only $10. Many even have the $1,000 but feel that $10 is all they should give. It's better to give the $10 and experience the joy and blessing of God than to give the larger amount and not receive the commendation of God. The same holds true if you know you should give the $1,000 and give only $999. Your gift will bless the recipient, but you, on the other hand, have not pleased God. Do what's in your heart to do, and in the absence of a clear directive from the Lord, do what you can and still have peace and joy.

Questions for Reflections

1. Express a time when you gave more than you should
and gave less than you were led to give?

2. How did you feel in both situations? How did you feel when you
did exactly what you thought you should have?

3. Do you have a giving plan?

Morning Decree #351
Start with The Harvest

"[Remember] this: he who sows sparingly and grudgingly will also reap sparingly and grudgingly, and he who sows generously [that blessings may come to someone] will also reap generously and with blessings." 2 Corinthians 9:6, AMP

A farmer determines the minimum amount of their projected harvest. They decide this long before planting season because they will need to acquire the land and the seed necessary. If they want to plant 40 acres of tomatoes, they need 40 acres of land and enough seed to cover the entire acreage. This calculation isn't made the day of planting or even during planting, but instead months before.

If you sow abundantly, you will reap abundantly. If you sow sparingly you will reap sparingly. This law is one of the most exciting, I believe, for it puts back under your control the amount of harvest you receive. Sowing and reaping from a biblical perspective is as predictable as planting seeds in a family garden. The more you plant, the more you will reap. The less you plant, the less you will reap.

Therefore, when you give financial seeds, based upon your available resources, decide how much harvest you want to receive before you plant. The amount, in comparison to others, may not seem to be much. The ultimate judge whether what you're sowing is in the abundant category is God. Don't compare, just do what's in your heart and within your capability. God sees, knows, and will multiply you accordingly.

Questions for Reflections

1. What are some of the harvests you need in your life in the next twelve months?

2. What resources do you think you need to acquire in order to meet your harvest goal?

3. Where will you sow your seeds? Why in that ministry?

Morning Decree #352
Leftovers Matter

"For if the [eager] readiness to give is there, then it is acceptable and welcomed in proportion to what a person has, not according to what he does not have."
2 Corinthians 8:12, AMP

There are times when you just don't have the money you wish to give. I've been in many church meetings when I didn't have the asked-for amount. I felt defeated, less than, and condemned. It wasn't that the minister was making me feel that way, but rather it was my own incorrect thinking. It wasn't until I realized God really didn't care about how much I gave, but rather was concerned with my heart or intention in whatever amount I decided to give. My pride at times caused me to either give more than I could afford or not give for fear of embarrassment. In either case, I missed out on the blessing.

Therefore, I've learned to listen to God within my own circumstances. I believe, according to the Scriptures, that God would not require something of you that you don't have ability to deliver, nor would He hold you accountable. God gives you credit for your intention in each case rather than what you actually put in the offering plate. Giving is a heart matter, not a math problem.

Questions for Reflections

1. Can you recall times when you felt God was asking something of you that you knew you had no way of doing?

2. When did you realize it wasn't God after all?

3. Why is it important to have the right heart when it comes to doing anything in Jesus' name?

Morning Decree #353
Work Your Dirt

"And God blessed them and said to them, Be fruitful, multiply, and fill the Earth, and subdue it [using all its vast resources in the service of God and man]; and have dominion over the fish of the sea, the birds of the air, and over every living creature that moves upon the Earth." Genesis 1:28, AMP

Understanding the awesome responsibility you have to determine what your future look like is critical. While God's sovereignty is without question, His influence is limited. This limitation, however, is by choice. He has given much leeway to His creation. From the beginning of creation, humans were given the responsibility to take care of their environment. This is still true.

You have the wonderful opportunity to determine what type of garden grows in your life. By the seeds you sow or don't sow, you craft what will be the fruit you enjoy. This doesn't factor God out by any stretch of the imagination, but rather it is a demonstration of God's decision to make you the chief steward.

Decide today by choosing the right seeds, efforts, actions, and words with which you will seed your life. The seeds you plant are under your complete control. What you speak is a seed, what you do is a seed, even how you think is a seed. As cliché as it sounds, "Sow it to grow it" is nevertheless as true today as it was since the beginning of time. You need to work your dirt to obtain the harvest and future you desire.

Questions for Reflections

1. Have you ever noticed weeds growing in a garden and wondered how they got there? What did you conclude as possible answers?

2. Who decides ultimately what kind of garden grows in the garden in your yard?

3. How can you change the type of plants you grow?

Morning Decree #354
Sow This, Harvest This

"And God said, 'See, I have given you every plant yielding seed that is on the face of all the land and every tree with seed in its fruit; you shall have them for food.'"
Genesis 1:29

Seedtime and harvest are in full effect (see Genesis 8:22). This law is working, just like gravity, regardless of one's geographic position, socioeconomic status, or gender. The universal Law of Seedtime and Harvest cares nothing about your race, nationality, or religious views. Essentially, if you sow pumpkin seeds, you will grow pumpkins. It's just that simple.

As you enthusiastically navigate your day, do so with the full knowledge that everything, absolutely everything, is a seed. Every action has a seed-like impact. What you do will produce a predictable outcome over time. If you act carelessly with your time, for instance, you will reap the fruit of poverty. If you fail to sow energy by way of proper and appropriate exercise, you will produce a health profile that is considered unhealthy. If you want something, you must sow that kind of seed. If you want more energy, you must plant exercise seeds. If you want this, whatever your "this" is, you must sow that type of seed. Everything is a seed.

Questions for Reflections

1. Describe an area of your life as a garden. What are you growing in that area that you didn't plan to grow?

2. What actions did you plant to grow that fruit in your life?

3. What type of fruit do you want more of in your life? What seeds do you need to sow?

Morning Decree #355
Pruning

"Any branch in Me that does not bear fruit [that stops bearing] He cuts away (trims off, takes away); and He cleanses and repeatedly prunes every branch that continues to bear fruit, to make it bear more and richer and more excellent fruit."
John 15:2, AMP

Pruning is necessary for more growth. This is true for plants and people. The cutting away of dead branches is essential to further healthy plants. To ignore the pruning process is not an act of mercy but of neglect, a dereliction of duty.

Clipping the dead, non-productive branches helps a plant bloom to its potential. Jesus mentioned that growth, in a spiritual sense, is directly tied to the degree of pruning to which a disciple submits. Your desire to be more effective must include periods and seasons of pruning or chastening. It is during those periods that the most important facets of development actually occur. Therefore, instead of avoiding the pruning process, rather seek it out. Look for opportunities to stretch and grow.

Questions for Reflections

1. What pruning experience or source are you avoiding?

2. What areas in your life are failing to see new growth?

3. What should you do to ensure that you experience timely prunings?

Morning Decree #356
First Pain, Then Progress

"If you live in Me [abide vitally united to Me] and My words remain in you and continue to live in your hearts, ask whatever you will, and it shall be done for you."
John 15:7, AMP

I'm not referring to pain that requires medical attention or prescription medications. Instead, I'm talking about the pain that often follows physical exercise and the pain that accompanies making a difficult, emotionally charged decision. That kinds of pain should be expected, anticipated, and embraced. It's the avoidance of this kind of pain that results in retarded growth.

Making difficult choices, like breaking away from an unhealthy relationship or choosing to be alone because of your personal convictions, can be painful. However, this pain is temporary—especially when you consider the prolonged dysfunction that accompanies failure to make that tough decision.

Embrace your situation knowing, though it's painful now, that the progress will ultimately produce results worth every single minute of emotional or physical discomfort.

Doing the best thing is always the right thing even though it feels like the wrong thing to do in the moment. Progress is awaiting you.

Questions for Reflections

1. Name three moments when you balked at making the best decision because you didn't want to embrace the pain that would follow?

2. Looking back, would you make a different decision today? Why?

3. What advice would you give someone who is facing difficult decisions in their life?

Morning Decree #357
Some Movement Required

"For physical training is of some value (useful for a little), but godliness (spiritual training) is useful and of value in everything and in every way, for it holds promise for the present life and also for the life which is to come." 1 Timothy 4:8, AMP

The Bible does not say that physical exercise is unnecessary; it simply asserts that it's not the most important factor in life or health. The point of this specific devotional, however, is to point out that—just as in the case of physical exercise—spiritual disciplines are necessary for optimum health.

What are the spiritual disciplines that you regularly practice? My most productive workout sessions at the gym are those that I do both consistently and with forethought.

I don't base my workout routines on my feelings on specific mornings because most mornings I simple don't feel like working out. I commence the trainings regardless of how I feel due to the fact that it is part of my personal disciplines—and I have a plan.

Your spiritual life is more important than your physique. It takes serious planning and determination to properly develop spiritually. The idea behind being a disciple is that of disciplined practice. To grow in Christ is more than knowing Scriptures or even agreeing with them. To develop properly requires the daily practice of certain key disciplines.

Questions for Reflections

1. What are the spiritual disciplines you practice daily?

2. Why do you feel the need to employ these practices?

3. What are your strongest disciplines? What are the areas in which you struggle the most?

Morning Decree #358
The Fine Print

"Jesus answered him, I assure you, most solemnly I tell you, that unless a person is born again (anew, from above), he cannot ever see (know, be acquainted with, and experience) the kingdom of God. You search and investigate and pore over the Scriptures diligently, because you suppose and trust that you have eternal life through them. And these [very Scriptures] testify about Me!" John 3:3, AMP

I miss many details when I read things that I think I already know. That it is even true when I read, of all things, the Bible. There are things we've heard about since we were young children in Sunday School. things like Jesus saves, Jesus is a healer, or Jesus will be a friend who sticks closer than a sibling—to name few. However, the reality is we often miss the truth behind the truths we read because we are either too familiar with them or quite frankly too lazy to dig deeper.

The Word of God is not something that can be understood, let alone embraced, without intentionality and effort. Simply put, if you're not hungry for truth, you won't be fed! There are details, (the fine print) that unless you're looking for them, you won't see them. What you don't know, or in this case don't see, will hurt you by default.

One such fine print is that Jesus Christ came to completely, totally, and irrevocably remove the destructive impact of the devil. Did you know this? Can you find those the details of that truth in the Word of God?

Questions for Reflections

1. Recall a time when you failed to understand the fine print in the assembly directions of a project and as a result it didn't work?

2. On a scale of 1–10, 10 being red hot, what is your intensity level when it comes to studying the Word of God?

3. What changes can you make to your daily routine to intensify your study opportunities?

Morning Decree #359
Benefits

"Blessed be the Lord, who daily loadeth us with benefits, even the God of our salvation. Selah." Psalms 68:19

The long–held idea that following Christ means living in poverty (physically, financially, emotionally) in every way except spiritually is not what the Bible teachers nor is it the will of God for anyone's life. A benefit is defined as something that is advantageous or good—an advantage. Benefits are advantageous; they are good. Poverty, brokenness, and lack are not good.

Taking a fresh look at the Scriptures—understanding what Jesus Christ actually purchased for us—one can't help but conclude we are loaded down with blessings. As a Good Father, God wants our lives to be full of beneficial things that fulfill us.

These benefits are part of our Salvation. They are not extra add-ons for a select few, but instead they are available to all who have the faith to receive them. It's a tragedy to live without that which Jesus Christ has died for you to have. Benefits are your inheritance as the heirs of God, according to the Scriptures (*Romans 8:17*).

Questions for Reflections

1. Why do you think many people equate Christianity with poverty?

2. List some benefits a person receives from their employer?

3. What would a person be losing out on if they were not aware of their benefit plan?

Morning Decree #360
Specific Prayers, Specific Answers

"If you then, evil as you are, know how to give good and advantageous gifts to your children, how much more will your Father Who is in Heaven [perfect as He is] give good and advantageous things to those who keep on asking Him!"
Matthew 7:11, AMP

A breakthrough is a result of sustained, focused pressure on a barrier. From a spiritual perspective, faith pressure breaks down doors, walls, and moves mountains. All hindrances must succumb to faith pressure. The more focused your prayers are, the more pressure is released, which means you need to be intentional about exactly what and for whom you are praying.

God is really into the details and specifics. Pray about matters with as much specificity as you can. You're not directing or bossing God around when you pray specifically. Rather, you are merely expressing the desires of your heart. Your Heavenly Father likes to hear directly from you.

If you want a specific blessing, be specific in your request. General prayer requests don't seem to get answered in my experience. God knows what you need before you even ask, but He still wants to hear your heart.

Questions for Reflections

1. What exactly do you want God to do for you?

2. What are your most sincere prayer requests?

3. How can you know if God answered your prayers
if you weren't specific when you prayed?

Morning Decree #361
Making Preparations

"And Joshua said unto the people, 'Sanctify yourselves: for tomorrow the Lord will do wonders among you.'" Joshua 3:5

By fasting with prayer, you are making your intentions known to the Father that you are serious about the things for which you are praying. I don't think anyone fully understands how fasting works. It's somewhat of a mystery, but the power of it cannot be denied. Fasting reveals the hindrances within and around you that must be addressed by your faith-in-action.

Fasting has a unique way of preparing you for what is to come or what should happen in the future. During times of intense prayer and fasting, listen for the correcting voice of the Holy Spirit. The Holy Spirit will work on the matter for which you are enduring hunger pains, but the process will also detox your life. Keep praying for your family and others too, but keep in mind God is preparing you for much more than you are presently experiencing.

Questions for Reflections

1. What is it about the preparation process that frightens you?

2. Can you remember an event in your life for which you were underprepared?

3. How do you feel knowing that you are well-prepared rather than under- or ill-prepared?

Morning Decree #362
You've Come Too Far to Quit Now

"Then he said to me, 'Fear not, Daniel, for from the first day that you set your mind and heart to understand and to humble yourself before your God, your words were heard, and I have come as a consequence of [and in response to] your words.'"
Daniel 10:12, AMP

The power of fasting with prayer is incontrovertible. It simply works! However, the waiting period between the time you make the request and your prayers getting answered can be challenging to negotiate and requires patience. Take solace in the fact that Daniel prayed for twenty-one straight days before getting a response from Heaven. Precisely, as the angelic messenger stated, ". . . from the first day . . ." Daniel's prayers were heard—your prayers are listened to as well.

Do not give up because the answer has yet to be revealed. Press forward. Stay on your knees. Regardless of the circumstantial evidence, keep praying! Continue to thank God for the breakthrough you seek. Your sacrifice will surely be rewarded.

Questions for Reflections

1. What are some practical things you can do to stay encouraged?

2. What are the reasons many people give up too soon?

3. Can you recall a moment when quitting would have been easier but you didn't?

Morning Decree #363
Unbroken Focus

"Looking to Jesus, the founder and perfecter of our faith, who for the joy that was set before Him endured the cross, despising the shame, and is seated at the right hand of the throne of God." Hebrews 12:2

When I lose focus on why I'm fasting, it becomes such a chore. Each hunger pain reminds me of what I'm losing out on rather than what I'm gaining. By staying focused on the reason I'm fasting, "my why," I almost look forward to fasting with prayer. There's much power in fasting. It's somewhat mysterious, not knowing how it changes things, people, and situations, but somehow it does. As you focus on the one for whom you're fasting and praying, you will discover a determination that will push you through the uncomfortable moments. It takes a vision of what can be that gets you through to what is.

I recall what is said about Jesus Christ in the book of Hebrews: "How He endured the Cross because of a future joy." I believe the joy "set before Him" was you and I—safe and secure, prosperous and healthy, joyful and peaceful. I thank God for Jesus' sacrifice. His focus is what got Him through. Keep in the forefront of your mind for whom and what you're sacrificing. There is incredible power within a focus that is unbroken.

Questions for Reflections

1. How does what you see affect your motivation?

2. What is the "joy" that will cause you to push past the difficulties of prayer?

3. What have been the distractions that have broken your focus in the past?

Morning Decree #364
It Waits for No One

"To everything there is a season, and a time for every matter or purpose under heaven." Ecclesiastes 3:1

"Neither time nor the tides of the ocean are waiting on you. They move as they have been designed regardless of your wants, needs, or desires. Both time and tide have power. Depending on how you use them, they can be assets or signal your demise."

Everyone one of us is given the exact same allotment of time each day when twenty-four hours are deposited into your life account. Regardless of our race, gender, nationality, or spiritual state, we all get the same amount of time. What differentiates people is how they invest their twenty-four-hour allotment of time. For the most part, you determine how your time is spent.

Time is a gift. It doesn't stop for anyone. It doesn't discriminate or show any favoritism. As you endeavor to discover the best usage of your time, consult the Creator of time, first and foremost. Every day is a gift from Him. He knows the best and most judicial use of the time with which He has graced you. Be a good manager of time and you will be rewarded in this life and the next most handsomely.

Questions for Reflections

1. What grade would you give yourself for your time management?

2. Name a few instances where you didn't manage your time well and it cost you something important.

3. What are some of the ways you can improve the usage of time, starting today?

Morning Decree #365
The End of Self

"Looking away [from all that will distract] to Jesus, Who is the Leader and the Source of our faith [giving the first incentive for our belief] and is also its Finisher [bringing it to maturity and perfection]. He, for the joy [of obtaining the prize] that was set before Him, endured the Cross, despising and ignoring the shame, and is now seated at the right hand of the throne of God." Hebrews 12:2, AMP

The end is nearer than you think. I know that sounds ominous, but I'm not talking about the end of the world. What I am referring to is the end of the trial you're facing—the fruit of your tears released in prayer. Anyone who tells you victory comes swiftly and easily all the time has never been in a real trial. It takes faith, vision, and a willingness to endure until the breakthrough comes.

Still, there is one way to make even the most difficult journeys a bit easier and that's by realizing God is the ultimate finisher. Therefore, when you come to the end of yourself, then you will find God. You will see His power, His wisdom, and His grace. He will do what you cannot. "The end of self is the beginning of God."

Questions for Reflections

1. How does focusing on Jesus help you in your faith?

2. Why does joy matter?

3. How does remembering the sacrifices of others form and inform your faith?

About the Author

Jeffery A. Williams, D.Min., MPA, is the founder and chief empowerment strategist of The Williams Empowerment Group LLC, whose sole mission is to help others achieve their dreams. Having coached more than 1,500 students through multiple coaching programs, live presentations, and interactive webinars, Dr. Williams has earned the reputation of "The Chief Empowerment Officer." A dynamic catalyst to corporations, nonprofit organizations, and entrepreneurs, Dr. Williams draws on his years of experience, education, and insatiable desire to see others "win" to show them how to change the trajectory of their life and business to previously unreached levels.

Dr. Williams has an earned doctorate from Gordon-Conwell Theological Seminary (Urban Complex Settings), a Master's in Public Administration from the Harvard Kennedy School of Government, and a bachelor's degree from Brown University in Social Environmental Analysis. In 2016, Dr. Williams was consecrated a bishop in the Covenant Fellowship Alliance. He and his wife, Lelani, live in Rhode Island and parent two young adult daughters, Joy Victoria and Grace Noelle.

In addition to being a sought-out advisor to members of government, Dr. Williams has been a regular chapel speaker for both the National Football League and Major League Soccer (2005-12, 2014). Dr. Williams is a trained mediator and has published six books: *Knowing Why: The Key That Unlocks Your Full Potential* with a workbook journal (which is used as a college textbook), an ebook entitled, *Resurge: From Disorder to Divine Order in 7 Steps*; and *The Morning Decree Devotionals Journal*-- originally published in four volumes.

With a strong desire to educate and elevate members of the community at large, Dr. Williams has dedicated his life to serve as both a spiritual guide and social change advocate. His work as a faith leader began with a nine-person congregation and has since grown to include several hundred members. Internationally he serves as the General Overseer of The Global Ambassadors Leadership Network through which he oversees 60 congregations in twelve nations, including local churches and ministries. His ministry is viewed in 182 nations of the world.

Through both his teachings and his actions, Dr. Williams always leads by example, helping others understand the connection between principle and practice. In 1999, he founded the Cathedral of Life Christian Assembly, renamed The King's Cathedral. He is also the founder of "The Well-Life Project," a funding agency with a mission to create twelve fresh water wells in the African nation of Zambia.

He is the husband of the beautiful Lelani Williams and they are enthusiastic parents to two young adults, Joy Victoria and Grace Noelle Williams. You can learn more about Dr. Williams at www.drjeffwilliams.org. You can also reach Dr. Williams through Facebook @williamsglobal777 or via email at williamsglobal777@gmail.com.